WILLIAM VAN HORN, M.D.

The 7 Steps to Passionate Love

Why Men are NOT from Mars & Women are NOT from Venus

from another book:
every night hold her in your arms,
end every night in love
never go to bed angry

©2000 William Van Horn, M.D.

ISBN 0-9677358-0-7

Publisher: Dunn Publishers
            240 Corporate Center Drive, Suite F
            Stockbridge, GA 30281
            www.vanhornmd.com

Cover design Andrea Perrine Brower
Inside book design by Dawn Grove
Printed by Health Communications, Inc.

I dedicate this book

to the committed lovers in my life:

My beautiful wife, Tamara,

who is my most intimate friend and lover.

My six, precious children.

My intimate friends in my personal support group.

The many wonderful people who have

attended my workshops and continue

to maintain a commitment to passionate love.

FOREWORD

In *The 7 Steps to Passionate Love*, you will learn to reach a higher level of intimacy and love than you ever knew existed. You will be challenged to become a more effective communicator, a more sensitive person, and a more intimate lover. If you are searching for a way to energize your relationship and to reach a new level of fulfillment, you found what you have been looking for, just as I did.

My wife and I have been friends since high school. We married in our early twenties with a tremendous sense of commitment and a desire to experience life together. We loved each other, but 23 years later we found our relationship in serious trouble. The pressures of building a company and raising children stripped our relationship of the joy and love that brought us together over two decades earlier. Our interaction was reduced to petty arguments and constant bickering. We could not last one week without a devastating fight and we reached a point in which, although we loved each other, we did not like each other. Over 12 years we had seen four different marriage counselors and attended numerous seminars and retreats.

When no solution seemed to work, we decided to separate.

Sandy heard Dr. Van Horn on the radio and asked me if I would seek help with her one more time. I agreed to attend one of his four-day workshops. During that time, I witnessed a change in myself and in my wife that proved to stand the test of time and the test of love. For the first time, we were offered ways to get to the root of our problems and ways to solve them. We learned how we could begin to enjoy and love each other on a daily basis and how to bring the excitement back into our relationship.

Sandy and I are more intimately in love with each other now than we were on our honeymoon. We have finally moved past our history and into a new relationship based on unconditional love and mature understanding. I used to value work over my time with my wife; now my priorities match hers. She used to have trouble communicating with me; now she understands me on a whole new level. I used to be numb to her feelings as well as mine; now I can feel happiness and love in ways that I never knew existed.

Dr. Van Horn's principles and techniques revolutionized my marriage and my life. They completely changed the dynamics of our family and re-established an intimacy that had been missing for over ten years. I am thrilled that Dr. Van Horn outlined his principles on paper, and I encourage you to prepare yourself for an incredible journey into your heart and the heart of your partner.

—*Ron Dunn, Atlanta, GA*

CONTENTS

Step 6

Step 7

Summary

Introduction

Men and women are inherently the same:
sensitive, vulnerable spiritual beings
created to intimately experience
and share love in relationships.

STUCK IN OUTER SPACE

*I*magine that you are an alien professor sent to earth from another galaxy on a critical mission. Your orders are to return to your planet with a clear understanding of the keys to intimate, loving relationships between men and women on earth. You are to present your findings at a planet wide symposium in only ten days. You have specifically been chosen because of your proven ability to objectively and efficiently investigate data. Your conclusion will be accepted as truth by many of your colleagues.

Upon your arrival, you disguise yourself as a college student and enter the nearest bookstore. You begin your search in the periodical section. Immediately, you are struck by the abundance of articles on sex. One magazine after another gives detailed information on how to maximize the quality of your sex life.

- *Cosmopolitan*, British Edition, April 1999
- "Make Your Own Sexy Video"
- "Do You Plus Him Equal Great Sex?"

3

- *YM* Young and Modern, May 1999
- "Sex Secrets" (special pullout section)

- *New Woman,* June 1999
- "How Often Do You Have Sex? What Your Bedding Average Says About You"

- *Men's Health,* June 1999
- "High Voltage Sex"

- *Redbook,* June 1999
- "5,000 Married Men Confess: What Keeps Sex (with you) Hot"

- *Jane,* May 1999
- "Who Is Having the Best Sex?"

- *Woman's Own,* July 1999
- "Orgasms Guaranteed!"

You pat yourself on the back. You cannot believe that you have already found the answer: **"Great sex is the key to a loving relationship."** How fortunate you are. What an easy search. The first seven magazines you read have at least one article on sex. You could read articles on sex all night if you wanted. You decide to limit yourself to twelve. Now your job is simply a matter of reading a few more articles, organizing the information and heading home.

What? It is not possible! You cannot believe what you find in your twelfth article:

- *Self,* May 1999.
- "Is Sex Dead?"

"It used to be considered normal to be unsexy in long-term relationships," says New York City sex and marital therapist Sharon Miller, Ph.D. "Extremely turned-on couples with robust sex lives in long-term relationships are actually rare."

The *Self* article destroys your theory. Great sex does not last. At least, not by itself or for most couples. Self tells how it is normal for couples to go long periods without sex. Sex seems to be better at the beginning of a relationship and before marriage. You conclude that sex certainly is **not** the key to a loving relationship.

Your search continues. No more quick conclusions. You almost returned home with the wrong information. This time the search will be more thorough. You go back to the periodicals.

- *Vogue*—British, June 1999.
- "The 40 People You Need to Make You Beautiful"

- *Vanity Fair*, June 1999.
- "Julia Roberts—The world's only $20 million actress opens up about her loves, her life, and her tabloid lunacy"

- *Glamour*, "Shania Twain (From Poverty to Pop Star)"

- *Shape*, June 1999.
- "Look Great Naked"

- *People*, May 31, 1999.
- "Sophia Loren—Forever Sexy"

- *More*, June 1999.
- "50 Ways To Look Great on the Beach"

You observe another obvious trend. Magazines are filled with articles on the benefits of beauty, wealth, possessions and fame.

Beautiful women dominate magazine covers and advertisements even when articles and products have little to do with women. Handsome men are paired with articles about athletic, professional and financial success. Magazines are loaded with advertisements promoting the "value" of acquiring possessions. It would be easy to conclude that the keys to loving relationships are beauty, wealth and professional success.

You know it is only a theory at this time. You are committed to avoiding premature conclusions. Now you must look for contradictory articles. You find them easily.

- *Ladies Home Journal*, 1999. "100 Most Important Women of the Twentieth Century—Jane Fonda"
  "Fonda, the daughter of the revered actor Henry Fonda, emerged as an international sexpot in 1968's "Barbarella," directed by first husband, Roger Vadim . . . left playboy Vadim for left-wing radical Tom Hayden and won critical praise (and two Oscars) for such films as "Klute" (1975) and Coming Home (1978). In 1991, two years after divorcing Hayden, Fonda tackled her most unlikely role yet as wife of billionaire media baron Ted Turner."

- *McCall's*, June 1999. "A frank talk with Kathie Lee"
  " . . . when her husband, Frank Gifford, 68, was caught by the paparazzi with another woman."

- *Mirabella*, June/July 1999. "Michelle Pfeiffer Opens Up"
  "Pfeiffer's marriage to thirty-something's Peter Horton, whom she met when they were acting students, ended amicably in 1988; she had to leave his force field to grow up. There followed a brief bad-boy period . . . a relatively peaceful interlude with the character actor Fisher Stevens . . . She broke up with Stevens and started adoption proceedings. 'I thought, this will separate the boys from the

men. And literally two weeks later I met David.'. . . They married at Claudia's christening."

- *TV Guide*, May 22-28, 1999. "Daddy Dearest?"
  "It's all part of a complex- and at times unflattering portrait of his late father, Michael Landon Sr., one of the most beloved figures in television history. And though Landon Jr.'s TV movie shows his father to have been a warm and loving man, there are enough dark moments particularly depicting Landon Sr.'s infidelity. . . . Though Landon, Sr., by all accounts, believed firmly in family values, he was also a man who married three times . . ."

- *Ladies Home Journal*, 1999. "100 Most Important Women of the Twentieth Century—Marilyn Monroe"
  ". . . the most enduring sex goddess of all time. Born in Los Angeles . . . Monroe lived mostly in orphanages until she was 14, when she married for the first time. . . . Her high profile marriages to powerful men (baseball great Joe DiMaggio and playwright Arthur Miller) ended in divorce. . . . In 1962, six weeks after being fired by Fox, she died, naked and alone, of a sleeping-pill overdose in her Los Angeles home."

- *TV Guide*, May 22-28, 1999. "Signing Off."
  "Allen has been married for 14 years to Laura Diebel, who is now CEO of Tim Allen Signature Tools, the tool line that bears her husband's name. Allen admits that the demands of a hit series have an effect on his home life. 'The people around me, my wife and [adolescent] daughter [Kady], were not too happy sometimes,' he says. 'Because I forgot them. This has been highly stressful for my wife. . . . So much is asked of me, and there is little time left for her.' "

After reading these articles, you know for sure that beauty, wealth and success do not guarantee love. Now you are more confused than ever. Your search is becoming much more difficult. When you eliminate articles on sex, beauty, wealth and success, little relevant information remains in magazines.

There were a few articles where the reference to love was puzzling for you:

- *Cosmopolitan,* British Edition, April 1999.
- "Women Who Love Men Who Love Drugs"

- *Teen People,* May 1999.
- "Suicidal Nightmare (Why one young couple decided to die for love.)"

- *Seventeen,* May 1999. "My Dad Had an Affair"
  "My parents never did get divorced. You can't know exactly what exists between two people in love. You have to let them play it out, even if they recklessly hurt each other . . ."

You are now dumbfounded by all the conflicting opinions about love. Your time in the periodicals has not been helpful. You still don't have your answer. You believe your answer is going to require more information than any single magazine can hold. You head for the book section.

As you enter the book section, you quickly observe that there are thousands of books written about relationships. How are you possibly going to discover the truth with so much information? Your time is limited. You decide to focus on the most popular perception of a loving relationship. With the help of a bookstore employee, you find the relationship book that has outsold all others in the past three years, *Men Are From Mars, Women Are From Venus,* by Dr. John Gray.

You are immediately attracted to the book because of the title. Finally, you have found someone, Dr. Gray, who has a broader view of life in the galaxy. Your hope is that he will also have a better-developed view of loving relationships. You already know that his book is an allegory. You have been to both Mars and Venus and know that no life exists on either planet. What you do not know is how Dr. Gray used this allegory to teach about loving relationships.

You also know that *Men Are From Mars, Women Are From Venus* has been purchased by millions of people and has been featured throughout the radio and television industry. If there is such a book as a Bible on loving relationships, you are holding it. It is your last chance to accomplish your mission. Your hope is that Dr. Gray will clearly show you the route to a loving relationship.

Your hope is immediately energized as you read the beginning of the book. Dr. Gray's advice is direct, easy to understand and applicable. He is not a theorist who talks about love without giving guidance on how to obtain it. Rather, Dr. Gray immediately establishes his belief that men and women are inherently different in the way they think, feel and relate. He then clearly states his solution, "When men and women are able to respect and accept their differences, then love has a chance to blossom."

You take notes as you study Dr. Gray's book:

- "A man's sense of self is defined through his ability to achieve results."

- "A woman's sense of self is defined through her feelings and the quality of her relationships."

- "A woman's self-esteem rises and falls like a wave. When she hits bottom, it is time for an emotional housecleaning."

- "Just as a man is fulfilled through working out the intricate details of solving a problem, a woman is fulfilled through talking about the details of her problems."

- "As a man under stress tends to focus on one problem and forget others, a woman under stress tends to expand and become overwhelmed by all problems."

- "To fully express their feelings, women assume poetic license to use various superlatives, metaphors and generalizations."

- "Women just haven't understood that men really do need to be alone or silent when they are upset."

- "The biggest challenge for a woman is to correctly interpret and support a man when he isn't talking."

- "Most women are surprised to realize that even when a man loves a woman, periodically, he needs to pull away before he can get closer. It is not a decision or a choice. It just happens. It is neither his fault nor her fault. It is a natural cycle."

- "The secret to empowering a man is never to try to change him or improve him."

Being a committed scientist, you want to thoroughly understand Dr. Gray's position before making a judgment on the quality of his relationship process. You read *Men Are From Mars, Women Are From Venus* twice. You listen to his tapes and study his follow-up materials and books. His description of intimacy and love is vastly different than how it is expressed on your planet in relationships between men and women.

On your planet, women prefer to solve problems rather than just talk about them. Women also communicate exceptionally well, rarely using superlatives or generalizations. You have female friends with high self-esteem, who handle stress well and rarely become "overwhelmed" by their problems. On your planet, women are very different than the women Dr. Gray describes.

The men are also different on your planet. They value relationships more than the ability to achieve results. They know that episodic distancing destroys intimacy and love and, therefore, consistently move toward their partner in love. Many of your male friends have come to you when upset, wanting to talk and be loved rather than to be alone. On your planet, men cherish friends and partners who love them enough to make suggestions and advise them on self-improvement. They want to regularly be critiqued in love to insure that they are maximizing their capability as a lover. Men on your planet are very different than the men Dr. Gray describes.

You are now totally confused. Men and women on earth relate so differently than you and others on your planet. Time is running out and you still do not have your answer. In the midst of your confusion, you recall a post-graduate history class about an ancient civilization on your planet in which men and women related exactly as Dr Gray described in his book.

Now you understand! Dr. Gray is working with a *primitive relationship model*—a model that has been replaced on your planet by a more advanced and enriching process. Dr. Gray's process is perfect for men and women who have come from generations of families in which true intimacy and love has long been lacking. Dr. Gray wrote a wonderful book for people who want to avoid the pain and effort required for personal insight and growth. His book is inspirational for the men and women who do not know any better than to settle for a very lonely relationship.

So now, finally, you have your answer. **People on earth do not know the keys to intimate, loving relationships.** *Men Are From Mars, Women Are From Venus*, the most successful relationship book in decades, simply teaches men and women how to accept an inadequate version of each other as they deny their innate desire for more intimacy and love. The outcome of Dr. Gray's relationship process is as lacking as the outcomes of those relationships in which the greatest emphasis is on sex, wealth, beauty or success. Each of these approaches fail miserably when it comes to the experience of true intimacy and love.

As an alien professor on a mission, you return to your galaxy. You are happy to have accomplished your mission but truly sad for all the lonely men and women on earth who are failing to find what they so desperately desire, true intimacy and love.

Back to Reality

Now, imagine that you are a man or woman living on earth and you come to my office. You have read *Men Are From Mars, Women Are From Venus* and you are considering a commitment to Dr. Gray's principles. You have also heard me say that people who believe men and women are from different planets will have relationships that are "stuck in outer space." You are well prepared with three specific questions.

I am also well prepared with three specific answers.

QUESTION #1: What is wrong with Dr. Gray's relationship process?

ANSWER # 1:

In his book, Dr. Gray described the "normal" male as insensitive and lacking in his capability of intimacy and love. Dr. Gray excused the inadequacies of the "normal" male by labeling those limitations as inherent and unchangeable. He then described a "normal" female as being very sensitive, emotionally labile and excessively verbal in her relationships. He also excused her inadequacies by calling them inherent and unchangeable. Once he established this limited and distorted perception of men and women, Dr. Gray presented an assortment of relationship principles that enable his "normal" man and his "normal" woman to tolerate each other. Unfortunately, his principles are fatally flawed.

- **Flaw A—Dr. Gray's explanation that men and women are inherently different doesn't hold water.** Dr. Gray presented a well-written argument outlining the differences between men and women, but those differences do not hold up across the population. Women who have the characteristics that Dr. Gray has isolated to men can be found all over the world. Men who relate like Dr. Gray's women are also abundant in many cultures.
  Dr. Gray's position that gender differences are inherent and universal is also refuted through the observation of children and non-traditional families. Younger children often display little or no gender differences while teenagers placed in safe, loving environments often quickly abandon gender differences. Among couples who establish non-traditional roles, gender differences often are reversed. Women who work in an insensitive, competitive environment become more distant and numb while men who stay home to care for children become more sensitive and intimate. These observations of children and non-traditional homes support the belief that gender differences are environmentally and culturally induced rather than inherent.

- **Flaw B—Dr. Gray's process results in tolerable rather than passionate relationships.**
  Dr. Gray's book teaches men and women how to develop "tolerable" relationships rather than passionately loving relationships. Dr. Gray teaches a process of acceptance and denial in which both men and women learn to accept the inadequacies of their partner as inherent and unchangeable and to deny their own need for true intimacy and love. In other words, he teaches couples how to put up with each other's limitations. The most limited person in the relationship, therefore, determines the quality of the relationship.

- **Flaw C—What about the men and women who do not "fit" Dr. Gray's stereotypes?**
  What does a sensitive, verbal man do? Should he listen to Dr. Gray and learn to numb and distance like the "normal" members of his gender? And what does a "numb," non-verbal female do? Should she follow Dr. Gray's model and attempt to become overwhelmed by problems and talk irrationally like the "normal" women around her? What is the plan for two sensitive, verbal people relating to each other? Should they both act like Dr. Gray's normal woman by taking turns being overwhelmed and hysterically rambling with each other? Dr. Gray's erroneous assumptions and model ignore these questions and many others.

QUESTION # 2: What can I expect with your relationship process?

ANSWER #2:
Imagine that you are a man or woman on earth living in an intimate and loving relationship—not a tolerable relationship

but a passionately loving relationship in which the highlight of your day is being with your lover.

Imagine a relationship in which sex is consistently great— not as the foundation to the relationship, but as a result of a foundation of true love. Imagine a relationship that involves two people committed to the hard work and personal growth necessary to achieve the highest level of intimacy and love. Imagine a relationship in which your partner's primary focus is helping you experience how wonderful, beautiful and precious you are. If you desire the relationship you are imagining, then *The Seven Steps to Passionate Love* is for you.

The underlying premise is simple:

Men and women are inherently the same: sensitive, vulnerable spiritual beings created to intimately experience and share love in relationships.

Both men and women have strayed from their inherent nature out of a need to survive in a world significantly lacking in love. Because men have drifted further from their true nature, it now appears to many that men and women are inherently different. The acceptance of these differences as unchangeable has further sabotaged the process of true intimacy and love. Consequently, we now live in a world where most couples have no idea of the quality of love that is available in a relationship.

The Seven Steps to Passionate Love will energize your relationships with the highest quality of love. No matter what your current relationship pattern is, you will learn how to passionately love your partner. You will be taught the truth about love and the process needed to experience it. You will learn how to overcome your developmental inadequacies and how to progressively mature in your capability of love. You will receive an in-depth and detailed description of a passionately, loving relationship along with a road map to experience it. In the end, you will think, act and experience like the passionate lover that you were created to be.

QUESTION #3: What inspired the development of the relationship process you teach?

ANSWER #3:

The development of the relationship model I teach was inspired by my personal experience in relationships and my professional evaluation of thousands of relationships. As a medical doctor and relationship therapist, my quest was to assist and inspire people to maximize the quality of their life. To achieve my goal, I had to first discover and define the keys to lasting value and fulfillment. I then had to develop a specific, objective process that would enable a committed person to achieve and maintain lasting fulfillment and value.

At the beginning of my journey, I had experienced the value of achievement, marriage, children and a committed religious life. I was satisfied and believed that I understood the keys to true fulfillment. My expectation was that I would be teaching people how to acquire what I already had. Working in an intensive treatment setting changed my whole perspective on life, love and relationships.

Daily, for over five years, I directed a two to three hour group designed to teach emotionally hurting people how to heal. My principle role was to push the participants to become sensitive, vulnerable and passionately intimate with each other. As the leader of the group, I also became more sensitive, vulnerable and intimate with the members of the group, many of whom would attend the group daily for six weeks and longer. I began to observe and experience a level of intimacy and love that I hadn't known existed. The experience was wonderful, powerful and more fulfilling than anything I had ever been involved in.

I also directed a weekly family group, consisting of as many as one hundred participants, focused on teaching families how to achieve the intimacy and love that I daily enjoyed in my treatment group. The family groups were so powerful that we would go for up to six hours without a break. Lives changed, healing occurred and my understanding of this unique experience of intimacy and love solidified.

The experiences in the intensive treatment process and the family group changed my life. I no longer was satisfied. I had discovered something far more valuable and fulfilling than my achievements, marriage, children and religious life. I wanted the daily experience of this passionate intimacy and love with my wife, children and friends. I also desired to share my discovery with others.

I am now ten years into my journey. I have watched thousands of individuals, couples and families change. I have experienced a new and markedly more fulfilling quality of life through relationships with my wife, children and intimate friends. I am more convinced than ever that I am living and teaching the truth. **This book is my opportunity to share the truth I now know and experience with you.**

What if you do not believe that it is possible to maintain passionate love in a long-term relationship? What if you believe that men and women are inherently so different that those differences cannot be overcome? In either case, I encourage you to take my one-year challenge: Live *The Seven Steps to Passionate Love* as defined in this book for one year. If at the end of that year, the quality of your relationship is not dramatically better, then decide this process will not work.

I guarantee that you will come to the conclusion that *The*

Seven Steps to Passionate Love does work. Having taught hundreds of couples to live passionately in love, I have never had a single couple who did not experience a dramatic improvement in the quality of their relationship after dedicating themselves to this model for one year. This process always works because it aligns you with the purpose of your creation as a **sensitive, vulnerable spiritual being prospering in love.**

This book teaches you the process in clear, consecutive steps and exercises:

Step 1: Know What Love Is:
Discover the full nature and qualities of love.

Step 2: Know Who You Are:
Learn the truth that you are a spiritual being experiencing the world through a body and mind and how to return to the spiritual state in which you were created to live.

Step 3: Love Factors:
Explore the five critical factors that determine the flow of love in your relationship.

Step 4: Establish A Foundation:
Take the steps to secure the foundation for your passionate, loving relationship.

Step 5: Communicate Love in Words and Touch:
Build on your foundation through the promotion of loving communication, the elimination of destructive communication and the consistent experience of daily touch and heavenly sex.

Step 6: Emotionally Heal Your Emotions:
Acquire a new view of feelings, thoughts and emotions and an effective plan to eliminate the emotional baggage of your past.

Step 7: Problem-Solving in Love:
> Protect your intimacy and love by turning relationship problems into an opportunity for maturity and growth.

It is important to understand that the purpose of this book is to change your life by changing the way you relate in your most intimate relationships. This is not a book on philosophy. This is a relationship manual where you will learn exactly what you need to do on a daily basis to experience and maintain passionate intimacy and love in your life. When you finish reading the book, you will be clear about what you need to be doing to live and relate as a passionate lover.

I emphasize this point because I often hear relationship therapists tell clients to love each other as if it happens naturally. Love does not happen naturally or spontaneously.

Love results from specific decisions made and actions taken by individuals in a relationship.
Love grows when individuals grow beyond their developmental issues.
Love matures when individuals mature emotionally and spiritually.

In this book, you will learn the decisions that you need to make and actions that you need to take to become a passionate lover.

You will learn what it means to love your partner, how to assess your capability of love, what to do to be a better lover and what to do if the process is not working. You will also be taught an emotional and spiritual maturation process that is necessary for your development as a lover.

The Seven Steps to Passionate Love empowers you with the specific steps to develop and maintain passionate intimacy and love in your relationships.

Whatever your current relationship status, you will benefit from this process.

$Step \quad 1$

*Love is an experience, a spiritual experience,
not a cognitive understanding.*

KNOW WHAT LOVE IS

"Dr. Van Horn, Sherry needs medicine. She has gone crazy!" John cried into the phone.

"Crazy? What do you mean, crazy?" I gently asked.

"She wants to talk—to talk about everything: our marriage, our children, our relationship. She keeps telling me that she wants to live The Seven Steps to Passionate Love *of yours." John paused for a breath. "Everybody thinks that she has gone off the deep end."*

"Who's everybody?" I interrupted.

"Me, my family, her family. She is telling everyone about this new kind of love. She just won't shut up with me. She's telling me that I need to hold her, talk nice to her, sit and listen to her. She's got this homework she wants me to do. Dr. Van Horn, she even wants me to cry-for no reason-just cry because you say it is good." John's voice grew louder with every sentence. "Cry? Me? That's crazy! I haven't cried in thirty years. That's crazy, right Dr. Van Horn?"

"Calm down, John," I softly said. "I can't evaluate Sherry by phone. If she needs medicine, I certainly want her

to have it." I could hear John nervously panting into the phone. He had awakened me at 6:30 AM, Saturday, with his call. "Where is she now?" I asked.

"That is just it, Dr. Van Horn. That is why I called. Sherry left me. Can you believe it? After twenty-five years, she left me last night. I thought for sure she was coming back. I sat up all night waiting for her. She is still not here. After calling everyone I know, I called you. I am really worried. I know she has lost her mind."

Although John was convinced of Sherry's insanity, I was equally convinced that her mind was fine. I had just seen Sherry on Wednesday during a follow-up group. I had also spent four days with her on the previous weekend during my intimacy and love workshop. Sherry had never displayed any signs of mental instability. I was more worried about John's state of mind at this point.

"John, it is obvious that you are really concerned about Sherry but there really is little you can do but wait for her to call. You can try to get her committed to a hospital but you need a doctor for that."

"That is what you are for, Dr. Van Horn."

"John, I couldn't commit Sherry at this point. The last time I saw her she was fine. If you find her this weekend, have me paged and I will talk to her. If you don't, call my office on Monday."

The weekend ended with no further calls from John; but, on Monday afternoon, he and Sherry were at my office for an appointment. It took less than two minutes to know that Sherry was not the problem. John looked exhausted, sitting in my office wearing a severely wrinkled, previously starched white shirt. His eyes were bloodshot, his hair

*matted and he looked like he hadn't slept in days. "John,"
I sympathetically said, "You look awful."*

*Struggling to keep his eyes open, John replied, "Dr. Van
Horn, I have not slept since Sherry left on Friday night. I
want her home. She refuses to come back home."*

*I turned to Sherry, smiled and asked, "Why did you
leave, Sherry?"*

*"Dr. Van Horn," Sherry firmly responded, "I am tired of
living in a lonely marriage. John is a good man but he is a
sorry lover. He thinks providing for my material needs and
listening to me talk are sufficient. John is often silent. He
acts like I am supposed to figure out what he is thinking
when he isn't talking. He often wants to be alone; and, even
when he is with me, it is like being alone. John doesn't want
me giving advice or suggesting ideas to improve our relationship. He simply wants me to be happy and appreciate
him for his accomplishments." Sherry paused, looked at her
husband, then continued, "John, I don't care about your
accomplishments. I want to be close to you. I want to get to
know you, to communicate with you, to love you for you. I
watched men change in Dr. Van Horn's workshop. They
came in numb and distant like you and left sensitive and
intimate with their wives. " Sherry moved over next to John,
took his hand, looked directly into his eyes and said, "If you
want me back, you sign up for the workshop today."*

*As Sherry was talking, I recalled the last thing I told her
as she was leaving the workshop, "Sherry, if you undertake*
The Seven Steps to Passionate Love, *you will start to value
yourself enough that you will not settle for a lonely marriage. John will never change unless you insist on it."*

*Three weeks passed. John and Sherry came to the workshop.
As with most second timers, Sherry was sensitive from the start,*

crying with every sad letter. John was as expected, polite, focused and numb. A bank examiner by profession, John looked the part. Neatly dressed with a freshly starched white shirt, John sat stiffly in his chair, periodically sharing a half smile with the group. My optimistic prediction was that John would need two to three workshops to achieve any breakthroughs.

The workshop proceeded in the standard manner, teaching the basics to The Seven Steps to Passionate Love *on Thursday, an evaluation of participants' families of origin on Friday, intimacy and sensitivity promotion on Saturday and wrap-up on Sunday.*

During the following Wednesday night follow-up group, I asked John and Sherry to stand. With Sherry and John weeping and tears streaming down my face, I addressed the over one hundred participants, "On Thursday, a stiff and stuffy bank examiner who hadn't cried in thirty years entered the workshop, hoping to save his marriage. On Sunday, a sensitive, wonderful spiritual man who had wept for over two hours on Saturday, went home passionately in love with his wife."

Sherry and John lived a distorted perception of love for twenty-five years. Sherry heard me talk about passionately loving marriages on my radio show. She wanted one. Sherry learned the truth about love in her first workshop. She wanted it so bad that she was willing to leave John if he would not change. John changed in his workshop.

Sherry and John attended follow-up groups for over one year. They continued to maintain passionate love in their marriage. I often had John stand up as proof of how men can become soft, sensitive and loving. Sherry and John no longer have a distorted perception of love.

All of his previous therapy had focused on changing Paul's behavior, as if his behavior was the issue. But it was simply a symptom of the real problem, which was that Paul was a lonely, empty young man searching for value in life.

As a child, Paul had been given everything—the finest clothes, the best toys, a beautiful home and the top schools. Yet he still hurt. As a teen-ager, Paul had what many considered the best things life had to offer, including pretty girlfriends, a "hot" car and a 40-foot yacht. Yet he still hurt. He sought relief for the pain and found it in a group of friends who dressed and lived as neo-Nazis.

When I met Paul, he was 16 years old, with black fingernails and a bald head, which he shaved daily. He wore black shirts, black pants and black combat boots. Paul had chosen my treatment program over jail after being caught in a felony theft with his neo-nazi friends. After brief introductions, I asked Paul what he thought about his life. He replied, "I think I have a great life Dr. Van Horn."

"Paul, I think you have a very lonely life, extremely lacking in quality and in love," I replied.

"How would you know, Dr. Van Horn?" Paul defended himself. "How can you say my life lacks love? You just met me. You're wrong! I have a lot of love. My friends love me a lot."

"Paul, you're right about me just meeting you," I replied. "But you are wrong about the amount of love in your life. I don't have to know a person very long to assess the amount of love in his life. I look at the fruit of his choices. Children who get a lot of love don't choose to commit felony thefts. You did."

"I only did that because my friends wanted to," he said.

I explained: "Your loving friends? Come on, Paul. Loving friends don't help you become a criminal. The fruit *of love is a life of true value and quality, not a criminal's life. The bad choices you've made are a reflection of the severe lack of love in your life, with your friends now and with your parents before.*

"While you are here at the center, I am going to introduce you to a new type of love, the kind of love that is a gift from God, the kind of love that brings lasting value to your life. You are going to learn how to experience love in relationships with your mom, dad and 'real' friends.'"

Paul sharply responded, "My mom, maybe, Dr. Van Horn," he said, "but no way, my dad or God. I hate my dad and his God. I'll never have anything to do with either of them. I've had enough of that kind of love to last me for my lifetime; As far as some 'real' friends, I have some now. They like me, they accept me, they don't complain; they don't push me to change; I think I get a lot of love from them."

I looked at Paul, smiled and proceeded with an analogy that I often use to help people understand what they are missing. "Paul, if I set a bowl of dog food on this table beside a big, juicy, well-cooked steak and then told you to eat one of them, which one would you eat? "

Paul looked at me and said, "That's a stupid question."

"Well, it may seem like a stupid question, Paul, but which one would you eat?" I persisted.

"Of course I'd eat the steak."

"Why wouldn't you eat the dog food, Paul?"

"Because steak is better. Everyone knows that. Dr. Van Horn, why don't you cut the bull shit. No one would eat the dog food."

I countered: "You're right, Paul. No one would choose the dog food over steak unless they had only been exposed to dog food. Once you have eaten steak, you know it is better than dog food. Since you have eaten steak, I have no doubt that you would choose it over dog food. "

Then I explained that Paul's choice for love was more like dog food than steak. I said he was choosing dog food because he'd never been introduced to true love. "Paul," I said, "When I see you choosing relationships that have the quality of dog food, it tells me that you're settling for the best relationships available. It is more fulfilling to hang out with accepting, neo-Nazi friends than to live the empty lie of your parents. On the other hand, true love is much better than anything that you've experienced. When I introduce you to true love, it will be as obvious to you as it is to me that you don't have love. It will be as easy for you to know the difference between true love and what you have now as it is for you to know the difference between steak and dog food."

Paul's problem was that he'd never been introduced to true love. He was introduced to the lie of an empty, lonely family, where he was forced to accept a perception of God without the experience of love. Consequently, he came to hate God and his father and believed he'd found real love and acceptance with the hate-filled neo-Nazis. What he was actually getting from his friends was not any closer to love than dog food was to steak. He was trying to fill the void in his life that can only be filled with true love.

Paul and his parents spent four weeks in the full-time intimacy and love program. Seven days per week, eight to ten hours per day, they learned about and experienced true love. Paul's distorted perception of love was corrected through a true experience of love. One year after leaving the center, Paul continued to live *The Seven Steps to Passionate Love.*

What is your perception of love? Are you settling for dog food?

Do you even realize that steak is available? In the following story, you will meet Lisa who, at best, was settling for dog food.

*"I know he loved me Dr. Van Horn. I know he loved me,"
cried Lisa as she sat in my group for the first day.*

*"Lisa, how could you say he loved you, when he's living
with another woman, sleeping in the same bed with her and
having sex with her? He lied to you for 12 months," I said.*

*"But Dr. Van Horn, we were so in love. I just can't believe
that this happened. How could his happen to me?" Lisa had
just come into the program that day. She was telling her
story about a three-year marriage to a handsome doctor
whom she had met as a 20-year-old college student. The
courtship had been deeply satisfying, with romantic trips,
tennis games and glamorous parties. Lisa claimed that she
had never met anyone who treated her better or who was as
exciting in bed. "I knew he was the right one for me from
the first week that we were dating," she said. Indeed, Lisa
and Steve married after only nine months of romance.*

*Lisa thought her marriage was perfect until a week ear-
lier, when Steve had announced he was leaving her for
another woman. She had been completely shocked. "I
couldn't believe it," Lisa shared with the group. "I didn't
even know there was anything wrong." The truth was that
Steve had been having an affair for a year with a nurse. At
the same time, he had maintained a romantic and sexual
relationship with Lisa. While he worked in his full-time
cardiology practice, she spent most of her time decorating
their home and playing tennis at the country club.*

*"I want him back, Dr. Van Horn. I don't want to lose
Steve. I've never had anyone love me like Steve loves me,"
she cried.*

"Lisa, let me ask you something," I said. "Picture another woman sitting here. I say to you that her husband had been having an affair for one year and had been lying to her day after day. As he used her sexually, he was having sex with another woman. How great a guy would you think he was?"

"Well, I know it sounds bad, Dr. Van Horn, but Steve really did love me," Lisa sobbed.

I looked around the group and began asking other women for their opinions.

"He didn't love her at all," said one woman.

"I think he's a bum, Dr. Van Horn, a total jerk and a bum," another woman said.

After listening to a few more similar comments, I said, "Well, if he's a total jerk and a bum, then why does Lisa want him back? Why Lisa? Why would you want Steve back when every other woman in this group believes he is anything but a lover?"

While sobbing with her hands covering her face, Lisa replied, "Dr. Van Horn, I want him back because he's the only man who ever really loved me."

Lisa, too, had a very strong perception of love. Again, like most people, her perception of love was distorted, and it motivated her to marry a philanderer who eventually left her for someone else. Her perception of love was based on the good feelings she experienced with a handsome, rich husband. Lisa was insensitive to her need for true love and had been raised to accept a superficial, empty marriage. Not only had she settled for dog food, she had settled for rotten dog food. Even sadder is the fact that when the rotten dog food was taken away, Lisa wanted it back.

What is your perception of love? Do you truly understand what love is? Are you like John and Sherry, perceiving love as stability and the absence of conflict? Were John and Sherry experiencing lasting value and fulfillment through the "love" they experienced in their marriage? Obviously not.

Do you have the same distorted perception of love that Paul and his parents had? Paul's neo-Nazi friends accepted him and didn't nag or push him to change. Paul's parents seemingly gave Paul everything a child could possibly want. Was Paul experiencing lasting value and fulfillment through the "love" that he received from his parents or his neo-Nazi friends? Obviously not.

Do you perceive love in the same distorted way as Lisa? Her husband provided good feelings, satisfying sex and material success. Was Lisa experiencing lasting fulfillment and value through the "love" she received from her husband? Again, obviously not.

Although it is easy to understand that John, Sherry, Paul and Lisa had a distorted perception of love, it is not easy to understand what love truly is. To successfully teach you how to achieve the benefits of love, it is necessary that you have an in-depth understanding of "true love." I say "true love" because millions of perspectives on love exist. I believe only one perspective of love results in lasting fulfillment and value in life. That perspective is what you will learn in this book.

As you read Step 1, you will discover that love is a nurturing spiritual energy that enables spiritual beings to experience lasting fulfillment and value. You will explore the characteristics of love:

Love is not a cognitive understanding; it is a spiritual experience.

Love is not simply a choice; it is a capability.

Love is not an exchange system; it is a gift.

Love is not a feeling state; it is a spiritual state.

Love is not simply a romantic experience that fades

over time; it is a growth experience that improves in quality and character over time.

Love does not arise out of a vacuum; God provides it.

Love is not judged by what someone says; it is judged by its fruit.

As your perspective of love solidifies, you will know that:

Love is the Spirit of God
flowing between two spiritual beings.

Love Is A Spiritual Experience

Imagine meeting someone who has never been in water. He comes from a part of the world where water is extremely scarce. Never has he bathed, showered or swam in water. You are given the responsibility to help him understand what it feels like to be in water-to float, to swim, to dive-the full experience. You are not allowed to use water as you pursue your responsibility. Imagine how difficult it would be to relate the full essence of an experience of water to a person who has never been through the experience. That is my dilemma as I teach you about love.

Love is an experience, a spiritual experience,
not a cognitive understanding.

You can only know the full essence of love through the experience of love. I taught a more shallow process of love for years not knowing the full depth of love. Why? Because I could only teach what I had experienced. I have now experienced a depth of love that I never imagined existed. I am teaching you a process designed to assist you in experiencing that depth of love.

I have found that people have an easier time moving into the experience of love if they first have a firm understanding of love; therefore, I have chosen to present an understanding of love before I discuss the process necessary to achieve the experience.

As you read about the following characteristics of love, remember that love is not found in reading. Love is ultimately discovered through experience.

Love Is Nurturing Spiritual Energy

Think about a plant sitting in a room—a large, leafy plant that requires water, nutrients and, most importantly, an energy source, if it is to grow. That energy source is the sun. If the plant receives an insufficient amount of light, either its growth will be retarded or it will die. If the plant receives proper nutrients and sufficient energy from the sun, it will thrive.

Love is to a person as sunlight is to a plant.

At your birth, two beings were born: your flesh and your spiritual self. Your flesh was created to house your spiritual self. Your spiritual self was created to be the center of your life experience. Your spiritual self is YOU. You are not your flesh. You are not a physical and mental being. You are a spiritual being. Your body and mind simply make up the house in which you live and through which you experience the spiritual dimension. As a spiritual being, you were created to experience and relate in the spiritual realm. True intimacy and love can only be experienced through your spiritual self.

Both your spiritual self and flesh enter the world as newborns. Both must grow up. Your physical flesh is nourished with food and nutrients. Your mental flesh is nourished with education and information. Your spiritual self is nourished with love.

Love is the spiritual food that is required for spiritual beings to thrive and mature.

It is common to receive nourishment for your body and mind while your spiritual self starves for love. Your flesh then matures into an adult while your true self, your spiritual self, remains a baby. You are forced to experience life and relate to others through your flesh, not through your spiritual self. You learn to see your flesh as your true self. You lose your ability to experience and share love intimately in the spiritual realm. Your quality of life is dramatically reduced as you are limited to experiencing and relating through your body and mind.

Like a plant without sunlight, your true self withers and the growth of your spiritual life is stunted. Your life lacks the quality and value that only can be found in the spiritual realm. Your false self, your flesh, becomes YOU. You learn to get your sense of value through your flesh. You relate to people who also get their value through their flesh. You raise children who are forced to find value through their flesh. This vicious curse of spiritual emptiness is passed from relationship to relationship, generation to generation.

Love is the spiritual energy that can stop this curse.

Think of love as energy, *spiritual energy,* which you cannot see or touch but can truly feel and experience. Like sunlight, love can flow. If you are in relationships that are flowing in love, you share and experience the spiritual energy and the warmth and soothing power of love. The result is spiritual nourishment for you and the others involved in the relationships.

Through the experience of the spiritual energy of love, your spiritual self matures. You mature in your capability of experiencing life as a spiritual being. You learn to see yourself as your spiritual self. You relate as a spiritual being. You experience lasting value and fulfillment from your spiritual life. Your spiritual self thrives. You choose relationships with people who intimately relate spiritually in love. You raise children who intimately relate spiritually in love. The blessings of love are passed from relationship to relationship, generation to generation.

Nothing but the spiritual energy of love can bring true empowerment to your relationships. Romantic and sexual love do not last. Sacrifice, care taking and role-playing eventually become empty, unrewarding experiences. Respecting and accepting gender differences limits spiritual growth. Only the experiencing and sharing of the nurturing spiritual energy of love brings lasting quality and value to your life.

I have been in groups where the vulnerability and intimacy are so strong that love begins to flow in abundance. There is nothing more wonderful than sharing in and experiencing the warmth and power of love. If you commit to this process, the spiritual energy of love will transform you and the people you love. You will become more sensitive, honest, open and loving. Your relationships will blossom and your generations will be blessed.

Jill was a 26-year-old wife of a music minister in a large Oregon church. She came into the treatment program because she was obsessed with a belief that her husband, Steve, was sexually abusing their 2-year-old child. No practical or suggestive evidence supported her obsession, but she could not get the thought out of her mind.

Jill was raised in a traumatizing home with frequent fighting between her abusive father and her sad, lonely mother. During long walks with her mother, Jill learned how "all men are selfish and abusive." To her parents and society, Jill had always been the "happy, well behaved" child.

She had effectively learned to stuff her emotional pain. The pain was just waiting to come out in her marriage.

When the emotional pain did emerge, it manifested itself through obsessive, irrational thoughts about her "unfaithful and abusive husband." In the second year of marriage, Jill became obsessed with the thought that her husband was having a homosexual relationship with his best friend. Jill would go into screaming fits, accusing her husband of an adulterous lifestyle. The accusations of Steve's infidelity finally stopped with the birth of their daughter. But Jill's screaming outbursts did not stop, and new accusations arose, namely that Steve was sexually abusing their daughter. Nothing worked to eliminate the obsessions or accusations, so Steve and Jill sought professional help.

In truth, Jill was married to a quiet, even-tempered man and a committed husband and father. Steve had never been unfaithful and had never been abusive to his daughter in any way. The abusive person in the relationship was Jill. She was verbally abusive with her unfounded screaming accusations. She perceived the world through the mind of a traumatized little girl who had been taught that all men were selfish and abusive.

Jill ended up coming into the treatment program on three different occasions, each time staying for approximately four weeks. In the center's environment of love, Jill blossomed. She began the slow process of emotional healing, learning how to grieve in an atmosphere of love. Within about two weeks of each stay at the center, Jill's obsessions faded as she intimately experienced love. Unfortunately, the joy did not last and the obsessions returned after Jill left the center.

Jill could not fully emotionally heal in only a few weeks. She could begin the process, but true emotional healing and spiritual growth require years of work in an environment of love. After each stay, Jill would return to a caring but typical church system that covered up emotional pain with smiles. Jill had no place to cry, to be real or to openly talk about her abusive childhood. Members of her church community, many of whom were friends, talked about love but avoided the intimacy and honesty necessary for love to flow. Her husband was kind and caring, but he, too, avoided the vulnerability necessary for love to be shared in its fullness. Within six to eight weeks of leaving the center, Jill's obsessions returned. The pain in her life became unbearable. The screaming outbursts again became a major part of her life. Instead of continuing her healing at home, Jill deteriorated in a life lacking true intimacy and love.

During her third visit to the center, Jill expressed her frustration with the lack of intimacy and love at home. "Dr. Van Horn, every time I come here, I meet the most wonderful people that I have ever met in my whole life. Both the clients and staff are so open and loving. I cannot seem to find people at home who are as loving as the people here. Where do you find all these wonderful people?"

I replied, "Jill, I don't go out looking for wonderful people. Typically, the people who come to me are hurting. Often, they are selfish and blaming in their hurt. I introduce them to love. They become a member of an intimate, loving community where grieving, honesty and vulnerability are encouraged. They learn how to access and share the spiritual energy of love. A wonderful, precious spiritual being begins to emerge and thrive. The outcome is a community of wonderful people intimately relating in love.

"Look at your own life, Jill," I continued. "When you come into the center and engage in The Seven Steps to

Passionate Love, *you are bathed in the nurturing, spiritual energy of love that flows in our center. Your sick thinking and emotional pain stop dominating your life. Your focus becomes flowing in love. The 'real' Jill, the wonderful, loving, spiritual being thrives. The same thing is true for the other people that you have met."*

Finally, Jill understood that she needed a better foundation of love when she returned home. She insisted that Steve start a relationship group with her, teaching people how to live The Seven Steps to Passionate Love. *One year after leaving the center for the third time, Jill and Steve were thriving in their community of love.*

Love is truly a nurturing spiritual energy—a spiritual energy that will transform your life. As the spiritual energy of love flows, your emotional pain and unhealthiness will start to fade. Your personality and talents will blossom as they are energized by love. Your capability of intimacy will mature and you will become the lover you were created to be.

You were also created to live in a community of love—a community where the nurturing spiritual energy of love freely flows—a community where men and women are distinctly similar in their sensitivity, vulnerability and honest communication, and capability of intimacy and love.

The spiritual energy of love cannot flow in a community if men relate one way and women another.

Whether you are a man or a woman, you can choose to value love and intimacy more than anything else in your life. You can choose to overcome the unhealthy relationship patterns you

were taught. You can learn to intimately share the nurturing
spiritual energy of love.

Love Is A Capability

*"Dr. Van Horn, what happened?" Lynn asked. " I worked
so hard at loving Peter, and I know he worked hard at loving me. We were both so committed. We came from broken
homes and we swore we'd never end up divorcing like our
parents did. And now I'm sitting here watching my 10-year
marriage end. I couldn't have tried any harder. Believe it or
not, I also don't think Peter could have tried any harder.*

*"But it just didn't work. We spent time together, we
learned to communicate, and we went out on dates, but the
feelings died away. Peter was just so numb. At first, it was
nice having someone who never screamed, who never yelled,
who was "safe." After all the other men I had dated, many
of whom were abusive, I really felt secure with Peter. He was
so quiet and calm and steady. Then after five years, Dr. Van
Horn, it was boring. I almost wished I could go back to my
boyfriend who used to beat me up, because at least when
he wasn't beating me up, there was someone there to be
intimate with. And I know Peter was trying. I just don't
understand why it didn't work. He was trying. I was trying.
I just couldn't stand it anymore. I had to leave."*

*Lynn was a 34-year-old woman who had met Peter after
breaking up with an abusive, alcoholic boyfriend, whom she
had dated for about two years. When she got up the courage
to leave him, she quickly fell in love with Peter, who
inquired about her bruises at work. Rather than lie to him,
Lynn revealed the truth. Peter seemed so compassionate and
kind that Lynn could not resist his invitation for a date. The*

romance grew, and, within one year, they were married. Now, ten years later, the divorce would be final in one week.

Sadly, what happened to Peter and Lynn is not an unusual story. The first time I had a woman tell me that she'd rather be with an ex who beat her up than with her present numb husband, I was surprised. But after hearing that story hundreds of times, I'm no longer surprised. There is nothing significantly more miserable than being a sensitive person in a relationship with a caring, committed and numb individual.

Peter was caring and committed, but he was significantly incapable of relating on a sensitive level. Lynn was more than caring and committed; she was capable of relating on a deeper, more sensitive level. She desired true intimacy and love. Peter was not capable of either.

If love were simply a choice, Peter and Lynn would have had a great relationship. They not only chose to be lovers, but they worked extremely hard reading countless books, attending multiple seminars and seeing several therapists. But none of the books or therapists ever showed them how to grow in their capability of love. No one taught Peter how to be more than kind and caring. Despite all his efforts, Peter never learned how to intimately relate.

It is extremely important that you understand that you can't simply choose to be a lover. Becoming a lover is a growth process, and it has to be the right growth process. One of the saddest observations I've made as a doctor is couples who've spent years and sometimes decades choosing to love each other, but who haven't come close to experiencing the depth of intimacy and love that is attainable. These couples have done everything they have been taught through the many books and authors who write about love being a choice. These couples have been told that they simply need to choose love for it to happen. Sadly enough, that is not true.

Love is a capability—not simply a choice.

If love were simply a choice, then almost everyone would be a great lover. Even in very unhealthy relationships, I typically find two people who say they love each other. Each has made a choice to love so they assume that love is present. In reality, very little love is present because neither person is capable of much love.

It appears much easier to believe that love is a choice because a choice results in an immediate outcome as a reflection of your will. You choose, therefore you have your outcome and you don't even have to work at it. Sounds easy and simple, but it doesn't work with love.

The development of your capability of love requires hard work. You must work at the process of love even when it hurts and you don't feel like it. Becoming a good lover requires an understanding of *The Seven Steps to Passionate Love* combined with a consistent disciplined effort to be a lover. If you commit daily to the process you are learning, you will see progressive growth in your capability to love.

On the other hand, if you commit years of your life to being a lover, but don't understand how to mature as a lover, the fruit of your work will be lacking. Sadly, most men and women do not understand the process of love and are, therefore, very lacking in their capability of love.

You can be an exception. You can move beyond gender issues, developmental losses and past relationship failures. You can perceive love as a capability. You can learn the steps needed to mature as a lover. You can overcome your deficits and grow in your capability of love.

Will you immediately become a great lover? No, but will your capability of intimacy and love improve over time? Absolutely. Whether you are male or female, you were created to be a channel of love. Being that channel of love is a capability that is available to anyone who is willing to understand and live *The Seven Steps to Passionate Love.*

Love Is A Gift

"How could Nick do this to me? How could he hurt me like this? I can't believe he left me," cried Patricia. "After three years of dating, I thought we were going to get married. I thought we were going to live together forever. I put three hard years of work into the relationship and now he's gone. He just used me. It's not fair. He owed me more than this".

"But Patricia," I replied, "Why did Nick owe you? What did you give him?

"I gave him my life," Patricia screamed. "I gave him all the love I could."

"Love?" I questioned. "You gave Nick Love? It couldn't have been love. It's not love if you expect something in return. Love is a gift. When you expect something in return, your relationship becomes an exchange system, not a gift. What did you think, that for your three years of commitment, he owed you a lifetime?"

"Yes, Dr. Van Horn. I did expect Nick to marry me. I wasn't in the relationship for nothing. I could have been working on a relationship with someone else. Nick just used me."

"In other words, you were exchanging services with

Nick," I answered. "You were doing the work based on what you would get in return. Nick wasn't the only one using someone. In fact, it seems to me that you got a fair exchange: three years of his life for three years of yours. You just wanted more, and he got tired of being used."

Patricia's perception of love is not an unusual one. She perceived love as an exchange system. If Patricia gave in the relationship, she then expected something in return. Many people perceive love in the same way. They believe that if they put time and effort into a relationship, their partner owes them something in return. If they spend money in a relationship, they expect gifts in return. If they are nice to the other person, they expect to be treated nicely in return. If they commit to loving their partner, then certainly, they are entitled to love in return. All these perceptions would be true if love was an entitlement or an exchange program, but it is not. Love is a gift.

What do I mean when I say that love is a gift? I am not talking about the basic expectations and responsibilities that must be met by each partner for two people to co-exist together. I am talking about two specific areas of the relationship.

Area One: The choice to be in the relationship. For a relationship to prosper in love, both individuals have to choose to be in the relationship because they are motivated by love. Your motivation for being with your partner must be that you would rather be passionately in love with him or her than anyone else. Your decision to stay in a relationship cannot be based on your need, your partner's need, your children's needs or an obligation owed. For the relationship to be based on love, both you and your partner must know that there is no one else you would rather be with and have the freedom to leave if you change your mind.

Love is the free gift of the spiritual energy that resides within you that you share with another person. If you are truly in a loving relationship and the other person wants out, that person is taking nothing from you that is yours. If it was a gift to begin with, then it is the choice of the giver—not the recipient—to determine when the gift ends. By the same principle, the giver expects nothing in return for what he or she has given. If you truly perceive love as a gift, then if the gift is taken away, you will not respond by blaming. Instead, you will be thankful for the period of time during which you were loved.

A person is clearly not for you when he or she no longer desires to be in an intimate, loving relationship with you. The last person you want in a relationship is someone who would rather be with someone else. You want a person who knows how uniquely special and wonderful you are and wants to spend his or her life giving love to you. You do not want to be in a relationship with someone because he or she is afraid of hurting you by ending the relationship. Neither do you want a relationship with someone who is motivated to stay because of a perceived debt or obligation. If you have established a relationship based on fear or debt, then you do not have a relationship based on love. For love to flow in the relationship, both partners need to be motivated by the spiritual energy of love.

Envision a man who is dying of thirst in a desert. He comes upon an oasis owned by another man. He finds that water in the oasis is typically sold at $50 a gallon because water is scarce in the area. He indicates to the owner that he has no money to pay for any water. The owner chooses to give him water free of charge for a period of time.

What if the owner stops giving the water after five minutes when the man is still dehydrated and has a high risk of dying? Would he then have cheated the man? What if he stops giving the water after several hours when the man now has enough energy to travel to the next oasis? Would he then have cheated the man? What if he chooses to give the man water until the man is fully hydrated and then request that the man move on? Would he then have cheated the man by not allowing him to stay forever?

Most people would agree that in all three cases, the owner would not have cheated the man. He owed the man nothing to begin with, and the water that the dying man received was a gift.

Like the water in the oasis, love is a gift. If you are truly in a loving relationship, the recipient of your love owes you nothing in return. If you "love" with the expectation of a return, then you are not loving. You are exchanging. If you are being loved by another person, your lover has the freedom to leave whenever he or she chooses, not when you choose. Your lover owes you nothing.

Why would you want to be in a relationship where you give your partner the freedom to leave at any time? Because the freedom to leave is an essential aspect of a loving relationship; it confirms that the relationship is based on a gift, not an entitlement. In addition, when the relationship is truly loving, people don't leave; they stay. They stay because there is nothing more enriching and fulfilling than a loving relationship where the love is truly a gift. They stay not out of fear or obligation but out of the desire to love and be loved.

If you want to have lasting, secure relationships, then become a true lover, a giver. You will be like an oasis to people dying of thirst. People will move toward you, seeking the love you give. Match up with a person who is also committed to being a lover, a giver. If you both commit to a lifestyle of love, you will have the secure, loving relationship you desire.

Area Two: The perception of your lover. The perception of your partner as beautiful and wonderful must be a gift that is determined by the spiritual energy of love within you, not any external factor outside of you. You cannot base your perception of your lover on his appearance, performance, treatment of you or any other external factor. If your perception of your partner is not a gift energized by love, you will not maintain a loving relationship.

Why is it critical that your perception of your partner be determined by the gift of love? Because the gift of love comes from a perfect source and your partner's external appearance, performance and treatment of you are going to be very imperfect. If the foundation to your perception of your partner is love, you will have a consistently loving perception despite his imperfections. The more capable you are of sharing love, the more you will be able to maintain a loving perception despite his mistakes. Instead of blaming him for his failures, you will be loving him as you help him overcome them.

Does the gift of love mean staying in a sick relationship and ignoring the problems? Absolutely not. The gift of love means **staying in love** with a committed partner and helping him with his problems. The gift of love also means **leaving in love** if your partner is not committed to both loving you and addressing his issues. Unhealthy people typically either stay and blame their partners for the problems or stay and enable their partners by ignoring the problems. Lover's either stay in love or leave in love.

Love is the gift of the spiritual energy within you shared with your partner. As you and your partner intimately share the gift of love, you will both progressively become more capable of perceiving the other as beautiful and wonderful despite the imperfections of his or her flesh. The gift of love will also energize the relationship so that both you and your partner are with the person of your dreams.

Love Is A Spiritual State, Not A Feeling State

"But we're in love, Dr. Van Horn. I know it is love. John is the most wonderful, loving man I have ever met in my life. He has big blue eyes and beautiful brown hair. When he touches me, I tingle all over. I feel so warm inside and so complete when I'm with John. I've never felt like this before, and I've never felt this wonderful before. We love doing things together, going places together. I could spend all day with John, every day, for the rest of my life, and never get bored. It is so wonderful being in love." Erica was working hard to convince me that her relationship with John was a satisfying experience.

"Erica, let me make sure I understand this," I responded. "You're telling me that John, the father of three children and husband of eight years, who is going to motels to have sex with you, his secretary, and then going home to live a lie with his wife—you're telling me that he is a great lover to you. Erica, do you really think that's love?"

"But Dr. Van Horn," she protested. "It feels so good. I know it's love. I've never been in love like this before. It has to be love."

"Erica, how capable of love could a man be if he is also capable of lying to his wife and his children? How capable of love is a man who could cheat on a woman to whom he has committed his life? Erica, who are you kidding? How could it be love?"

"Dr. Van Horn, I'm telling you it's love. It has to be love. I've never felt this good before."

Erica was being deceived by the intense feelings she was experiencing with John. In the moment, Erica seemingly had more quality and value in her life than she ever had before.

However, it was not destined to last. It never does when the relationship is based on a lie. Erica simply was involved in the feelings of "falling in love."

If I truly believed that the feeling state of falling in love was true love, I would be teaching people how to pursue that feeling state. Falling in love is a *feeling state* that typically fades over time. **True love is a *spiritual energy state* that matures and intensifies over time.** Falling in love produces intense, temporary pleasure while true love results in lasting value and fulfillment.

Erica had fallen in love with John, but the relationship was based on deception and dishonesty. Consequently, no true love was flowing in the relationship. Love does not flow in a relationship based on a lie. Erica believed that she had the love of her life. In reality, she had a relationship of the moment. The intimacy and feelings of being in love could not last because true love was not there. It was simply a matter of time before the good feelings were replaced with the emotional pain of two lonely people. Erica had fallen in love but had not learned to stay in love.

Is it possible to fall in love and then stay in love? Yes, but only if the intense feelings of falling in love are supported by a daily commitment to *The Seven Steps to Passionate Love.* If your initial falling in love feeling state does not lead to a daily commitment to the principals that promote true love, then the intimacy and intense feelings will gradually fade.

One of my first goals in assisting a couple in their experience of true love is to have them do homework promoting the falling in love experience. Once the sensitivity and intimacy of being in love are established, the couple learns specific steps designed to energize the relationship with the spiritual energy of love. As each person's capability of love grows, the passion and intimacy mature. If the couple maintains their focus on and value for true love, they will not only fall in love and but will also stay in love.

It is the spiritual state of true love—not the feeling state of falling in love—that guarantees lasting quality and value in your relationships. Falling in love is a great place to start, but it cannot be the foundation of relationship. With true love as the foundation, your feeling state of falling in love will be nurtured and maintained over time.

The Power Source

"Dr. Van Horn, say whatever you want to say, but don't tell me that I don't love my wife."

"Mike, if I define love as the spiritual energy that nurtures spiritual beings, is love what you give your wife?"

"No, Dr. Van Horn, that's not what I give her, because I don't believe in such a thing as a spiritual realm, but I do love her."

"What if I say God is the power source for love? Do you have an intimate relationship with God?

"No, Dr. Van Horn, I don't even believe in God," Mike adamantly responded.

"Well if you don't believe in a spiritual realm or God, how could you believe that you are giving your wife the spiritual energy that results in spiritual growth?"

"I don't believe that I am giving her any of that spiritual stuff, but I do believe I love her. I would die for her. I'm committed to her. I work hard for her. I provide for her. She has everything a woman could want in her life. How can you say I don't love her, Dr. Van Horn?"

"She has everything a woman could want? Come on, Mike. Everything except what she desires the most, intimacy *and love with her husband. You work all the time, make a lot of money and you're busy. You do give a lot to your wife, but you don't give intimately, and you don't give her love."*

Love is the spiritual energy that nurtures spiritual beings. The source of love is God. God is love, and without God in your life, you cannot love. You can care deeply about, be committed to, be willing to die for, provide well for, cry with, laugh with, hold and make love with your partner. But without God in your life, you cannot love. Without God, you cannot experience lasting quality and value. Without true love in your relationships, you will always have a void in your life.

The source of love is God. God is love, and without God in your life, you cannot love.

Love is not from a human or earthly source. Love comes from heaven, if we define heaven as the home of God. A person who pursues an intimate relationship with God gains access to God and, as a result, to love.

Think of love as water flowing between two hoses. Go out and buy two of the prettiest, strongest and best quality hoses that can be made. Join the hoses using the ultimate connector. How much water would flow between the hoses?

If the hoses were not connected to a water source, the quality of the hose and connector would mean nothing. Men and women were created to be hoses through which God's love would flow. We were created to be channels of his spirit.

If you and your lover are not connected to the power source—God—then love cannot flow in the relationship.

You can develop the prettiest connection by doing everything right in your relationship, but if you do not have the source of love in your life, the fruit of your relationship will not be lasting quality and value.

What about all the people who claim to know God and are obviously sorry lovers? In my personal search to discover true love, one of the biggest roadblocks was the lack of love within the religious community. Love was not the essence of the religion I encountered and participated in. Knowledge, judgement, inhibitions and emptiness are better descriptions of the religion I knew.

Most religious people have a firm knowledge of God but very little intimacy with Him. The power source I am talking about only comes through a sensitive, vulnerable, intimate relationship with God. Do not bias your perspective of the love described in this book by viewing the lives of the people you know who represent God. Most of them are not accessing the power source and are significantly incapable of true love.

Skip had everything as a child, a beautiful home, academic and athletic success, and parents committed to doing anything and everything to give their child the best chance in life. As a pastor's son, Skip also received a thorough understanding of God. His parents "loved him with God's love" throughout his development.

So why is it then, that when I met Skip, he was a handsome, athletic, 28-year old prospering stockbroker spending an average of $10,000 per month on cocaine? That's right. Skip was risking his life daily to get high.

Believing that Skip had everything he needed to experience fulfillment in life, other doctors concluded that Skip's use of cocaine was due to a genetic predisposition to addiction, triggered by Skip's first use of cocaine. In other words, they believed his addiction was due to a chemical problem in his brain. Skip and his family liked the explanation.

I knew different. I could not buy that explanation. Genetics does not explain why Skip tried cocaine the first time. A man whose value in life is based on intimacy and love would not use drugs. He would not even think of using drugs. You cannot be both a lover and a cocaine addict. Inside every cocaine addict is a lonely, empty spiritual being who did not receive the love he needed as a child. Skip was no exception. Skip, like other cocaine addicts, had been raised in a family where intimacy and true love were seriously lacking.

How could a young man who appeared to receive so much from his parents get so little true love? It happens frequently in the "fake food family." Skip was a product of a fake food family.

What is the fake food family? Think about two children fed two different types of food. One child is fed perfectly fake food. It looks like food, tastes like food, smells like food and even fills you up like food, but the fake food has absolutely no nutrient value. The food is fake, but the child does not know it is fake. The second child is fed rotten food. It smells, looks, and tastes rotten. Like the fake food, the rotten food also has no nutrient value. But, because it is rotten, the child knows it is rotten.

Which child is worse off, the fake food child or the rotten food child? The answer may not be obvious to you, but one child is clearly better off—the child who received the rotten food. Why? Because he would know something is wrong. Both children would receive no nutrient value from the food, but the rotten-food child would have an explanation for his nutritional lack. By knowing what is wrong, the rotten-food child could pursue a reasonable solution.

The child fed the fake food would be in a much worse situation. He would perceive that he had all the nutrition he needed. When his mental and/or physical health began to decline, the fake-food child wouldn't suspect his perfect food. He would be looking for solutions believing he was receiving all the nutrition he needed.

The fake food family also applies to spiritual food. Love is the spiritual food that nurtures spiritual beings. In the fake food family, everyone seems loving but there is no true love. Mom and dad don't fight. They care for, provide for, encourage and are there for their children. But they do not share the spiritual energy of love with their children. Mom and dad are not channels of God's love. On the outside, they are very pretty hoses with very pretty connectors attaching them to their children; but, on the inside, there is no substance, no water, no flow of love.

An extremely talented youth, Skip was one of the top golfers in the United States. His father was his coach and most avid supporter. At age 20, Skip, on a full college scholarship, married the prize "catch" of his school. She was beautiful, talented and pursued by all the "hot guys." He now had it all—a gorgeous wife, tremendous athletic success and a future career as a professional golfer.

Everything changed during his senior year at college. Skip was involved in an auto accident that resulted in an injury severe enough to end his golf career. Devastated, Skip dropped out of school for a semester. Supported by his family, he attempted to refocus his life. Skip then returned to college, got his business degree and put his energy into a

new career as a stockbroker. Although he was extremely suc-
cessful, proving to be as talented in business as he was in
sports, Skip's real dream was lost. As he said to me, "I never
could reproduce in my work the 'high' that I had found in
golf." But Skip did reproduce that high. This time, it was
with cocaine.

Skip believed that he was loved. He was cared for as if it was love . . . Still, he did not receive true love.

How could that happen when both of Skip's parents claimed to have the power source? Although they believed in God, neither parent knew how to intimately relate in the spiritual realm. They had a cognitive understanding of God but not an intimate spiritual experience. Skip learned to pursue value and pleasure through his many accomplishments and successes. He prayed to God, thanked God, and talked about God but never intimately experienced God. Skip received an imitation of love, fake food for his spiritual growth.

Skip believed he had everything, a loving family, tremendous talent and a beautiful girlfriend. He never considered the possibility that love is what he needed. After four weeks at my treatment center, Skip was pursuing a new "high," the wonderful, energizing, fulfilling experience of love.

Picture a large, beautiful lake, so large that you cannot see the opposite shore. Imagine the water being perfectly clear, crystal clear, where you can easily view the bottom of the lake at any depth when light is available. Now taste the water—crisp, pure and immediately refreshing.

God is the lake. The water is love. Through an intimate relationship with God, we become like small streams feeding off the lake. We become channels for God's love. God is the reservoir of love. We are the

channels for the dispersion of His love.

Are you currently hooked into the source? You cannot be a lover without the power source. You also cannot be a lover without intimately relating to the power source. Knowledge of God is not sufficient. Spiritual intimacy with God is necessary. You and your partner must first individually attach to the power source, God; and then, together learn how to access and grow in love.

Flow of the Spirit of God

So what exactly is love? You have learned that love is a spiritual experience, not a cognitive understanding. It is the spiritual energy that nurtures spiritual beings. It is a capability, a gift, and a spiritual state. You have learned that the source of love is God and that you are a spiritual being, created to be a channel of God's love.

As you progress through this book, I want you to have a simple, workable understanding of love.

Love is the flow of the Spirit of God
between two spiritual beings.

Think of a man and a woman standing facing each other. Imagine that inside the man is a sensitive, vulnerable spiritual being. Inside the woman is a sensitive, vulnerable spiritual being. Now imagine energy flowing between them. You may imagine it as heat, as waves or as light radiating from inside each of their bodies. The energy is being shared and experienced by both of them. Love is that spiritual energy that is flowing between the two spiritual beings, housed in different bodies.

Sound strange? It certainly would to me if I was hearing it for the first time. I have had many people leave my groups perceiving me as a "nut." Those same people often ended up perceiving me as a genius after experiencing the love that I am describing. I am neither a nut nor a genius; I am simply a person who has experienced a power that will change your life—the power of love.

Remember that love is a spiritual experience. You cannot simply understand a spiritual experience; you must experience it. The purpose of this part of the book is to give you a cognitive understanding of what you soon will be experiencing. Don't make your final judgement until you and your partner have had the pleasure of the experience.

"Dr. Van Horn," Pete was obviously angry, "I am fifty years old and very successful. I don't need any of this spiritual energy garbage that you been putting in my wife's head."

"Pete, you are talking to the wrong person," I firmly but softly responded. "Right now, you and Sarah are paying me to teach you about this so called 'garbage.' You need to complain to Sarah not me."

Pete was even more frustrated after my response. He had already tried to talk Sarah out of coming to my office . . . They arrived on time.

"Sarah," I questioned as I turned to her, "Why do you want Pete here?"

Sarah started crying as she replied, "Dr. Van Horn, Pete is very successful. We seemingly have everything. But . . . you know that spiritual emptiness that you are always talking about; I feel it all the time. I live in this big beautiful home, can fly anywhere I want to, can buy anything I desire . . . and I hate it. I want some passionate love in my life and if Pete doesn't want it with me, I am through with this relationship."

"Pete, what do you think?" I asked.

Pete, sitting with his arms crossed over his chest and a tense frown on his face, replied, "I want Sarah but I don't want any of this crap that you are offering,"

I paused, smiled at Pete and then said, "Pete, what I am offering is a relationship where you and Sarah are passionately in love—where you come home to a woman who sees a beautiful, wonderful man when you walk in the door—to a woman who would rather be with you than anyone else in the world—to a woman who wants to passionately make love to you every day. What is so bad about that?"

"That sounds great!" Pete, now smiling, replied, "But what about all of this spiritual energy stuff."

"That spiritual energy stuff is what enables the passion to stay. Without it, the passionate feelings will fade."

The outcome of this process is not you and your partner sitting around repeating prayers and chants. The outcome is a relationship where you and your partner passionately love each other as you pursue professional, personal and recreational interests. It is love—**the flow of the Spirit of God between two spiritual beings**—that maintains the passion.

In Step 2, we are going to pursue a deeper understanding of what it means to be a spiritual being living in a flesh.

Step 1 Exercises

• Both you and your partner independently make a list of what you believe are the five most significant characteristics of love. Also, in one sentence, write your definition of love. Compare and discuss your perceptions.

• Make a list of the characteristics and definition of love presented in Step 1 and compare it to the characteristics you listed. Study the list daily until you can easily recall each characteristic and the definition.

$Step$ 2

*You are a spiritual being
and your true self is your spiritual self.*

KNOW WHO YOU ARE

*J*f men and women are truly similar in nature—spiritual beings who thrive in the presence of intimacy and love— why do they appear so different in life? Why does it seem that men avoid their feelings at all cost and women get stuck in their feelings? Why does it seem that men shut up in their pain while women seem to never stop talking? Why is "the guys" hanging out so different from the "the girls" hanging out? Why do so many more women get their value from raising children and homemaking while the majority of men get their value from work?

In discussing "why men and women seem so different," the answers often revolve around genetics, brain development and hormones. Many would argue that men and women simply have a consistently different genetic blueprint. Other specialists argue that sex-related hormones alter the development of the male and female brain and psyche. I am convinced that neither genetics nor hormones are the answer. *Rather, it is the socialization process that is promoting the gender differences.*

What evidence do I have to support my position? The most

conclusive evidence is my personal and professional experience. Since learning to live *The Seven Steps to Passionate Love,*
I am much more like Dr. Gray's woman—sensitive, verbal and
desiring to be loved when I am hurting or upset. My sense of self
is not defined through my ability to achieve results; the intimacy and love in my life define my sense of self. I actively pursue advice and criticism from my wife on how I can be a better
lover. I don't need to pull away before I can get closer. I consistently desire to be intimate and in love with my wife. Through
living *The Seven Steps to Passionate Love*, I have become a much
more capable lover.

My personal experiences as a parent also support my belief that
relationship patterns are not inherent and gender based. I have
observed my nineteen-year-old son transform from a significantly
numb, performance based and pleasure-seeking teenager into a
sensitive, loving young man. I have watched my seventeen-year-
old son openly cry while sitting on the sofa intimately holding
hands with his brother. I have regularly enjoyed the blessing of my
fifteen and eleven-year-old sons cuddling up next to me on the
couch as we watch a movie or sporting event. I observe my daughter and realize that she is no more verbal, sensitive, or desirous of
intimacy than my sons. The lives of my children clearly support
my position that gender differences are not inherent.

My professional experience is equally convincing. I have
helped hundreds of numb, distant, performance-based men
change their values. I have also helped hundreds of women
understand their sensitivity and become passionate lovers
instead of blamers. I have yet to have a man or woman commit
to *The Seven Steps to Passionate Love* and fail to significantly
change. My professional experiences have validated for me that
the differences between many men and women are not inherent
genetic or hormonal differences.

Recent changes in the roles played by both men and women also strongly support my position. You now find many less sensitive women who do not cry easily, who do not want children and who get their value through work rather than homemaking. You also do not have to search far to find sensitive men who prefer talking to hiding and who find much more value in raising children than in making money. Women are taking on roles considered masculine while men are engaging in activities traditionally viewed as feminine. Without a change in genetics or brain development, the sensitivity and lifestyles of many men and women have been reversed.

I am also convinced that any man can attain the sensitivity level of any woman and become as capable of intimacy and love as his female companion. The process I teach does not alter genetics, hormones or fundamental brain development. Nevertheless, it results in relationships where there are no gender differences in sensitivity, capability of healthy, nurturing communication or commitment to the pursuit of passionate intimacy and love.

I do not disagree with the observation that men and women often approach relationships differently. I disagree with the belief that it is inherent and unchangeable.

The purpose of this step is to teach you why men and women appear so different. We are going to explore the relationship between the three dimensions of self, the true purpose for your creation and how childhood relationships influence your choices and experiences in adult relationships. As you gain this understanding, it will become clear to you that men and women are inherently similar in nature.

Men and Women are Body, Mind and Spirit

You are a spiritual being. Whether you are male or female, your true self is your spiritual self. You are not your body. You are not your brain. You are not a well-developed member of the animal kingdom. You are a spiritual being who was created to relate intimately with God and other spiritual beings.

Understanding that your true self is your spiritual self, not your body or mind, is absolutely critical to your pursuit of true value and fulfillment. It is your spiritual self that enables you to relate intimately with God and other people. It is your spiritual self that enables you to experience and share love and to maintain lasting self-esteem and self-worth. It is your spiritual self that ultimately enables you to experience the highest quality of life possible.

You are a spiritual being
and your true self is your spiritual self.

If you are a spiritual being, then what is it that you see in the mirror? What you see in the mirror is your flesh. Your flesh is the house for your true self, your spiritual self. You, a spiritual being, live in your flesh. You are not your flesh, but you do live in your flesh and experience the world through your flesh.

Your flesh has two components: your body and your mind. Your body is the part of you that you can physically touch, your tangible flesh, internally and externally. Your body includes your arms, legs, chest, head, heart, lungs, stomach and brain— anything and everything about you that is physical and tangible.

The second component of your flesh is your mind. Your mind is not part of your body. It is not tangible or touchable. Your mind is an information processor for your thoughts and feelings. It is the home for your emotions.

It is important to understand the difference between your brain and your mind. Although both are part of your flesh and are significant to your experience of life, they are not one in the same. Together, your brain and mind form your emotional computer. The hardware of the computer, your brain, works off chemicals and electricity. The software of the computer, your mind, is the programming recorded in your brain. Thought and feeling patterns of the mind are programmed in electrical/chemical circuits of the brain. The significance of the difference between your brain and mind will become very clear as you progress in your understanding of love.

---

*You are a spiritual being living in
and experiencing life through your flesh.*

The Black Box

To help you understand the relationship between your body, your mind, and your spiritual self, I use the analogy of a black box. Imagine your flesh being like a black box where all of the sides are opaque, except one, which consist of two windows. On the inside of the windows is a set of shutters.

The physical box represents your body. The outer window represents your brain, the physical organ that uses chemicals and electricity to operate like the hardware of a computer. The inner window represents your mind, the software containing the programming for your thoughts and feelings. The cleanliness of your windows correlates with the health of your mind and brain while the openness of your shutters represents your sensitivity to the spiritual realm. In other words, the healthier your brain, the cleaner your brain window; the healthier your mind, the cleaner your mind window; the more sensitive you are to the spiritual realm, the more open your shutters.

The interior of the box is part of the spiritual realm where you, a spiritual being, live.

You are a spiritual being who lives in a body and experiences the world through a brain window, mind window and set of shutters.

Using the black box analogy, you can better understand the relationship between your spiritual self, your flesh and the Spirit of God. You, a spiritual being, experience the world through your brain window, mind window and set of shutters. If you have the power source for love, the Spirit of God, it is represented by an illuminated light bulb, also located in the interior of the box. Therefore, your capability to experience and flow in the Spirit of God is also affected by your windows and shutters.

I will be referring to the black box throughout this book. You will learn how to keep your windows clean and shutters open in later steps. At this time, I would like you to clarify in your mind that you are a spiritual being living in a body and experiencing the world through two windows and a set of shutters.

Spiritual Maturity

When you were born, two beings were born: your spiritual self and your flesh. Your spiritual self, your true self, entered the world as a sensitive, vulnerable spiritual baby housed in your flesh. You were both a physical baby and a spiritual baby. Both your flesh and your spiritual self needed to mature and develop. You probably understand what it means to mature physically and mentally. The purpose of this section is to help you understand the dynamics of your spiritual maturity.

***Spiritual maturity is your ability to experience
true value and fulfillment through accessing
and flowing in love.***

The greater your spiritual maturity, the better your capability
to flow in the Spirit of God and the more you experience the
fruits of true love. The more you experience the fruits of love,
the higher your quality of life. Spiritual maturity is, therefore,
the key to lasting quality and fulfillment in life.

***Spiritual emptiness is your
inherent spiritual void that is present at birth.***

Spiritual emptiness is the opposite of spiritual maturity.
While spiritual maturity reflects your ability to access love,
spiritual emptiness reflects your inability to access the Spirit of
God. In other words, when you are experiencing the fruits of
love in your relationships and life, it is a sign of your spiritual
maturity. When you are upset, lonely or hurting, you are experiencing your spiritual emptiness—you are experiencing your
inherent spiritual void because of your inability to access and
flow in the Spirit of God.

Vessel

***Spiritual maturity can be compared
to an empty vessel filling up.***

At birth, you had no spiritual maturity. Like your flesh, your
spiritual self was a little baby. Your spiritual self was just beginning to develop. You had no ability to access and flow in true
love or to experience true value and fulfillment through the

experience of the Spirit of God. You were born with an inherent spiritual void. You were an empty vessel.

You did not spontaneously spiritually mature. The spiritual void inside of you did not simply disappear. Your vessel did not automatically fill. Spiritual growth does not happen spontaneously; an active process is necessary for your vessel to fill.

Church attendance does not fill the vessel. The presence of caring, committed, "Godly parents" does not fill the vessel. An intimate relationship with God does not by itself fill the vessel. The absence of abuse does not fill the vessel. Religious education does not fill the vessel. Achievements and successes do not fill the vessel. Affirmations, compliments and "I love you" do not fill the vessel.

**The only thing that fills your vessel
is the intimate experience of true love.**

Your mom and dad were your initial channels of love. In a **perfectly loving family**, your parents would be perfectly flowing channels of love. They would flood you with the Spirit of God through intimate, loving relationships. Your vessel would gradually fill. You would progressively mature in your ability to access and share love. You would develop a value system that places the pursuit of intimacy and love above all other values.

As you experienced love, you would develop from the state of a spiritually immature child who had no capability of accessing and sharing love—*an empty vessel*—to a spiritually mature adult who could consistently flow in love, a *full vessel*. As a full vessel, your experience of value and worth would be based on the love that you experience from God and people. You would surround yourself with people who were equally committed to and capable of truly loving relationships. If you were raised in a ***perfectly loving family***, as an adult, you would consistently experience the value and fulfillment that you were created to experience.

Would it not be wonderful if we had all been raised in a ***perfectly loving family*** and were now full vessels, spiritually mature and consistently flowing in love? **Obviously, none of us were raised in a *perfectly loving family*. Sadly, most of us grew up in homes markedly lacking in the flow of love.**

What are the repercussions of being raised in a family lacking in love? The lack of love in your home made it impossible for you to fully mature spiritually. To some degree, you remained an empty vessel, a spiritually immature person. You were forced to seek value from a source other than love because true love was not consistently available. Your capability of true intimacy and love never fully developed.

Growing up in a home lacking in love, you acquired a distorted perception of love. You learned to accept, as normal, relationships lacking in true love. You never gained your full ability to access the Spirit of God. You were deprived of the lasting value and fulfillment that can only be found through love. Ultimately, you were destined to live an adult life significantly lacking in the fullness of love.

Not everyone's life is equally lacking in love. Nor is everyone's vessel equally empty. The fullness of your vessel is somewhere between 0 and 100 percent. Your spiritual maturity is somewhere between experiencing none of your value through love to obtaining most of your value from love.

Is it necessary to know exactly how full your vessel is? No, but it is important to know that your vessel is somewhat empty, that you are not experiencing everything that you were created to experience. Why? Because *if you are not aware of the emptiness in your life, you will not know that something better is possible.* If the best food you have ever tasted is dog food, you will be unaware of the value of steak. Likewise, if the highest quality of life you have experienced is a 50-percent loving one, you will be unaware of the value of a life full of love.

My professional experience has proven to me that most people are significantly spiritually immature and, therefore, significantly empty vessels. They have not experienced any-where near the fullness of love and are settling for dog food when steak is available. Their lives are very ***spiritually empty*** and are dominated by very lonely relationships. Most people relate in their flesh and avoid the vulnerability necessary for spiritual growth. Consequently, most adults are adults in the flesh only.

Most adults are still spiritual babies.

You may be thinking, "I'm not a spiritual baby. I received plenty of love and intimacy growing up in my family. My vessel was filled and I have very loving relationships."

If you are doubtful that I am correct, ask yourself the follow-ing questions:

- Do I obtain my value from intimacy and love?
- Is intimacy and love with God and others more important to me than anything else?
- Can I hug, lovingly touch and cry easily with both men and women?
- Can I openly and honestly communicate about all aspects of my life, both good and bad, with my family and intimate friends?
- When I am hurting, do I go to someone and cry in his or her arms?

- Would I enjoy intimately relating to my partner more than engaging in fun activities?
- Do I feel just as good when I fail as I do when I am successful?

If you answered "no" to any of the questions, you can be assured that you are not fully spiritually mature. You also have something in common with most everyone you know. You did not experience the fullness of love in your childhood and you need more intimacy and love in your life today. Having assessed thousands of families for the quality of love in their home, I can assure you that the vast majority of families are significantly lacking in true intimacy, love and spiritual maturity.

Understand, I am not saying that you did not have caring, kind and committed parents. I am not saying that your parents did not try to give you everything they possibly could. **I am saying that you did not consistently receive the nurturing spiritual energy that comes only from God and brings the highest quality of life.** You did not consistently receive the fullness of love.

You may have grown up a home that presented a facade of love, what you believe to be love, but lacked the consistent flow of the Spirit of God. If so, it will be very difficult for you to accept that love was lacking in your childhood. You will want to defend your family to prove me wrong. You will want to prove that your parents were the loving people you knew them to be.

Before you make your final judgement, read this entire book. Then decide if true love was, to some degree, lacking in your home. If I am right and you do not realize it, you will miss out on the opportunity to experience the love for which you were created.

The exciting perspective is that if you become aware of the love you have missed, aware of the spiritual emptiness in your life, you can still fill it. You can develop relationships dominated by true intimacy and love. You can be passionately in love with your partner. You can have a quality of life that few experience.

Covers

If everyone has some degree of spiritual emptiness, then why isn't everyone hurting? Why can one person in a relationship be content with the level of intimacy and love while the other person desperately wants more? Why can two children come out of the same family, seemingly receiving the same amount of love, and one appear satisfied while the other is lonely and needy? If true love is so critical to quality of life, why do certain people who clearly lack love seem so pleased with their life? Understanding the answers to these questions requires that you learn two new concepts: sensitivity and covers.

Sensitivity is the capability to experience
on a spiritual level.

Covers are whatever you use
to numb yourself to the spiritual realm
or to gain a sense of personal value.

Sensitivity and covers are opposing concepts. The more sensitive you are, the less covered you are. The more covered you are, the less sensitive you are. In other words, covers keep you from being sensitive to the spiritual realm: both your spiritual emptiness and the Spirit of God.

Understanding sensitivity is critical to your development as a lover. You were first introduced to sensitivity when you learned about the black box. The shutters on the black box are a parallel analogy to the covers for your vessel. Both the closing of the shutters and the covering of the vessel are analogous to a loss of sensitivity. Sensitivity is not a complicated concept, but it is, nevertheless, often misunderstood. A major part of this step is dedicated to fully explaining the concept of sensitivity. For now, understand that the more covered you are, the less sensitive you are.

Your covers developed automatically to protect you from the lack of love in your childhood. Your covers temporarily enable you to avoid your spiritual emptiness while living a life lacking in the fullness of love. Covers give you a false sense of worth that feels good in the short run but never results in lasting value.

Most people have a variety of covers. People seek value from multiple sources other than love, such as performance, education, religion, work, children, entertainment and materialism. People also use many covers to numb themselves to their need for intimacy and love, including isolation, drugs, alcohol and empty relationships. Often, covers provide both a source of value and a way to numb.

Covers can be categorized as pretty or ugly. In general, pretty covers are acceptable in most walks of life and do not result in obvious harm to you or the people around you. Pretty covers may include work, performance, parenting, hobbies, academic degrees, financial success, status, and religion. Ugly covers, on the other hand, are not acceptable in many walks of life and often prove destructive. They may include sick relationships, sexual promiscuity, and addiction of any kind.

Traditional male and female roles are simply covers acquired during early childhood and adolescence. Common covers for women have been children, homemaking, and church. Common covers for men have been work, money, providing for the family, sports and sex. Distancing, adultery and superficial male relationships also are common among traditional men while intimate female relationships, gossiping and blaming are more common among traditional women. If you simply view men and women by their traditional covers, you easily could be deceived and conclude that men and women are inherently different.

Why do I refer to "traditional" men and women? Because covers have changed dramatically in recent years. Today, men talk and cry more while women compete and numb more. Many women now seek value through career success and sports. Many men now focus on parenting and spending time at home. Drug addiction and alcoholism are common with both genders and the rate of female addiction is on the rise. Recent changes in behavior patterns of both men and women demonstrate that the supposed inherent gender differences are actually differences in covers.

The supposed inherent gender differences are actually differences in covers.

Whether a cover is considered ugly or pretty is subjective and is significantly influenced by cultural standards or norms. In the last several decades, the acceptance of alternative lifestyles has blurred the difference between pretty and ugly covers. For example, two generations ago, sex before marriage would have been considered an ugly cover by a much greater percentage of people than it is today. In certain parts of our country, smoking marijuana would be an ugly cover. In other areas, marijuana use is an acceptable personal choice. Covers, therefore, are considered pretty or ugly based on cultural standards, not absolute standards.

Although the value of covers is subjective and transient, the value of love is absolute and permanent. Only love brings lasting quality and value to your life. Covers can temporarily numb you to your need for love or give you a false sense of worth, but only the consistent experience of true intimacy and love brings lasting satisfaction to the spiritual void that you were born with.

As you will learn, the process of spiritual growth entails the gradual loss of your covers as you progressively mature in your capability of love.

Losing covers is necessary if you want to open up to a greater experience. With a foundation of intimate, loving relationships, you can gradually lose your covers, regain your sensitivity and mature into the beautiful, wonderful spiritual being you were created to be.

Under the Covers

Mike and Tom were identical twin brothers raised in a home dominated by the daily screaming of their parents. If they were not fighting with each other, Mike and Tom's parents were yelling at the two boys. Although their parents were committed caretakers, dad working two jobs so mom could stay home, the screaming and yelling destroyed the sensitivity and vulnerability required for true intimacy and love to flow. Consequently, both Mike and Tom grew up in a home significantly lacking in love.

Mike was valedictorian of his high school class, an All-American football player granted a full ride to the University of Alabama, and the boyfriend of the head cheerleader. Everyone who knew Mike regarded him as an All-American kid and a healthy, young man headed for a great career.

Tom, on the other hand, drank heavily in high school, spending most of his time partying with different girls. Everyone who knew Tom considered him a troubled youth, who needed to make significant changes to prevent his life from ending in disaster.

How could two completely opposite young men come out of the same family? Was it genetics, personal determination, peer pressure or alcoholism that resulted in the dramatic lifestyle differences? Did Mike get what he needed to have a productive life while Tom got cheated? Was it simply a matter of free will, with Mike making healthy choices and Tom opting for a self-destructive path? Was Mike truly healthier than Tom?

To answer the above questions, it is necessary first to define "health." Most people define health based on external factors, such as career, financial and personal success and the absence of illness and failures. The problem with this definition is that external success and the good feelings resulting from success is temporary and often masks underlying emotional pain and spiritual emptiness. People or families may appear successful and productive on the surface, while emotional pain and the generational curse of the family are very evident on a more intimate level.

In developing a definition of health, I wanted to know what was necessary for an individual to maintain the experience of true value and fulfillment in his life and the lives of his offspring. After studying thousands of family systems and observing at least three generations of each family, I found that "health" is synonymous with "spiritual maturity." Only through the consistent experience of true love can an individual maintain the experience of true value and fulfillment in his life and family. The definition of heath is, therefore, the same as the definition of spiritual maturity:

***"Health" is the capability of experiencing true value
and fulfillment through accessing and flowing in love.***

Using this definition of health, now ask yourself who was
healthier—Mike or Tom? Was Mike truly more capable than
Tom of experiencing and sharing love in intimate relationships?
Was Mike experiencing his value through intimacy and true
love? Or did Mike simply have prettier covers than Tom?
Although Mike appeared to be headed for a more productive
life, was he truly going to find lasting value and quality of life
through all of his accomplishments and successes?

Most psychologists and psychiatrists would say that Mike was
the healthier of the two. These experts would argue that Mike
had adjusted to and overcome the pain of his childhood while
Tom had made life choices based on the pain of a hurting little
boy. I would agree that Tom's choices were destructive and definitely reflected the emotional pain of his development. But I
would disagree with the perception that Mike had overcome his
emotional pain. Mike had simply covered up his pain.

From a perspective of true health, both Tom and Mike were
unhealthy. Neither received much love growing up in an abusive family. Neither experienced true value and fulfillment.
Both were empty vessels, spiritually immature and incapable of
flowing in love.

The difference between Tom and Mike was not their health
but their covers. Mike moved toward the pretty covers of performance, education and sports. Tom moved toward the ugly
covers alcoholism and sex. While Mike was thriving at athletics
and academics, Tom was drowning in his emotional pain and
failures. Neither Mike nor Tom was capable of accessing and
flowing in true love. Both were empty vessels draped with
covers.

You might be thinking that although Mike was not healthy, he certainly was a lot better off than Tom. From a practical perspective, Mike was doing well. But would it last? Would Mike be able to keep his emotional pain and spiritual emptiness covered up forever? Would he be able to experience the full quality of his life? Would he be able to stop the emotional curse that had obviously affected his parents and his brother? The answer to all these questions is no. Mike's emotional pain and spiritual emptiness eventually would show up. Emotional pain always comes to the surface in the absence of true healing. Even if Mike were able to stuff his emotional pain, it would seep into his marriage and into the lives of his children.

Mike would not be able to "cover" the emotional curse that runs through generations of his family. Mike was destined to have significant problems experiencing and maintaining intimacy and love with his spouse and children. I have worked with many "Mikes"—hard driving, successful workaholics, married to lonely women, with rebellious children. The only way to end the curse is to uncover the emotional pain and resolve it through emotional healing in love. Mike was doing well covering not loving.

For healing to last, it must be based on your capability to love, not your capability to cover.

What about Tom? If Mike was in bad shape, then Tom had to be in really bad shape. Right? In truth, when it comes to teaching men how to become passionate lovers, it is easier to work with a committed. "Tom" than a committed "Mike." Sound crazy? It may seem crazy, but it is consistently true.

Critical to *The Seven Steps to Passionate Love* is uncovering your spiritual emptiness—uncovering the emotional pain that you have stuffed—uncovering the spiritual void with which you were born. You cannot become a passionate lover if you do not get in touch with your spiritual emptiness.

Both Mike and Tom were empty vessels, spiritual babies, loaded with emotional pain. Neither had received the love necessary to spiritually grow. Both needed to uncover their spiritual emptiness if they were to heal emotionally and grow spiritually. Who was the most covered of the two? Obviously, Mike. Who would have the most difficult time becoming aware of his need to heal? Again, Mike. And who would have the most difficult time removing the covers and facing his emotional pain and spiritual emptiness? Again, the answer is Mike. Having worked with hundreds of men like the two brothers, I can assure you that it is definitely easier to help a lonely, empty spiritual being with ugly covers, such as Tom, than it is to help the "Mikes," who have no idea they have a problem.

Does that mean that Tom would become a passionate lover? No, it means that Tom would have an easier time becoming sensitive to his emotional pain and aware of his need for help. Knowing that you are hurting and need help is the starting point for healing, but it is not a guarantee of spiritual growth. Tom's healing would occur only if he were willing to do the necessary work. In the short run, it would be easier for Tom to stay sick because true healing requires many painful but healthy decisions. In the long run, living *The Seven Steps to Passionate Love* would be the easiest way for Tom and his future generations.

What about covered-up Mike? Is he a lost cause? Absolutely not. Initially, it would be difficult to convince Mike that he has covered-up emotional pain. The key for Mike would be his realization that experiencing the true fullness of love is better than all his accomplishments. Once he committed to becoming a lover, Mike's ability to accomplish goals would be a great asset. In the end, Mike's commitment would determine the outcome.

**The power of love is so great that you can heal
no matter how bad your past has been,
how horribly you have failed as a lover or how many
unsuccessful relationships you have endured.**

With *The Seven Steps to Passionate Love*, your personal health
entering is not nearly as important as your commitment to
growth. The power of love is so great that you can heal no matter how bad your past has been, how horribly you have failed as
a lover or how many unsuccessful relationships you have
endured. What matters is your commitment to doing the work
that will empower your life and relationships with love. Love,
the flow of the Spirit of God, will do the healing and produce the
quality of life for which you were created.

*Halfway through the interview, I still did not understand
why Paula had come to see me. She had beautiful brown
hair and big blue eyes. Her smile beamed as she sat and
answered my questions. Up to this point in the evaluation,
there had been no indication of pain or illness in Paula's
life. Looking at her, I certainly could see nothing wrong. It
was not until the end of the evaluation that I became aware
of her issue. I asked the question, "Paula, do you ever feel
so bad that you wish you could die?"*

*Paula answered, "All the time—I can't seem to stop
thinking about it. For the past six months, I haven't stopped
thinking about killing myself."*

*Shocked, I inquired, "What do you mean you haven't
stopped thinking about killing yourself?"*

*"I mean that about 95 percent of my thoughts are about
different ways that I can take my life."*

I sat there stunned. I asked myself how someone who

seemingly had everything could be suicidal.

Paula had been raised in a caring, kind, pastor's home. Her mom was a homemaker, dedicating all her time to rais- ing Paula and her brother. Paula's father was as proud of his daughter as any father could be, bragging to everyone who would listen as he described his beautiful and talented daughter. Paula, a talented singer, had performed in church since the age of five. The apple of her parents' eyes, she had never been in any kind of trouble.

When I looked for the patterns of abuse that I often see with suicidal patients, I consistently found none. Paula was never sexually, verbally or physically abused, nor had she been significantly neglected. In fact, Paula could objec- tively point out how she was complimented daily for her looks, behavior and talent. She recalled regular hugs and kisses from both parents. Paula had what appeared to be the "perfect family."

If Paula was raised in the perfect family, how do you explain her suicidal obsession? Could it be explained by a chemical depression? No, Paula's medical evaluation revealed that her brain was chemically healthy. Could it simply be a "bad" chromosome? No, there is always much more than genetics involved when someone is suicidal.

At this point in the evaluation, I did not know why Paula was suicidal so I decided to ask her, "Paula, why do you want to die? Why would such a talented, beautiful young woman in her first year of college be obsessed with thoughts to take her life?"

Still with the same beautiful smile seemingly pasted to her face, Paula replied, "I don't know, Dr. Van Horn. That's why I'm here."

If spiritual maturity is the capability to experience lasting value and fulfillment through accessing and flowing in love, how spiritually mature was Paula? How full was her vessel? Paula experienced so little true value and fulfillment that she was obsessed with thoughts of suicide. She was basically incapable of accessing and flowing in love. Rather than being consumed with the Spirit of God, Paula was consumed with the emotional pain of a traumatized little girl. Obviously, Paula was an empty vessel and a spiritually immature woman.

If you accept the premise that one's spiritual maturity is determined by the experience of love as a child, what can you conclude about the amount of love that Paula received as a child? The answer is obvious. Paula could not have received much true love as a child. Her spiritual immaturity proved that her childhood was significantly lacking in love.

How can you know for sure that Paula received so little love in a home that seemed so loving? You do not judge love by the external appearance of a family. You judge love by its fruit. The fruit of a family's love is the spiritual maturity of its children.

The ***fruit of a loving home*** is that the children from that home, the recipient of the love, mature in their capability to experience lasting value and fulfillment through accessing and flowing in love. The ***fruit of a loving home*** is that the recipients of the love, the children, become capable of seeing themselves as beautiful, wonderful creations of God.

Paula was the fruit of her parents' love. Paula was a lonely, scared, suicidal young woman. Paula was incapable of experiencing lasting value and fulfillment through love and incapable of seeing herself as a beautiful, wonderful creation of God. The fruit of Paula's home was a lonely little girl who wanted to end her life. Paula, obviously, did not grow up in a loving home.

Since Paula obviously did not grow up in a loving home, what kind of home did she grow up in? It was not an overtly abusive or alcoholic home. It was a religious home with a pastor as the head of the house. It was a home with caring and committed parents—Paula was their only daughter and she was their life. Paula grew up in a "good" home that looked like a loving home, but the fruit was sour.

Remember, love is the flow of the Spirit of God. People can be kind, caring, committed and willing to die for one another and still not be loving. Working with families like Paula's is how I discovered the essence of true love. All the crucial ingredients of a "good" home were in Paula's family, yet true love was missing. Paula's parents could not have consistently empowered her with the Spirit of God. That is obvious. But what may not be so obvious to you is why. Why didn't Paula experience true love from her parents?

Once you understand the principles of a loving relationship, it will be easy for you to discover why love is lacking in a home. You will be able to evaluate a family system and follow the generational curse of emotional pain. As you gain a more in-depth perception of love, you will realize that easily recognized patterns of spiritual emptiness exist in most family systems.

Paula's family displayed a pattern of spiritual emptiness that I often see in religious homes. Instead of learning to pursue value through the experience of love, Paula was taught to obtain value through performing for mom, dad and God. Instead of her parents bringing value and fulfillment to Paula by acting as channels of love, Paula was given the responsibility of bringing value and fulfillment to her parents' lives through her performance. Paula did not grow up experiencing her value through love. Rather, she spent her childhood pursuing a false value through making her parents proud.

Paula was her parents' cover. Instead of being loved by her parents, Paula was used by them. Rather than receiving value through a relationship with her parents, Paula gave her parents value. Paula took on the burden of being the "perfect little girl" for mom and dad.

Of course, her parents treated her special. She was their prized possession. You do not abuse your most valued possession. You care for it. You admire it. You value it. Paula's parents did not know that they were using her. They thought that by caring for Paula's every need that they were loving her.

Paula's mother and father knew nothing about true intimacy and love. They knew not to abuse their daughter, how to care for her and how to be proud of her. But they knew nothing about spiritual intimacy and flowing in the Spirit of God. What Paula's parents perceived as love was, in truth, simply Paula being used to keep her parents happy.

Paula was also given the responsibility for keeping God happy. She was taught that when she performed well, God was pleased. When she made a mistake, God was sad. Paula learned to feel good avoiding sin and feel horrible when she did sin. Eventually, Paula learned to keep God happy all the time by not sinning or, at least, by not being aware of her sin.

Paula grew up with a very distorted perception of God. She did not learn that God was there to make her happy through the gift of His Love and Spirit. Rather, Paula was taught that it was her job to make God happy through her gift of her "sinless and talented performance." Instead of learning that the love of God was the foundation for her experience of value, Paula was taught that her performance was the foundation from which God gained value. She was raised to believe that when she made a mistake, she was hurting God and her parents. ***Paula's cover became "perfection for God."*** She performed for God, used her talents for God and avoided sin to keep God from hurting.

Paula's cover came crashing down in her sixth month of college. Paula was dating a handsome young freshman at a religious university. On her third date, Paula's young suitor shocked her by placing his hand down her shirt and massaging her breast. After the experience, guilt consumed Paula because not only had she committed a sin but also she had enjoyed it.

Now, she had done the ultimate wrong. She had betrayed God and her parents. She had lost the purity she had vowed never to relinquish until marriage. In Paula's mind, she was as evil as a person could be and deserved the ultimate penalty, the death penalty. From the day of her breast massage until the day I met her six months later, Paula had been obsessively planning her suicide.

What a sad story? As I write this, I think about Paula and how traumatized she was when I met her, how little she experienced her true value. How much love had Paula experienced in development? Almost none. How much true value and quality of life did Paula have? Almost none. How capable of experiencing value through intimacy and love was Paula? Almost none. How much fullness was in Paula's vessel? Almost none.

Paula was a lonely little girl in a talented earthly body, but she had lost her ability to "cover" with perfection. Without her cover—from which she experienced a false sense of value—Paula experienced no real value. A sensitive, vulnerable, sweet little baby had been turned into a miserable, suicidal woman while growing up in a caring, "Godly" home.

I wish I could say that Paula's story is an unusual one, but the truth is that performance and the avoidance of sin are common covers in religious homes. A value system of love has been replaced by a value system of performing for God. The children in these homes remain empty vessels and are cheated out of the lasting value that comes from relationships with true love. The families appear loving while spiritual emptiness and emotional pain flow from parent to child, generation to generation.

Under the covers is the real health of a family. The façade of love means nothing. Accomplishments, rewards and success have little long-term value. A committed religious life without true love will manifest in the fruit of the family—the children. Only passionate intimacy energized by the Spirit of God will stop the emotional curse of a family and produce the blessings of love for many generations.

If you are like Mike, Tom and Paula and did not get the love that you needed to spiritually develop, then your vessel is significantly empty. Your true self, your spiritual self, is a lonely little boy or girl in an adult flesh. You developed covers to survive and your relationships are significantly limited by your lack of capability of love. But you do not have to remain a covered-up spiritual child. You can begin the process of spiritual maturity by shedding your covers, uncovering your spiritual emptiness and pursuing *The Seven Steps to Passionate Love*.

Sensitivity

Sensitivity is your capability to experience on a spiritual level—the capability to experience as your true self, a sensitive, vulnerable spiritual being.

Understanding the concept of the "spiritual realm" is important to your understanding of sensitivity. The spiritual realm is a dimension of reality that is distinct from the mental and physical. All spiritual beings, including God and Satan, live and operate in the spiritual realm. Your true self, your spiritual self, also lives in the spiritual realm.

Many members of the scientific community actively resist the concept of a spiritual realm. They want scientific proof, "facts," before they will believe in the existence of another dimension. Proving the existence of the spiritual realm is not my goal. You do not even have to accept its existence to benefit from this relationship process. Simply, engage in the process of love and enjoy the experience. Over time, the experience of true love will validate its own existence and that of the spiritual dimension.

The spiritual realm is the dimension where the Spirit of God flows. True intimacy and love can only be experienced and maintained through the spiritual dimension. Any pursuit of passion and love that does not include the spiritual realm will fail over time. The intense feelings of passionate love can only be maintained with the energizing power of the Spirit of God.

Sensitivity is, therefore, your ability to experience the dimension of reality that is the home of God, Satan, spiritual beings and love.

Sensitivity is not simply your ability to feel. Feelings can be a fruit of spiritual forces, but they also can originate and be experienced in the flesh only. If the origin of your feelings is limited to your flesh, you are lacking in sensitivity. If the energy behind your feelings is coming from the spiritual realm, it is an indication of sensitivity. Typically, there is both a flesh and spiritual component to the origin of your feelings.

Sensitivity also is more than your willingness to be kind and caring. As I will discuss in detail later a person can be kind and caring and still be very insensitive. Why? Because you can be kind and caring in the flesh without being in touch with the spiritual realm. And if you are not in touch with the spiritual realm, you are not sensitive.

An atypical example of sensitivity can be seen with physically abusive men. Men who "beat" their wives are often very sensitive. Sound ridiculous? Not if you understand sensitivity. Abusive men experience on a spiritual level; and, by definition, are therefore sensitive. The spiritual experience is one of spiritual emptiness and pain. In the midst of their pain, they chose to blame and abuse their wives. Consequently, these men are both sensitive and abusive.

Sensitivity, therefore, is not always a good thing. If you are sensitive to the spiritual realm and do not have enough love in your life, your sensitivity will result in pain. You will experience the pain of a lonely, spiritual being whose need for love is not being fulfilled. You are better off maintaining covers. Uncovered people who do not have enough love in their lives experience a tremendous amount of emotional pain in the midst of their sensitivity.

On the other hand, covered people who attempt to intimately relate are sorry lovers. Sensitivity is necessary if you want to maximize the experience of love in your relationship. Your covers prevent intimacy and love from blossoming. You have to lose your covers and regain your sensitivity to the spiritual realm if you desire to experience the fullness of love.

Were you ever fully uncovered—fully sensitive to the spiritual realm—completely open to the full experience of love? Yes. You were born fully sensitive, totally open to the experience of spiritual intimacy and true love. Your shutters were wide open. Your vessel was fully uncovered. You were a sensitive, vulnerable, spiritual being who needed to be loved. Your mother and father were supposed to be your channels for love. You were supposed to be bathed in love by parents who were flowing in the Spirit of God.

A child who is loved maintains his/her sensitivity. There is no need for covers because true value and fulfillment are being experienced through love. Spiritual maturity is gradually acquired. Talents are maximized as a reflection of the love being experienced. Loving relationships are valued above everything else because nothing is more satisfying. Intimacy with God occurs naturally because God is the source of all love. A child who is fully loved matures into an uncovered, sensitive loving adult.

What about life in the real world, where all of us were raised in homes lacking the fullness of love? Life in a home lacking in love is a very different experience from the life described above. To survive your childhood lack of love, you automatically lost some of your sensitivity. If your dad was a workaholic, you became insensitive to your need for intimate time with a father. If mom was critical and demanding, you became numb to your need for intimate, loving communication. If hugs and kisses were infrequent in your home, you learned to survive well without intimate touch. Ultimately, your sensitivity and vulnerability diminished to the extent needed to tolerate the lack of intimacy and love in your home.

Instead of experiencing value and fulfillment through love in the spiritual realm, you learned to find value through pleasure and success in your flesh. You learned to feel good by achieving in school, competing in sports and having fun with friends. Instead of being spiritually intimate with your parents, you learned to please them through your obedience and talents. You learned to relate superficially in a world of superficial relationships. You may have been introduced to God, but never have fully experienced the God of love, the God that can only be found through sensitivity to the spiritual realm.

**When you were raised without the fullness of love,
the real you, the spiritual being,
never had the chance to fulfill your true purpose
as a sensitive, passionate lover.**

Bill grew up in a "screaming" family. He could not remember a single day when his mother and father were together that they did not scream at each other. Verbal abuse of the children was equally common. Bill spent years crying himself to sleep, wishing his parents would stop fighting. But the fighting continued. No matter how much Bill cried or hurt, the fighting continued. Finally at the age of ten, Bill no longer hurt. The fighting continued, but the hurting and crying stopped.

As a confident, energetic 10-year-old, Bill would leave his screaming parents, walk into school and feel like the happiest kid in his school. The fights no longer bothered him. Sure, Bill still wished his parents would stop fighting, but he knew there was nothing he could do. Bill also knew that he enjoyed playing sports, getting straight A's, and being one of the toughest kids in his school. Sports, school and fighting were something he could control. His parents' problems were out of his control. Bill took control of what he could, learned to enjoy life and prayed daily for his mom and dad, all by the age of 10.

Bill grew up without enough love. For the first decade of his life, he was sensitive to his need for love. He hurt because he was experiencing life on a spiritual level. The spiritual experience in his home was one of spiritual emptiness, not love. Bill hurt because he needed true intimacy and love, which his parents were unable to give him.

After 10 years, Bill stopped hurting because he stopped being sensitive to the spiritual realm and his need for true love. Bill learned to find value in his flesh through his covers of performance, athletics and fighting. He stopped hurting because he no longer sought from his parents what they could not give him, spiritual intimacy and love.

What happened to Bill happened to you to some extent. You lost your sensitivity and you stopped hurting. Does that mean you became totally insensitive to the spiritual realm? No, but it does mean that you became less sensitive than you were created to be.

Your loss of sensitivity was an issue of survival. You survived the lack of love in your life. You developed covers that enabled you to feel good without love. Covers are good for surviving a lacking childhood, but they are damaging to your efforts to experience the fullness of love as an adult.

To understand how a loss of sensitivity in childhood affects your ability to experience and share love as an adult, you need to be clear on the definitions of sensitivity, intimacy and love.

Sensitivity, as you have learned, is the capability to experience on a spiritual level. A loss of sensitivity correlates with the closing of the shutters on your black box and the covering of your vessel. In other words, the more closed your shutters and the more covered your vessel, the less sensitive you are. The less sensitive you are, the less you experience and relate as a spiritual being and the more you experience as your flesh.

Intimacy is two people relating on a spiritual level.

The least sensitive person in your relationship determines the intimacy. If you are a 100-percent sensitive woman relating to a 50-percent sensitive man, the maximum intimacy you will experience is 50 percent. Until your partner improves his sensitivity, your intimacy will be limited.

Love is the flow of the Spirit of God between two people who are intimately relating.

In other words, love is the Spirit of God flowing between two sensitive people who are relating on a spiritual level. You can have sensitivity without intimacy—a person can be experiencing on a spiritual level but not relating to anyone. You can have intimacy without love—two sensitive people can be relating to each other on a spiritual level without doing what is necessary to establish the flow of the Spirit of God. You cannot, however, have love without intimacy. Nor can you have intimacy without sensitivity.

A "fire hose" analogy is beneficial when considering the relationship between sensitivity, intimacy and love. Consider men and women to have been created to function like 4-inch fire hoses, open channels for love to flow through. Sensitivity would be analogous to the openness of each hose. The more open the hose, the greater the sensitivity. At birth, each of us was a fully open 4-inch hose. During our childhood, our hoses slowly filled with calcification in response to the emotional pain and lack of love in our homes. As adults, we have varying degrees of calcification. The more calcified our hose, the less our sensitivity.

Picture you and your partner as two 4-inch fire hoses. You, a 25% calcified hose, are 75% sensitive and can flow with a 3-inch stream of water. Your partner, a half-clogged hose, is 50%

sensitive and can flow with a maximum of a 2-inch stream. Intimacy in your relationship can be understood by matching the open ends of your hoses together. Your intimacy is analogous to the largest opening that the two hoses have in common, which in this example is 50% because of your partner, the half-clogged hose. Without an increase in your partner's sensitivity, you could not improve the intimacy in the relationship.

Let's also use this same example to better understand love. Love is analogous to the flow of water between the hoses. The maximum flow of water is determined by the largest common opening which, again, is limited to 50% by your partner's sensitivity, the half-clogged hose. The maximum flow of love, therefore, is limited by the maximum degree of intimacy, which is determined by the least sensitive person.

To solidify your understanding of how your sensitivity affects your ability to flow in the Spirit of God, look again at the analogies that you have learned: the black box, the vessel with covers and the fire hoses. In these analogies, the loss of sensitivity can be correlated to the shutters closing on the black box, the development of covers on the vessel or the calcification of the fire hose.

The more the shutters on your black box close, the less sensitive you are and the less the light of God can flow to and from your spiritual self. The more extensively you develop covers to your vessel, the less sensitive you are and the less you experience life as a spiritual being. The less you experience life as a spiritual being, the less you are open to the experience of true love. The more calcified your hose, the less sensitive you are and the smaller the opening for love to flow through. The smaller the opening for love to flow through, the less capable of intimacy and love you are. Using any of these three analogies, it is easy to see that sensitivity is critical to *The Seven Steps to Passionate Love.*

Impact of Decreasing Sensitivity

The loss of sensitivity and its detrimental effects are obvious in many different areas of society. The most glaring example is the significant insensitivity of most men. In general, men tend to loose their sensitivity more extensively than women and earlier in their development. Boys are taught to be tough, strong, and independent. They are taught to be brave and not cry. Boys are taught that their role in society is to take care of and provide for the "weaker" members of the family. Boys are taught how to survive in a competitive world. Most boys learn their lessons well. By the time they are adults, most boys have become significantly numb.

Equally sad and even more detrimental is the recent movement to help girls be more like boys. When women were predominantly homemakers, some degree of sensitivity was maintained through the mother-child relationship. Sensitive, caring mothers were admired. Intimacy with children and girlfriends enabled women to tolerate their numb husbands. As women have entered the workplace and taken on the role of co-providers, sensitivity has significantly decreased in the home. Now, girls are encouraged to harden themselves so they can compete in the workplace and are learning to perceive insensitivity as a sign of strength, not as the curse it truly is.

With both parents working, the lack of spiritual sensitivity in the home has increased, devastating family systems and undermining social values. A loss of sensitivity to the spiritual realm means a loss of sensitivity to true love and an increased need for covers. Children are being forced to acquire covers earlier in development and more extensively than ever before.

Currently, the most popular covers are associated with the experience of pleasure. Parents have taken on the role of providers of pleasure rather than channels of love. The average child spends far more time being entertained than being loved. Proof of this can be seen in the success of the entertainment and retail industries. Children thrive on all forms of entertainment including computers, the Internet, television, radio, books, movies, sports and music. Children also spend more money on retail purchases than ever before. The high of entertainment and materialism temporarily enable children to avoid the spiritual emptiness in their lives. But it doesn't last. As the thrills of "healthy" entertainment wear off, more destructive and perverted forms of entertainment are pursued.

Sex, drugs, alcohol and violence are some of the more prevalent and destructive forms of entertainment that have become covers in many of our children's lives. The recent high school shootings stimulated a new focus on these destructive behaviors, but the true cause and answer are being missed. The cause is a lack of sensitivity and love in the homes of these children. The answer is sensitive, intimate, loving relationships.

The lack of intimacy and love in homes creates a vicious generational curse. When a child learns to survive without love by numbing through covers, his lack of spiritual sensitivity prevents him from finding true love as an adult. He develops relationships in the flesh with people who are equally lacking in spiritual sensitivity. He raises children who learn to survive by becoming spiritually numb. Each generation becomes less in touch with the spiritual realm and less capable of love. We are now many generations into this cycle. Consequently, it is difficult to find spiritually sensitive families where intimacy and love are the primary values.

What about religious families? Religious people claim to be sensitive, caring and intimate with God. Are they truly? After studying hundreds of families, most of whom were religious, I am convinced that the vast majority of religious homes are markedly lacking in spiritual sensitivity and true love. Religious people talk love while living materialistic and performance-based values. Parents in religious homes place much greater emphasis on education for their children than intimacy with their children. Religious people also value church attendance and righteous performance for God far more than spiritual intimacy with people and God. Most religious families have a commitment to love but lack the spiritual sensitivity necessary to flow in love.

Can the generational curse be stopped in your family? Absolutely, but only if you and your spouse are willing to do the work necessary to stop the curse. You cannot continue to live in a spiritually insensitive relationship. You must learn and apply the principles that will enable you to get your shutters open, your covers off and your hose wide open. You must return to the state of a sensitive, vulnerable child, the state in which you were created to live. You must learn to live a life where true love, the flow of the Spirit of God, is the foundation to your existence. If you do so, your loving home will be the first of many generations of truly loving homes.

What is the cost?

If being sensitive and vulnerable in *The Seven Steps to Passionate Love* is so wonderful, why is it so rare to find a couple who are sensitive and vulnerable? Why not return to that state of a newborn child and become fully sensitive again?

Why not? Because it hurts. Regaining your sensitivity is a painful process. It is painful to be vulnerable when you have been hurt in the past. It hurts to trust when you have been betrayed in the past. It is painful to give up covers when those covers have enabled you to survive for so many years.

Remember, the reason you lost your sensitivity and developed covers was to stop hurting. The closure of your shutters enabled you to numb to the emotional pain and spiritual emptiness that existed in your childhood home. As you have learned, the loss of sensitivity reduces both your experience of emotional pain and your capability to experience the fullness of love. It would be reasonable, therefore, to conclude that an increase in sensitivity would be a wonderful experience. Ultimately, that conclusion is true. Initially, an increase in sensitivity is painful and difficult.

The loss of sensitivity reduces both your experience of emotional pain and your capability to experience the fullness of love. Initially, an increase in sensitivity is painful and difficult.

When your shutters first open, you are opened up to emotional pain that has been covered up since your early childhood. You are exposed to pain that you may not even know you have, pain that you stopped feeling as a young child. When you take off your covers, what is revealed is a lonely, hurting child who desperately needs to be loved.

Jack was a 35-year-old medical doctor, father of three children and husband of 10 years. He worked as a family practitioner in a small town in California. Jack had the typical profile of a medical doctor, hard working, intelligent, competitive and successful in many areas of his life.

Jack enrolled in The Seven Steps to Passionate Love *workshop upon the request of his wife, Mary. For years, Mary had complained that Jack was emotionally numb. Jack did not agree. He did not perceive himself as numb.*

Rather, he believed that the problem was that Mary was "too sensitive." Jack came to the workshop hoping to fix Mary's sensitivity.

During the second day of the workshop, Jack read the story of the "highs" and "lows" of his life. Jack described a childhood family loaded with emotional pain. His father was an alcoholic. His mother was a rage-aholic who regularly screamed at Jack and his two siblings. The curse of the family was evident in the adult lives of Jack's siblings. His brother was actively abusing drugs in his second marriage. His sister had divorced her alcoholic husband, only to marry an emotionally and verbally abusive man.

Jack, on the other hand, never used drugs or alcohol. He excelled both athletically and academically. Jack married his high-school sweetheart, Mary, earned a full academic scholarship to college, finished in the top ten of his medical school class and was immediately successful as a family doctor.

Even at home, Jack was a success. Although Mary believed Jack was numb, she readily acknowledged his many wonderful attributes as a father and husband. He never yelled. He was a great provider. Jack coached his children in soccer and basketball. He was sexually faithful to his wife despite daily offers from attractive nurses. Overall, Jack was a committed father and husband.

So what was the problem? Since Jack had apparently overcome the emotional pain of his unhealthy family, why not leave him alone? The problem was that Jack had simply stuffed the pain. Jack was numb and he did not know it. But Mary did. Every day, Mary experienced the loneliness of being married to a numb husband. She wanted more. Mary was willing to give up the big house, the nice cars and the prestige of being a doctor's wife. She wanted passionate love, and she decided to find it with or without Jack. Mary saw the workshop as their last chance.

The third day of the workshop was the day for uncovering. It was time to find the "real" Jack, the lonely, empty spiritual child who had been cheated out of love. As requested, Jack read a letter describing the worst fight he had ever witnessed between his parents. At the beginning of his letter, Jack calmly described the horrible experience of being a little boy watching the two most important people in his life verbally rip each other apart. As he read about the their fight, Jack recalled looking out his living room window to watch his father drive down the street after announcing that he was going to "end his miserable life."

As Jack remembered that experience, an amazing transformation took place. The calm, confident, adult Jack broke down into a sobbing, needy little boy. Jack pulled his legs to his chest, stuck his head between his knees and sobbed for the next 45 minutes as other group members lovingly touched him.

What happened to Jack? The incredible sad memory of watching his suicidal father leave home ripped away Jack's covers. Underneath the covers was the "real" Jack, a sensitive, vulnerable, hurting spiritual being who had been cheated out of a childhood of intimacy and love.

Jack's grieving was the beginning of a transformation in his marriage. In just four days, his sensitivity dramatically improved. For the first time, Jack and Mary were truly intimate. Their shutters were open and their vessels uncovered. Both Jack and Mary had become two wide-open fire hoses learning to flow in love.

It hurts to become more sensitive, to uncover pain you worked so hard to survive. Nevertheless, the hurt is worth the reward. If you become more sensitive in an environment of love, the emotional pain will slowly heal and the spiritual emptiness will gradually be replaced by the experience of true love. You, your spouse, your immediate family and the generations to come will all have a much greater quality of life. In the short run, regaining your sensitivity is a painful process. In the long run, the benefits of the increased sensitivity far outweigh the initial cost.

Are You Numb and Caring?

Betsy was truly stuck despite more than five years of individual therapy and three years of marital therapy. Betsy could not stop hurting without medications that made her feel drugged. Both her doctor and husband wanted her to stay on the medications. Betsy wanted off the medications, but every time she tried, she became overwhelmed with emotional pain. Betsy concluded that she had no choice: she would have to live a life of a "medication zombie."

Remaining a "medication zombie" made perfect sense to her doctor. That was his business. Betsy's husband, Mark, was willing to take a "zombie" over a "crazy wife" any day. He could not handle any more volatile outbursts. Mark was elated that the medication had worked. A mildly drugged wife was just fine with him.

Finally, Betsy had to agree. She, too, hated the emotional outbursts. She hated the screaming. She hated acting like a "crazy" person. She hated herself after the episodes.

Nothing had worked except medication. Three months of intensive therapy in the hospital had failed. Five years of outpatient counseling had been unsuccessful. Thousands of dollars and ten years of treatment had not eliminated the emotional pain. The drugs were successful in two weeks.

Betsy came to my clinic for an evaluation because she wanted a local doctor to prescribe her medications. An out-of-town specialist had stabilized her on the medications. Now she needed regular refills.

After I completed her initial evaluation, I agreed with Betsy's perception that she was "stuck." Not because she had to take medications but because she was an extremely sensitive woman married to a kind, loving but "numb" caretaker.

If you met Mark, you would think Betsy had it made. Mark appeared to be very sensitive. He was always watching over Betsy, taking care of every detail of her treatment. But sensitivity is not how well you care for someone. Sensitivity, as you have learned, is your capability to experience and relate on a spiritual level. Mark was superb at caring for Betsy's physical needs, but he was pathetic at meeting her need for spiritual intimacy and love.

Because a raging, alcoholic father physically and verbally abused him, Mark lost his spiritual sensitivity early in life. By the age of 6, he no longer cried during severe beatings. Mark's cover became protecting and caring for his sisters and his mother. He swore to himself that he would never yell or hurt anyone when he grew up.

After marrying Betsy, Mark's primary cover became providing for and taking care of her needs. He was attracted to Betsy's "wounded" spirit. Betsy was attracted to Mark's emotional stability. Their covers matched. As long as Betsy stayed "sick," Mark had a purpose. His vessel remained covered.

Although Mark was a kind, committed man in the flesh, the real Mark, the sensitive, vulnerable spiritual being, was long gone. Mark was numb. He was incapable of relating on an intimate, spiritual level. When Mark related to Betsy, it looked like love, but in reality, not much love was flowing. Mark offered Betsy security, not love, and security does not heal emotional and spiritual wounds.

So, where did that leave Betsy? Betsy was extremely sensitive. She was very much in touch with her spiritual self, a lonely little girl who had been raised by a sexually abusive father. Betsy was capable of intimately relating on a spiritual level. She was sensitive to her need for love.

To professionals who do not understand true love, it appeared that Betsy had all the love a woman could possibly need. Everyone, including Mark and Betsy, perceived Mark as a great lover. In truth, Mark was a pathetic lover and Betsy was starving for love.

That is why Betsy was "stuck." Not because she had to take medicines. Rather, Betsy was stuck because she was a lonely woman in a lonely marriage. Mark was covered, while Betsy was wide open. Everyone thought she had love when she had almost none. Her emotional outbursts were a result of loneliness, not a need for medication. When everyone was blind to the real problem, the quick fix was drugs. I recommended a different approach.

On the first night that Mark and Betsy came for counseling, I asked them how much real love did they think they had in their relationship on a scale from one to 10.

After they thought for a moment, Betsy reported a number of 9 and Mark a number of 8. I looked at Mark and said, "Now truthfully Mark, how much intimacy and love can you get from a woman who is drugged all the time?"

Mark immediately defended Betsy, "Well, Dr. Van Horn, it is not Betsy's fault that she has to take medications."

"Mark, I did not say it is her fault," I replied. "I simply asked you how much intimacy and love can you get from a woman who is drugged all the time. She cannot have sex with you. She is often too drugged to sit down and talk to you. You cannot go out on dates. You basically cannot go anywhere together. So how much love do you really get?"

Mark again went to Betsy's defense, "But she's still a wonderful person, Dr. Van Horn."

But I persisted in making him see the reality of what was going on. "I didn't ask you if she is a wonderful person, Mark. I know you care about her. I know you take care of her. I know you want to say nice things to her and about her. But is this really what you expected when you married her? Did you expect to be spending all of your time taking care of her and receiving little in return?"

Betsy interrupted, "Dr. Van Horn, I can answer your question. Mark gets essentially no love from me. I am a sorry lover. I can't believe he stays with me. I can't stand how I feel. I can't stand who I have become. I certainly know that I don't give Mark much love at all. '

"What do you say now, Mark, do you still think it's a nine?" I asked.

"I guess not, Dr. Van Horn. I guess it's more like a one or a two."

"Okay, I will agree with a two," I responded. "Now let me ask you this Mark. How much do you hurt living with Betsy?"

"Not very much. In fact, almost none."

"Do you spend much time with other friends?"

"No, between caring for Betsy and working, I am busy all the time."

"Why is it then, that with so little love in your life, you are not hurting all the time?

Mark paused, looked away, and then said, "I don't know, Dr. Van Horn. I guess I just don't need that much love to function."

I looked at Mark, eventually making eye contact, and questioned, "You don't need much love to function? When do you think you stopped needing love to function?"

"To tell you the truth, Dr. Van Horn, it has been so long I don't remember."

"Mark, it would probably be fair to say that you are numb to your need for love. Would you agree?"

"Dr. Van Horn, I guess you are right. I am numb to my need for love."

I looked at Betsy who had started to cry and asked, "How good a lover is a numb man, Betsy? Do you think Mark can be both numb and a good lover?"

Betsy sobbed and replied in a broken voice, "I can't talk bad about Mark. He has been so good to me."

"Betsy, it is not talking bad about someone if you help him see his needs. Mark needs love, yet he will never receive it as long as he is numb."

Betsy had stopped crying when she said, "Of course, Mark is numb. You can look at him and see it. I know he is not a good lover, but it was easier to stay sick than to try to make him change."

When you are numb to your need for love, you can be sure that you have lost your spiritual sensitivity. When you have lost your spiritual sensitivity, you have lost your capability to be intimate. When you have lost your capability to be intimate, you have lost your capability to flow in love. You can be kind and caring, but the recipient of that care will not experience true love.

Betsy was clearly sensitive and needy. Her need for true love was not being met. Mark was getting value through caring for her. She was surviving by taking drugs. Once Mark did the work to regain his sensitivity and they both did the work to establish a loving relationship, Betsy began to heal without medication.

Sensitivity is the ability to experience on a spiritual level. For you and your partner to be intimate, both of you have to be sensitive. Regaining your sensitivity is painful, but the rewards are tremendous.

The Biggest Lie

Although it has been 10 years since our first meeting, it is easy to remember my introduction to Max Jones. He introduced himself in a dramatic fashion. Max walked up to the second floor of the hospital where my treatment program was located and requested a brief meeting. Because his wife had been admitted to the program on the previous day, I agreed to the meeting.

As I walked into the conference room, I quickly observed two things. First, Max was a large man, much larger than I. He was at least 6 feet 5 inches tall and weighed a good 250 pounds. Secondly, he was really upset. As Max stood there glaring down at me (I am only 6 feet tall), he angrily announced, "Dr. Van Horn, I have a shotgun in my car. You have two choices. Discharge my wife or die. I am going to kill you if you do not discharge my wife immediately."

My immediate thought was to call security and get as far away from Max as I could. My second thought was that Max was clearly a hurting man and needed help. Since I was in the business of helping hurting people, here was an opportunity. Obviously, I was not going to be able to help him if he killed me. But on the other hand, his shotgun was in the car. That gave me the window of opportunity I needed.

I quietly asked, "Max, why do you want your wife out of the hospital?"

Max immediately went into a verbal tirade, "Why? Why do I want her out of here? Maybe, because I have spent over $100,000 for her treatment in the last 10 years. What do you think, Dr. Van Horn? Is that a good reason? What about the fact that she is sicker than she was ten years ago? Is that enough reason for you? Or would you rather hear that the last quack like you had an affair with my wife?" Red-faced with his fists clenched, Max yelled, "It is your choice. You pick the best reason and get her out of here now."

While waiting for Max to calm down, I sat down at the conference table. I then looked up at Max and said, "Max, I am really sorry that you and your wife have been through such horrible experiences. There are a lot of quacks in this field." I paused to observe Max's response. "Please sit down so we can talk."

To my surprise, Max followed my suggestion. I continued, "Did you really spend over $100,000? That is crazy." Max nodded in agreement. "Did the doctors include you in the process?"

"No," he said. "In fact, the last one tried to get her to divorce me, at the same time he was screwing her." Max started to cry.

I placed my hand on Max's arm and said, "That's really sad, Max. It is good to cry. Obviously, you care a lot about your wife."

"Care a lot?" Max responded, weeping openly. In a broken voice, he said, "She is my life. She is everything to me."

Duncan was a typical accountant, stiff, distant and intelligent. He was also insensitive and numb. His attendance at The Seven Steps to Passionate Love *workshop was a result of blackmail. "Attend or be divorced" was his wife's ultimatum. Duncan and Patty were in their 25th year of marriage when she announced her condition for continuing the relationship. Patty was loaded with sensitivity and tired of being married to a numb man.*

Duncan arrived at the workshop, angry and skeptical. Four days later, after participating in a 40-hour process that included six hours of grieving in an environment of love, the "real" Duncan, the sensitive, vulnerable spiritual being, had returned. The stiff, numb bank accountant was gone. The transformation was amazing. Patty was ecstatic, having finally found the sweet, sensitive husband that she had always wanted.

Joe could not recall crying for more than 40 years. "If I cried, my dad smacked me across the face, so I stopped crying," he said. When he talked about his dad beating him, Joe didn't cry. When he talked about watching his mom get beat up by his father, he didn't cry. When Joe talked about the death of his only brother, he didn't cry. Even when he talked about losing "the love of his life," his 5-year-old daughter from his first marriage, Joe didn't cry. But when he talked about his only dog, Fluffy, who would lick the tears off his face after his daily beatings, Joe cried.

Joe sobbed like a hurting little boy when he recalled that, as a 5-year-old, he had to bury Fluffy in a backyard grave. The letter about Fluffy produced the first tears that Joe had cried in more than four decades. It was only the beginning of many tearful letters.

As Joe progressed in his sensitivity, he eventually cried for the lonely little boy who was abused by his father. He sobbed while remembering his mother being repeatedly beaten and for his only daughter that he no longer knew. An insensitive man who had not cried in 40 years walked into our center. Three months later, a sensitive, vulnerable spiritual being walked out.

The **biggest lie** regarding sensitivity is that men were created to be less sensitive than women. Men were not created to be numb. Women were not designed to be more sensitive than men.

Men were created to live as sensitive, vulnerable spiritual beings.
No woman is inherently more sensitive than any man.

Max, Duncan and Joe are not the exceptions; they are the norm. Behind every male flesh, no matter how numb or unloving he may be, is a sensitive, vulnerable spiritual being created to intimately relate in love. I have worked with hundreds of men who initially lacked sensitivity but became sensitive, passionate lovers.

Am I saying that men are typically as sensitive as women? No. The average man has lost his inherent sensitivity and is much less sensitive than the average woman. Most men lack the sensitivity necessary for truly loving relationships and are uncomfortable in an environment of love. The majority of men also avoid crying, particularly in the presence of another person, and are poor at communicating intimate thoughts and feelings. The reason most men appear less sensitive than women is because, typically, they are less sensitive.

The fact that the average man is less sensitive than the average woman does not mean that the lack of sensitivity is inherent or irreversible. Take a group of newborn children. Put diapers on them. Can you separate the boys from the girls? No! Can you pick out females based on sensitivity? Of course not! Newborn males are as sensitive as newborn females. Can you determine the gender of the newborns based on relationship patterns? Again, the answer is no. Male and female newborns are equally capable of sensitivity in relationships.

Take a group of teenage children. Can you distinguish between the boys and girls based on sensitivity? Yes, but many boys are still very sensitive at this age. If you have a group of teenagers living in an environment of love where sensitivity is promoted, the boys and girls are equally sensitive. How do I know? Because I have done it. I have worked with teenagers in an environment of love where sensitivity is promoted as a wonderful thing, not a girl thing, a sissy thing. Guess what happens? Teenage boys do great. They quickly learn to enjoy being sensitive. Clearly, males were created to live and relate as sensitive spiritual beings.

If males were created to relate as spiritual beings, then why do most men stay so numb? There are two main reasons.

1) *Sensitive men do not fit in our culture.* Think about it. Where do sensitive men fit in our society? Sensitive men certainly do not fit in with other men, most of whom are insensitive. They also do not fit with most women even though women claim to want a sensitive man in their lives.

   A typical woman runs from a man who is truly sensitive.

Women are programmed through the media to move toward the more macho, "strong" man. Women are typically uncomfortable with a man crying or demonstrating weakness. When women refer to "their man" as sensitive, they are usually referring to a kind, caring, numb man, not a truly sensitive man. Not that kind and caring is bad. Kind and caring is a whole lot better than mean and abusive, but it is nothing like spiritually sensitive and loving.

2) ***True spiritual sensitivity is rarely promoted among men.*** Many leaders in the religious community believe they are teaching men to be more spiritually sensitive. In truth, they are really promoting commitment to God and family, not spiritual sensitivity. Why would these religious leaders confuse commitment with sensitivity? Because they themselves are typically committed men living a life lacking in sensitivity. It is very difficult to understand the spiritual experience of sensitivity when you are numb; therefore, most religious leaders are unaware of the depth of spiritual sensitivity that is possible.

No matter how numb he is,
any man can regain his sensitivity.

The bottom line is that men were created to be as sensitive and vulnerable as women. Having spent years promoting sensitivity among couples, I have consistently found that behind any insensitive male flesh is a sensitive, vulnerable spiritual child who desperately wants and needs love. It is truly a wonderful experience to watch that sensitive, vulnerable little boy come forth and learn how to become a lover.

You Can't Be Too Sensitive

Zack was obviously upset when he turned to his wife in the middle of the group and said, "You are too sensitive, Lisa. You cry all the time. You get upset when I don't smile at you. You get upset if a pretty woman walks by. You always think that I am mad at you. You think that I think that you are ugly. You are just too sensitive. I'm so tired of your sensitivity. I can't stand it anymore. Can't we just have one day when you are numb and not whining about something?"

Lisa, with tears in her eyes, responded, "I'm sorry, Zack. I don't want to be so sensitive, but I can't help it."

I interrupted, "Lisa how many times have you been told you are too sensitive?"

"Hundreds, Dr. Van Horn. Ever since I was a little girl, someone has been telling me that I am too sensitive." Lisa openly wept as she answered my question. "My mom used to tell me I was too sensitive all the time. Any time I cried after she screamed at me, she told me that I was too sensitive. She said that I needed to get over it and stop crying. But I couldn't."

Turning to Zack, I asked, "Zack, how many times have you told Lisa she is too sensitive?"

Jack laughed, as he responded, "A couple of million."

"What is so funny, Zack? Do you think it is funny that your wife hurts all the time?" I was purposefully pushing Zack.

"What do you expect me to do, Dr. Van Horn? Cry with her?" Jack defensively replied. "At first, I just ignored it and went on my way. When I did, Lisa just whined more, cried more and complained more. Finally, I had to do

something. I learned to laugh and move on. She really is too sensitive. Nobody should feel so bad all the time and nobody should have to live with someone who feels so bad."

"Have you ever thought about comforting her, holding her and loving on her when she is feeling bad?"

"If I did that Dr. Van Horn, I'd be holding her all the time. I have to work. I have other things I want to do. I did not marry her to hold her while she cried. I married her to have fun with her."

I turned to Lisa and asked, "Was there ever a time, Lisa, when you didn't consistently feel bad?"

"The first six months that I dated Zack. I don't think I cried very much at all, Dr. Van Horn."

"Why do you think that you went so long without hurting? You can't seem to go a day now without crying."

"Well, Zack and I were together all the time. When we were together, he focused on me. He focused on loving me, giving me attention, telling me how beautiful I was. Now that I've put on 15 pounds, he doesn't even like to look at me."

"Were you just as sensitive during those six months as you are now?"

"I think so Dr. Van Horn, but I felt good then because I was getting so much attention."

Zack interrupted, "Lisa, nobody can give you that much attention. I've got to work and make a living."

"Zack, how did you do it back then? Didn't you have a job back then too," I asked.

"Well, I guess," Jack stuttered. "I did have a job."

I interrupted. "So you did have a job. And did you spend that much time focusing on Lisa or is she just making it up?"

"No, she's not making it up. I spent 40-50 hours, every week, with Lisa. I worked, but time with Lisa was a priority. I enjoyed it. It was fun. We had a great time together."

"So when did it stop," I asked. "Think about it, Jack and Lisa? When did you stop spending a lot of time together?"

Lisa responded first, "As far as I can remember, Dr. Van Horn, our time together stopped right after the honeymoon."

Jack joined in, "Yeah, I remember now. When we got back from the honeymoon, we were broke. To pay for the ring and the honeymoon, I had to work about 80 hours per week for about six months."

"If you were working 80 hours per week, you must have been exhausted when you weren't working. How much quality time did Lisa have with you then?" "

Zack thought for a moment and replied, "Well, basically none."

"So Lisa went from spending 40-50 hours per week with you for over six months to being alone all the time. Is that when the whining started?"

"No, Dr. Van Horn, the whining didn't start until about three months into our marriage. And once it started, it did not stop. The little time that I was at home was consumed with Lisa crying, complaining and whining. By the time I returned to normal working hours, I could hardly stand to go home. How would you like to go home to somebody who hurts all the time and blames you?"

Zack and Lisa's story is a fairly typical one. During the romantic phase of the relationship, both Lisa and Zack were experiencing tremendously good feelings triggered by the "falling in love" experience. Lisa's covers came down, her shutters opened and the sensitive, vulnerable little girl was intimately relating to Zack. Zack's shutters also opened; he was sensitive, vulnerable and "in love."

Lisa was able to stay vulnerable and not hurt because of the love she was experiencing from Zack. After the honeymoon, Zack went back to his covers of work, performance and making money. Lisa was left at home, uncovered, sensitive and significantly lacking in love. The end result was that Lisa hurt. Lisa was not spiritually mature enough to experience God's love on her own. She did not have relationships in her life to act as channels for God's love. Without covers, Lisa simply hurt.

As the hurt persisted, the complaining and blaming started. As Lisa blamed, Zack distanced. Even when Zack was home, he was numb and very little love flowed. As Zack distanced, Lisa hurt even more. As she hurt more, Lisa blamed more and Zack distanced more.

The **hurt/blame/distance/hurt more** cycle is fairly common in relationships where there is a difference in sensitivity between the partners. The more sensitive person blames in their pain and the less sensitive person distances in their pain. The more the sensitive person blames the more the insensitive person distances.

The problem was not Lisa's sensitivity. The problem was Lisa's unresolved emotional pain and the lack of love in her life. In *The Seven Steps to Passionate Love*, the goal is for every man and woman to become as sensitive as Lisa. She was fully sensitive, fully open to the experience of love. If you become fully sensitive, you must also value intimacy and love first in your life. As you experience the love that you need, your emotional pain will slowly be resolved and your ability to experience and share love will mature.

What about real life? Didn't Zack have to work? How can people live this sensitive, vulnerable life and still function in a harsh, insensitive world? These are questions I am often asked. The answer is found in a discussion of valusitive, fully open to the experience of love. If you become fully sensitive, you must also value intimacy and love first in your life. As you experience the love that you need, your emotional pain will slowly be resolved and your ability to experience and share love will mature.

What about real life? Didn't Zack have to work? How can people live this sensitive, vulnerable life and still function in a harsh, insensitive world? These are questions I am often asked. The answer is found in a discussion of values.

What do you value most in your life? If you value materialism and success more than passionate love, you are being cheated. If you value entertainment and superficial relationships more than passionate love, you are being cheated. If you value caring for your home and children more than you value passionate love, you are being cheated. If you value church attendance and ministries more than you value passionate love with your family, you are being cheated.

***You must value passionate love
more than anything else if you desire to experience
the highest quality of life possible.***

Why value passionate love more than anything else? Because a life of love is better than anything else. True love is the only thing that brings lasting fulfillment.

If you value true love more than anything else in your life, you will have time for relationships. You will also have time for work and dealing with the "real world." You may not be able to build that million-dollar company, have the biggest house on the block, save all the sinners in your town or be involved in every ministry at church; but you will be able to provide for your family and use your talents productively while you are spending time in passionate loving relationships. The issue is never one of time, work or dealing with the "real world." The issue is one of values.

Let's return to Zack and Lisa. After the honeymoon, did Zack have enough time for Lisa? You probably answered no, but the correct answer is yes. Zack did have enough time for Lisa, but he chose to spend that time at work. Does that mean he does not have to pay the bills that he accumulated for a ring, wedding and honeymoon? No, it doesn't. He was responsible for his debts, but he did not have to pay them off so quickly. He also didn't have to accumulate them in the first place. Zack and Lisa could have chosen to spend less on the ring, wedding and honeymoon. They also could have developed a plan to pay off their debts at a pace that would not damage the quality of their relationship. Again, the issue is one of **values**.

Were Zack and Lisa able to fix their relationship? Yes. Zack changed his work schedule so that he and Lisa could have consistent quality time together. Zack also began to work on his sensitivity. Lisa stopped complaining and blaming. She realized that Zack was responsible for being her lover, not for fixing her pain. Lisa also learned to move toward Zack for love when she was hurting instead of pushing him away with blaming. Finally, both Lisa and Zack developed an intimate, healthy relationship with a friend outside their marriage to strengthen their foundation of love. One year after committing to *The Seven Steps To Passionate Love*, Zack and Lisa were doing great.

You cannot be too sensitive.

Sensitivity is a wonderful and necessary aspect of a truly loving relationship. Lisa was not too sensitive; she simply was not receiving enough love. As a relationship specialist, I would always rather start with a sensitive person like Lisa than a more numb person like Zack. Why? Because regaining sensitivity can often be a very difficult task.

You live in a very insensitive world. There are very few places where you can go to work on your sensitivity, while there are unlimited opportunities to numb. A major part of my work is assisting people in returning to that sensitive, vulnerable state where true love can be experienced.

How do you regain your sensitivity once you are covered? There is a very specific process that must be undertaken. You will learn that process in Step 4.

Value sensitivity. Value sharing and experiencing in the spiritual realm. Learn to live and relate as the spiritual being that you truly are instead of the covers that you were forced to take on.

If you are presently sensitive, be thankful and energize your sensitivity with love. If you are hurting, know that it is not because you are too sensitive. You simply need more love. If you are lacking in sensitivity, realize that you are being cheated. A greater quality of life is available to you through the sensitive experience of love. Do the work to regain your full sensitivity. Get your shutters open, your vessel uncovered, your hose unclogged and fill your life with relationships flowing in the Spirit of God.

Motivated by Feelings

Have you ever wondered what motivated you to date a certain man or woman? To choose the partner you chose? Or what currently motivates you to stay with your spouse? To stay in a marriage that is not anything like you originally planned?

Most people believe the motivations for their relationships are unique, special or spiritual, deeper than mere physical attraction and more meaningful than simple feelings. Most couples want to believe love is the glue that holds them together. People will credit love for relationships no matter how lacking they are, such as workaholics and lonely spouses, alcoholics and enabling spouses, and husbands and wives tolerating each other for the sake of their children.

In truth, love has little to do with the origin and maintenance of most relationships. Rarely do you find couples who have matched up because of "true love." Even more rare is a couple still passionately in love after several years of being together. Most men and women are either **motivated by feelings or maintaining covers** when they pick or stay with a partner.

Motivated by feelings means you are either **moving toward pleasure or moving away from pain,** or a combination of both. Moving toward pleasure in a relationship simply means that you get good feelings when you are with your partner. The intensity of the feelings can range from mild to extremely pleasurable and sometimes euphoric. They are powerful enough to motivate you to choose that partner. Movement away from pain in a relationship, on the other hand, means that you get bad feelings when you distance from your partner. The intensity of the bad feelings can also range between mild discomfort to extremely painful. The bad feelings can occur even when you are leaving a very lonely and/or painful relationship.

Movement toward pleasure is almost always the dominant motivation during the beginning of a relationship—the "romantic stage." You go out with the person who makes you feel good. You date the person you find attractive, funny, entertaining or important. Your motivation is the good feelings that you experience when you think of being with your lover; looking at your lover; touching or holding your lover. The time-length of the romantic stage varies with each relationship, but it can actually last past the wedding and into the first few years of a marriage.

The good feelings of the romantic stage typically fade as priorities change. Time at work replaces time with your lover. Taking care of children becomes more important than making love to your spouse. The necessity of sleep supersedes the desire for late-night romance. The practical realities of your life progressively overshadow the pleasures of the relationship. Instead of living passionately in love, you settle for a passionless but comfortable co-existence.

Is it possible to maintain the feelings of the romantic stage forever, to be passionately in love every day of your life? Yes, it is! If the initial romantic feelings are energized by love and daily steps are taken to maintain that love, you and your lover can stay passionately in love throughout your lives.

Is it possible to maintain the feelings of the romantic stage without flowing in the Spirit of God? Yes, but only if you are willing to jump from one relationship to another. The "romancer" does just that, moving toward pleasure, motivated by the thrill of the "hunt." The intense pleasure of chasing and capturing the prize is what drives the romancer. He moves from one relationship to another as the romance dies. The romancer avoids, at all costs, the commitment and personal growth necessary for a truly loving relationship. The end result is a very shallow experience of romance that does not even compare to the fulfilling experience of true love.

The "lonely" and the "abused" are people who enter relationships without ever experiencing the romantic stage. Both are motivated by feelings, but in this case, the movement is away from pain, not toward pleasure. The "lonely" settle for a less-than-ideal person because the pain of being alone is so great that anyone is better than no one. They may not experience any romantic feelings with their partner. Their motivation is not romance; it is the avoidance of the pain of being alone.

The abused are also motivated by the avoidance of pain. The abused typically are women who marry to escape an abusive parent. The pain of living with an abusive parent is far greater than the pain of marrying a man whom she does not love. Unfortunately, most women who escape abusive fathers marry abusive husbands. As a result, the abused perpetually find themselves in abusive homes.

In addition to the "lonely" and "abused," many other people stay in relationships to avoid the pain of leaving. In a typical relationship, the good feelings of the romantic stage progressively fade and the relationship no longer is maintained by the experience of pleasure. Rather, it is the avoidance of the pain of separation and divorce that maintains the union. People stay together for the children, financial reasons, religious beliefs, their families or simply to avoid admitting there is a problem. Movement away from pain can be a powerful motivation to keep couples together, but it is a sad reflection of the depravity within the relationship.

If ***movement away from pain*** is such a powerful motivation, why is the divorce rate so high? The answer is rather simple. Divorce occurs when the pain of staying becomes greater than the pain of leaving. When divorce was a cultural taboo, couples stayed in their lonely, empty marriages for decades and called it love. Now that divorce has become more acceptable, the pain of ending a relationship has declined and people are much less willing to accept a lonely marriage. Divorce has become an easy escape.

Are you a romancer, lonely, abused or divorcee? Did you pick you partner based on moving toward pleasure or movement away from pain? Are you staying in a relationship significantly lacking in love because you do not want to deal with the pain of leaving? Or are you still unsure about what motivated you to choose your partner?

Whatever your current perception, the next section, Motivated By Covers, will strengthen your understanding of what inspired you to pick your partner.

Motivated By Covers

Motivated by covers means that people choose partners based on each other's covers. A single cover may determine the choice; however, more commonly, many covers are involved. Motivated by covers is intricately intertwined with motivation by feelings. I have separated the two simply to make it easier to understand.

We are going to study the covers and relationship patterns of four couples. These relationship patterns illustrate some of the most common scenarios that I see with men and women attracted to each other based on covers:

1) **A person chooses a partner with a matching cover.** Choosing a mate based on matching covers is by far the most common pattern. People who find value in appearance marry attractive people. Cheerleaders match up with athletes. People with money marry wealthy people. Traditional women marry hard working, committed providers. Traditional men marry pretty, submissive homemakers. People who use religion to avoid the emptiness in their lives select religious people. Artists choose creative partners.

The list could go on forever. The important issue is to

understand that most people are motivated to marry someone with similar covers.

2) **A person chooses a partner with the same cover as a parent who he or she admired.**

At some point in development, every child perceives mom
and dad like God: all- knowing, powerful and perfect. For
some, the illusion never dies. For others, the illusion is
gradually destroyed by obvious inadequacies. Many retain
some degree of respect and admiration for their parents.
Ultimately, many adults decide to marry someone just like
mom or dad.

3) **A person chooses a partner with the opposite cover of a parent who he or she disliked.**

Many parents fail miserably to love and nurture their children. Sadly, many children become painfully aware of this
failure. In their effort to recover from the emotional trauma
of childhood, it is common for people to decide never to
marry a person like their mother and father. In choosing
partners, they are motivated to seek the opposite of their
"sick" parent.

*John grew up with a workaholic father and a mother who
was impossible to please. John was constantly criticized by
his mother despite the fact that his primary cover was performance. John was the "All-American kid," popular with
friends while graduating from high school with excellent
grades and a college basketball scholarship.*

*John entered college and continued with his achieve-
ments as he pursued a legal career. In his sophomore year,
John decided that he wanted to get married. It was time to
find the woman of his dreams. John began his search by
listing the qualities he desired in a wife. At the top of his list*

was the criterion that his future wife would accept him no matter what. After years of living with a persistently critical mother, John was committed to marrying someone who would love and approve of him despite his failures. After two years of dating, John found the woman he wanted to marry.

Sally came from a very different type of home than John. She came from a family with parents who never yelled and rarely expressed displeasure. Sally was "Miss Perfect" in every situation, at school, church and home. She majored in elementary education at college and was a volunteer for several charities. Everyone who met Sally liked her and John was no exception.

John and Sally dated for one year, followed by a one-year engagement. They discussed their dreams, desires and "every possible problem" that could arise if they were to marry. John was as competent in this relationship as he was in all areas of his life. He treated Sally like the "princess" she was. Sally treated John equally well, always sweet and smiling, rarely making a mistake and never complaining or showing displeasure. John and Sally were in love. John had "covered his bases," spending two years with Sally, without a single argument.

They got married. Within the first week of marriage, Sally expressed her first displeasure. She didn't like John waking her up in the middle of the night to make love. Sally believed that lovemaking should be scheduled, not spontaneous. John adjusted.

By their second year of marriage, John had made many other adjustments for his perfectionist wife, who believed there was a right way to do things and a wrong way. Sally determined the right way. By the fifth year of marriage, her criticisms of John had increased to several per day. John simply was not meeting the standard that Sally's "perfect father" had displayed. Sally's constant disapproval eventually came between them. John could hardly believe it. He had married his mom.

John and Sally married because of **matching covers.** Both John and Sally pursued value through performing well and avoiding mistakes. Their cover, therefore, was ***performance.*** Remember, *a cover is whatever you use for a source of value or to numb yourself to your need for true intimacy and love.* Both John and Sally experienced value through personal and professional success. Neither came from a family where true love was the foundation of the home. Both John and Sally covered up their need for love by performing well in all areas of their lives.

In picking a mate, John and Sally sought someone who would reinforce their performance covers and would be respected and considered a "good catch" within their community. Neither John nor Sally would have been interested in a less attractive mate or someone who possessed obvious flaws. When your value comes through performance, you want people to like you, admire your success and approve of your spouse. Picking a spouse, therefore, is one of your most significant performances.

To perform your best, you will want to pick the "best" spouse. You will view the person you marry as a reflection of your worth. You will pick a person whom others approve and admire. John and Sally chose each other because each was a successful performer.

Although John desired to marry ***someone who would love him despite his failures,*** there was no way he was going to pick a tolerant, accepting person. Why? Because to accept a person despite their imperfections requires that you recognize and accept your own imperfections. The higher expectations you have of yourself, the less tolerant you will be of others' imperfections. Only by recognizing that you are significantly imperfect can you then love others who also are flawed.

John was a perfect fake; therefore his choice for a wife would also be a perfect fake. He was blind to his own weaknesses; therefore he was destined to pick a woman equally blind to her weaknesses. John was intolerant of imperfections; therefore he was guaranteed to marry an equally intolerant mate.

Sally was a woman who met John's standards for perfection. To Sally, John also was the "perfect" man or, at least, almost perfect. Prior to marriage, the fear of losing John kept Sally from mentioning what she saw as his minor flaws. She simply convinced herself that he would mature over time.

After they married, the threat of losing John no longer existed. He was now a committed husband. When John's maturation did not meet Sally's expectations, she began to express her concerns. Over time, her criticisms became more frequent, her complaints louder and her dissatisfaction more pronounced. Not only was John not "accepted despite his flaws," he was frequently criticized, despite his near perfection.

How could John end up marrying a woman as critical as his mom? Because he was motivated by his covers instead of love. John was not a lover; he was a user. He married a woman who gave him value, who reinforced his cover of perfection.

Being a user, John picked a user. The capability of seeing someone as wonderful and beautiful despite his or her flaws is a characteristic of a lover. John wanted to marry a lover but it was impossible. No lover would have settled for a user like John.

Patty's father was a raging, abusive drunk who frequently beat her mother and brothers. He never hit Patty because, as she said, "I was his little angel." Patty learned very early in life to shut up and do what dad said. When he was drunk, she knew to stay out of the way. As far back as she could remember, Patty swore that she would "never marry a man like her dad."

In Patty's third year of college, she met Larry. He was nothing like her dad. Growing up as a preacher's son, Larry never yelled, got angry or drank alcohol. Because he was the most quiet, committed "man of God" that she had ever met, Patty felt safe with Larry. After 18 months of dating, they were married.

After five years of marriage, Patty was ready to pack her luggage and move out, even though Larry was still the quiet, withdrawn and easygoing man with whom she had fallen in love. Patty had accomplished her goal not to marry a man like her dad, but her perception had changed.

Patty now saw Larry in a different light. "Larry is the most boring person I have ever met," she said. "I honestly think my mother had it better than I do. At least when my dad wasn't drinking and raging, he was somebody to have fun with. Larry is so numb. Its like he's not even in the room when he is with me."

Like most couples, Larry and Patty started dating based on the pleasure they experienced together. As the relationship progressed, Patty was attracted to Larry's *lack* of screaming, *lack* of aggression, *lack* of drinking and *lack* of instability. Patty wanted a man who *lacked* the covers of her dad. It is common for women with abusive fathers to use the avoidance of men like their fathers as covers. Patty's father was unstable, alcoholic and violent. Patty's cover became stability and the avoidance of alcohol, emotional outbursts and pain. Her choice for a mate was an expert at avoiding pain.

Larry grew up as a pastor's child where he was trained to avoid everything that was not pretty, nice and pure. In addition to his ability to avoid conflict, he also was skilled at denying unpleasantness and discomfort, expressing himself only if he had something positive to say. He never cried and was happy all the time.

The major problem with this excessively positive approach to life is that it is not real life. Real life includes joy and pain. If you become an expert at avoiding pain, you also become an expert at avoiding true love. Larry was an expert at living a truly numb life.

Initially, Larry's numbness—reflected in his ability to steer clear of pain—was attractive to Patty. Larry was the opposite of her chaotic, emotionally labile father. Stability combined with the good feelings of the romantic stage maintained the relationship at first. But the good feelings of the romantic stage eventually were replaced by the boredom of being married to a numb husband.

Patty felt like she might as well be married to an ice cube. She wanted passion. After five years of marriage to Larry, she was even willing to settle for "a little abuse" if it meant bringing passion back into her life.

Chris was the typical All-Star quarterback, leading his team to a state championship while dating Joyce, the head cheerleader. Chris and Joyce were the "dream couple," popular, talented and beautiful. Everyone wanted to trade places with Chris and Joyce. Chris went to Notre Dame as a prized recruit and Joyce followed her love interest to South Bend. Chris' college football career wasn't great, but it was good enough to enable him to obtain a nice start in the business world. During their senior years at college, Chris and Joyce got married in front of more than 1,000 guests. It was the "dream couple" beginning a "dream marriage" with one of the most extravagant weddings ever held in their hometown.

After 10 years of marriage, Chris and Joyce were the proud parents of an 8-year-old son and a 6-year-old daughter. Chris was a successful stockbroker; Joyce was a homemaker and on the board of several local charities. Chris and Joyce continued to enjoy the dream life, living in a million-dollar home overlooking the eighteenth green of the most exclusive country club in town. They appeared to have it all.

I knew it was just appearance when Chris asked me his final question at the end of his evaluation: "Dr. Van Horn, do you think my difficulty sleeping could have anything to do with the affair I am having with my secretary?"

Chris married based on the same motivation that ruled his life: ***moving toward pleasure.*** Chris' primary cover was pleasure—pleasure in winning, pleasure in conquering, pleasure in sex, and pleasure in materialism. His life had been shrouded in the pleasure of success in sports and the adulation that comes with it in our American culture. Chris found pleasure in dating the prettiest girls and "making it" with them when possible. He welcomed any challenge because he knew he would win. Chris was in love with himself and the pleasures of life.

In Joyce, Chris found someone who matched up with his cover of pleasure. He was thrilled when he "won" Joyce, competing with all the other "studs" at school. To Chris, sex with Joyce was the next best thing to throwing a touchdown pass; she was "great in bed." The ultimate woman: beautiful, fun loving and the "best lay in town." Joyce simply made Chris' life of pleasure more pleasurable.

What attracted Joyce to her playboy boyfriend? "He was just like daddy." Joyce's father was an All-American football player, handsome and admired, who had married the head cheerleader, her mother. How could Joyce go wrong marrying a man just like her wonderful dad?

What went wrong is that feelings did not last. Chris experienced what occurs in any relationship based on good feelings without true love—the pleasure dies. Chris did the rational thing; he found a new playmate. Joyce, though still beautiful, sexy and desirous to men, was no longer exciting to Chris, who needed a new thrill to maintain his arousal—the name of the game for this man of pleasure.

Joyce married someone "just like daddy," all right: tall, handsome talented and a sorry lover. Joyce had been raised to value the flesh: appearance, success and materialism. After 10 years of marriage, she was not bored. She had all her covers in place: a big house, prestige in the community, plenty of money and two beautiful children. Joyce was comfortable with an absent husband, for she had learned as a little girl that good men are handsome, successful and not home. In her own eyes, she had the perfect life.

Chris and Joyce bought into the materialistic, pleasure-filled life that dominates many homes. As long as she never found out about Chris' affair, Joyce would remain satisfied with her life. As long as he could get his sleep problem fixed, Chris would also be satisfied with his life. Sadly, both Chris and Joyce were both content to hide in the covers of a life focused on the attainment of immediate gratification. A lifestyle of pleasure does not even compare to a life energized by the Spirit of God. Both Chris and Joyce were being cheated and they did not even know it.

Melanie absolutely loved her father. As a little girl, she

*could remember waiting excitedly for him to come home,
knowing that soon, they would be playing games together.
Melanie knew that one day she would grow up and marry
someone just like her dad.*

*Melanie's early childhood admiration for her dad
changed to pity in her teenage years. Melanie watched her
father become progressively depressed under the barrage of
verbal abuse from her mother who was constantly yelling
and "bitching" about something. No matter what her dad
did, it was never enough. When mom had a bad day, dad
"got it."*

*Because Melanie knew the abuse was wrong, she did every-
thing she could do to make her sad father feel better. Nothing
ever worked. Even his multiple hospitalizations for depression
failed to produce long-term benefits. When she was 17 years
old, Melanie found her father dead of an overdose.*

*Melanie had been married for three years when she and
her husband, Mark, came to my office for help. On their first
visit, they told me in detail about their first day together.
Mark was sitting on a park bench near the university, obviously upset. Feeling sorry for him, Melanie sat down and
struck up a conversation where she learned that he had been
verbally and physically abused by his mother.*

*Melanie remembered falling in love with "this sensitive,
needy guy." Mark recalled being attracted to Mary's willingness to listen, her compassion and her sympathy. They
spent every day together for the next 30 days. Both recalled
those days as the most wonderful time of their life. Mark's
depression cleared; he felt safe and loved in Melanie's arms.*

*During the first year of their romance, Mark had one
brief depression for two weeks during the summer. Melanie
was there, and she helped him through it. During the*

second year of their dating, Mark suffered with several episodes of depression. Melanie spent approximately one to three weeks out of every three months helping Mark work through depressive episodes. By the third year of romance, approximately a third of their time together was spent dealing with Mark's pain and loneliness. Despite these repeated depressive episodes, Melanie chose to marry Mark because they "were in love with each other."

Now three years into the marriage, Melanie was tired of it all. "Dr. Van Horn, I am so sick of taking care of Mark," she said. "I support the family. I raise our child. Mark's the biggest baby of them all. I want out, but I feel so bad leaving him."

Melanie and Mark demonstrate a classic care-taking relationship. Melanie had grown up perceiving love as taking care of someone in need. As a little girl, Melanie had committed to marrying someone just like her dad. Mark was the perfect fit. He was a sensitive, lonely man who needed to be saved. Melanie was his savior.

After many frustrating years of unsuccessful attempts to help her abused and depressed father, Melanie was elated to find a man who not only needed her but who clearly benefited from her love. Mark was equally excited to finally have the supportive, nurturing care that he had never received from his mother. Melanie and Mark seemed to be perfectly matched as they entered marriage.

The perfect match started to unravel early in the marriage. Over time, all covers lose their effectiveness; Mark and Melanie's covers were no exception. Mark steadily gained less from Melanie's caretaking. The more he hurt, the less fulfilled Melanie felt. Finally, she grew tired of being responsible for

Mark. With the arrival of their child, Melanie had a new cover. It was time for Mark to grow up.

After three years of marriage, Melanie viewed Mark as an irresponsible headache for a woman already overburdened. The pain of taking care of Mark was exceeding the pain of leaving him and Melanie was ready to move on.

The purpose of the four previous stories is to emphasize three significant points:

- **You are being motivated by values and perceptions that you acquired as a child.** Unfortunately, when you are in the midst of intense feelings, it is difficult to know the truth. All of those couples thought that they were marrying based on love, but they were not. None of them knew much about true love. They married based on feelings and covers.
- **Lasting value can never be found in covers.** Many people are deceived by the temporary value found in covers. No matter how satisfying your life may seem, you are being cheated if that satisfaction is not coming from the experience of love.
- **No matter what inspired you to match up with your partner, you can develop a relationship based on love.** Even if you are currently "sick" of your partner, the power of love can transform the relationship. *The Seven Steps to Passionate Love* will enable both of you to overcome your emotional pain, move beyond your past mistakes and live a life energized by passionate love.

Most current counseling techniques focus on assisting couples in developing new covers for their empty marriage or teaching them how to co-exist without conflict. The process you currently are learning will enable you to uncover your true self, regain your sensitivity, experience the love of God, and live a life dominated by passionate intimacy and love.

In Step 3, we are going to explore the essential factors that determine the flow of love in a relationship.

Step 2 Exercises

- Stand in front of a double paned window. Observe the outer pane of glass and think of it as your brain. Observe the inner pane of glass and consider it to be your mind. Look outside through the two panes of glass and think of yourself, a spiritual being, viewing the world through a brain and mind window.

- Ask your partner to stand on the other side of a double pane window. As you look at your partner, think about the idea that you and your partner are relating through four panes of glass, two brain windows and two mind windows.

- Both you and your partner independently make a list of your covers, your parent's covers and each other's covers. Compare and discuss your perceptions.

$Step$ 3

Love requires not only the presence of the Spirit of God but also the capability to access and flow in the Spirit of God.

LOVE FACTORS

At this point in the process, you understand:

- Love is the flow of the Spirit of God.
- You were created to be a channel for love.
- Lasting value and fulfillment can only be found through the passionate experience of love in the spiritual realm.
- You are a spiritual being living in a flesh and experiencing life through a brain window, mind window and set of shutters.
- Your sensitivity, the ability to experience on a spiritual level, has been significantly influenced by the amount of true love that you have experienced to this time in your life.
- You develop covers to numb yourself to the lack of true love in your development.
- Between you and a greater experience of love is the emotional pain associated with losing your covers and increasing your sensitivity.

So what do you do now? You learn the five factors that determine the flow of love in a relationship and the practical steps for developing an intimate, passionate, loving relationship.

The Seven Steps to Passionate Love is not a philosophical understanding; it is an **outcome and experiential process.** An outcome process is focused on producing change, achieving an outcome. An experiential process results in an experience rather than simply an understanding.

The outcome of this process is the experience of the Spirit of God.

Why is it important to know this? Because many therapies and relationship programs focus on theory, not outcome. At this point, I have established a foundation of understanding from which you can move forward into the experience of love.

Moving into experience begins with an effective model of a relationship flowing in love. Picture two black boxes facing each other, one representing a man and the other a woman. As you have learned, the exterior of the black box illustrates the flesh of each person, with the outer window analogous to the brain, the inner window depicting the mind and the shutters representing sensitivity. The interior of the box is where each spiritual being lives. Both interiors also contain an illuminated light, indicating the presence of the Spirit of God. Between the black boxes is a bridge, representing an *intimate, healthy relationship (IHR)* between the man and the woman.

Love Factors (Model)

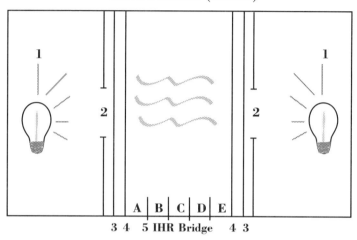

Factor 1	Power Source	**IHR Bridge**
Factor 2	Openness of Shutters	A – Time
Factor 3	Clarity of Mind Windows	B – Loving Communication
Factor 4	Clarity of Brain Windows	C – Loving Commitment
Factor 5	IHR Bridge	D – Loving Touch
		E – Loving Perception

Referring to this model, now think of love flowing between a man and a woman. For a man to love a woman, the Spirit of God must flow from his spiritual self through his open shutters, his mind window and his brain window, then across the IHR Bridge and through the woman's brain window, her mind window and her open shutters to her spiritual self. For a woman to love a man, the reverse must happen.

A loving relationship is, therefore, a dynamic process involving many factors that results in the Spirit of God flowing between two spiritual beings.

The five critical factors that determine the flow of love in a relationship are as follows:

- **The presence of the power source, the Spirit of God.**
- **The openness of the shutters.**
- **The clarity of the mind windows.**
- **The clarity of the brain windows.**
- **The quality of the IHR Bridge.**

If you desire to empower your relationship with passionate love, all five factors must be considered for both you and your partner. The five love factors are the same for men and women.

No significant gender differences exist between men and women when it comes to the love factors.

It is common for couples to engage in a process of love primarily focused on one factor of their relationship, the bridge between them. As you can clearly see with this model, if you simply focus on the bridge and ignore the other factors, the benefits will be limited. *You must address the emotional, physical and spiritual health of the individuals, in addition to the relationship bridge, if you desire to maximize the flow of love.*

Another common scenario is for one person in a relationship to become the identified "sick" person. As the sick person, he is required to participate in therapy while his spouse waits for him to get better. After a period of therapy, the sick person returns home to the empty relationship he left. Within a short time, the relationship issues and personal problems return.

There is never only one sick person in a struggling relationship. Both people are lacking in their capability of love. The wife of an alcoholic is as incapable of love as the alcoholic. The abused woman is as incapable of love as her abusive boyfriend. The numb, happy husband is as incapable of love as his crying, depressed wife. The blaming wife is as incapable of love as her adulterous husband. In any relationship that is lacking in love, both people in the relationship need to improve their capability of love.

Improving your capability of love requires both understanding the love factors and engaging in processes that will enable you to maximize the factors in your love life. Step 3 will help you strengthen the factors in your relationship by gaining a more in-depth understanding. In the following steps, you will engage in activities that promote personal and relationship growth.

You may be thinking that it is too complicated and difficult. It truly is not. It does require adapting a whole new perception of love. It also requires that you daily engage in activities that promote a passionate experience of love. However, once you are living *The Seven Steps to Passionate Love* and are enjoying the wonderful benefits of true love, your life will much simpler and markedly more fulfilling.

Begin, now, by solidifying your understanding of each love factor.

Love Factor # 1: *The Presence of the Power Source*

Love requires not only the presence of the Spirit of God but also the capability to access and flow in the Spirit of God.

As you have learned, love is the spiritual energy that nurtures spiritual beings. It is the flow of the Spirit of God. The power source for love is God.

No relationship can grow in love if there is no power source. If you have not reunited with your Creator on a personal level, then all your efforts at love will be fruitless. If you have the power source and your partner does not, at best, there will be a one-way flow of love. If neither you nor your partner has the power source, there is no possibility of love.

On the other hand, both you and your partner having the power source does not guarantee love. If you do not engage in the relationship process that enables the power source to be utilized and experienced, you and your partner will be as lonely and empty as if there were no power source. The vast majority of people who claim to have the power source are not intimately in touch with God. These "religious" people experience and share very little of the Spirit of God. They are as incapable of love as those who do not know God.

John and Sue were in their twentieth year of marriage when they first entered counseling. John and Sue had not made love in almost ten years. They spent less than five minutes a day talking to each other. For the previous decade, their typical daily routine consisted of John going to the church to perform his pastoral duties while Sue cleaned house and watched soap operas. On Sunday, they played the role of the happily married pastoral couple.

When I asked John why he stayed with Sue, John replied, "I love her."

When I asked Sue the same question, she responded, "He's my husband. That's why."

"John, what do you mean you love her," I asked. Somewhat sarcastically, I continued. "You don't talk to her. You don't hold her. You don't hug her. You don't lay with

her. You don't make love to her. You rarely even eat with her. You're calling that love?"

"Dr. Van Horn, I would die for Sue, and I have never considered leaving her for one moment," John responded emphatically.

"John, do you think that is love? Do you really believe Sue would be worse off if you left her?" I asked, challenging his ridiculous perception of love. John did not respond as he turned his eyes to the floor. I continued, "I think that she would be better off if you left her. It might force her to do something with her life."

I then turned to Sue and asked, "Sue, what did you mean by 'He's my husband'?"

"I mean, he's my husband," Sue sheepishly replied. "You don't just up and leave your husband."

"So, Sue, you stay no matter what. You stay in a relationship no matter how lonely and empty and sick it is? Where did you learn that?"

"That's God's love. He stays with us no matter what, and I am committed to John with God's love."

"Sue, that's not God's love. What you and John have is the opposite of love. You are two lonely, empty people living a miserable life and presenting a lie to your church and the world. God's love is available to you, but you and John are nowhere near it."

John and Sue lived a lie. Living a lie is far more common among religious people than most would believe. When I first started my medical practice, I was amazed to discover that the vast majority of marriages between people claiming to be close to God were lonely and very lacking in love.

**You can have the power source and be totally
incapable of accessing it.**

Having the power source simply means that you have the
potential for a life of quality and value through love. Living *The
Seven Steps to Passionate Love* will enable you to fulfill that
potential.

Love Factor #2: Openness of the Shutters

You have already been extensively exposed to the concept of
sensitivity; therefore, I am going to limit the discussion here.
Remember, sensitivity is the ability to experience on a spiritual
level. Intimacy is two people relating on a spiritual level. Love
is the Spirit of God flowing between two people who are relating
intimately on a spiritual level. You can only have as much love
as you have intimacy and you can only have as much intimacy
as you have sensitivity.

The following are three additional points I want to emphasize.

- A lack of sensitivity is one of the four major causes of the
  lack of love in relationships.
- Both men and women were created to be totally sensitive.
- All men and women are capable of returning to the highest
  level of sensitivity and vulnerability.

In Step 4, you will learn a strategy for regaining your total
sensitivity and vulnerability.

Love Factor #3: Clarity of the Mind Windows

Your mind is like a window through which you experience
and share love. Because it is the software for the thoughts and
feelings programmed in your brain, your mind is a significant

part of your emotional computer and is critical to your experience of life.

At birth, you have minimal programming in your mind. You have very little programming for feelings and no programming for thoughts. By the age of five, your mind has already been programmed with some of your most intense feeling states, many of which can profoundly affect your adult relationships.

Every time you emotionally hurt and every time you think, activity is taking place in your mind. Emotional pain and distorted thoughts fog your mind window and inhibit the flow of love. Because the mind window is frequently fogged in relationships, Step Six is dedicated to clearing your mind window through reprogramming your emotional computer.

For now, simply understand that your thinking and feeling patterns do interfere with your experience of intimacy and love in your relationships. Learning how to reprogram your mind and clear your mind window is essential to living *The Seven Steps to Passionate Love.*

Love Factor #4: Clarity of the Brain Windows

Tommy and Paula had a great relationship. They truly valued intimacy and love more than anything in life. Tommy and Paula were passionately in love with each other and were willing to do the work to stay "in love." Both had learned the keys to experiencing the flow of the Spirit of God in their relationship and they daily engaged in passion builders necessary to maintain it. Tommy and Paula were truly living The Seven Steps to Passionate Love.

Heading into his third year of marriage, Tommy was very thankful. He had found the quality and value in life that he had so desperately desired. He enjoyed being at home, spending time with Paula and daily making love to her. Most significantly, Tommy had an intimate friend whom he could trust and to whom he could turn when he was upset.

Tommy was thankful because he did not have to come home to a "nagging" wife. He was married to a woman who valued his preferences and respected his need for a life apart from her. Tommy was thrilled to have a wife who passionately loved him sexually. He did not have to fight for sex like so many of his friends. Tommy simply could not believe that living The Seven Steps to Passionate Love *could be so wonderful.*

Paula was equally excited. She had what all her friends wanted: a passionately loving husband who valued her more than anything or anyone else. Paula did not have to deal with a numb husband who defended his right to neglect her for work or play. She did not have to call a girlfriend if she needed someone to hold her while she cried because Tommy was always more than willing to fulfill that role. Paula did not have to fight for a few minutes of attention. She and Tommy lovingly communicated throughout the day. Paula did not have to wait for sex to be touched by her husband. Tommy lovingly touched and caressed her throughout the day.

But then something changed, rapidly and dramatically. It started with Paula having sleep problems, often waking up five, six, seven times a night. Within four weeks of the onset of the sleep problems, Paula struggled to stay asleep more than a few hours per night. Without sleep, she was so fatigued during the day that she was having a difficult time meeting responsibilities, even minor ones. Paula progressively became tired and lost interest in all activities, including sex. After two months of Paula's depression,

Tommy was coming home to a depressed wife either lying on the sofa or crying in the bedroom.

Tommy suggested that Paula seek help. Paula refused. Tommy begged. Paula was adamant that she wasn't a 'nut' and she wasn't seeing a 'shrink'. Paula's depression worsened. She accused Tommy of having an affair. Tommy assured her that he would never cheat on her and that he was totally committed to their marriage. Paula did not believe him. She became convinced that he was seeing another woman. Paula began questioning Tommy excessively. She threatened to leave him. Paula even hired a private detective to follow Tommy.

Tommy knew he was not having an affair. He knew that he still loved his wife. What Tommy did not know is what had happened to his wife and marriage. What was once a passionately loving, intimate relationship had become a relationship dominated by a paranoid, depressed woman.

As a medical doctor who specializes in brain illnesses, I am very aware of how the brain can affect the experience of intimacy and love. It makes sense to most people that your brain can affect your thinking, memory, mental activity and physical activity. Most of us know someone who suffered with a stroke. We have seen the mental and physical damage a stroke can cause. Most of us have also experienced how difficult it is to concentrate when we are tired. We understand mental fatigue. What is not so commonly understood is that your brain can also interfere with your experience of intimacy and love.

How does the brain interfere with the experience of intimacy and love? For a long time, I did not know the answer to this question. I believed in the concept of spiritual intimacy, but I did not understand the brain's influence on that intimacy. The black box analogy changed my understanding.

With the block box analogy, you learned that your brain is a window through which you experience life. You relate to God through your brain window. You relate to other people through your brain window. You experience and share love through your brain window. Ultimately, you experience reality through your brain window.

The clarity of your brain window ~ the health of your brain ~ is critical to your experience of life. If your brain is healthy and the window is clean, then life can be experienced in its fullness. With a clear brain window you can experience true intimacy and love and your perception of reality remains reasonably accurate. On the other hand, when your brain is chemically imbalanced, your window becomes fogged and your experience of life distorted.

With a fogged brain window, you can lose your experience of intimacy and love with God and others.

Paula not only lost her experience of intimacy and love; she also lost her capability to function in life. Her brain window was fogged. Her brain was chemically depressed.

As is often the case, Paula's brain illness started with a sleep problem. Sleep is an important time for the brain to chemically restore itself. Without proper sleep, you cannot maintain a fully healthy brain. As Paula's sleep pattern worsened, her daily functioning also worsened. She experienced many of the classic symptoms of a chemical depression: fatigue; a decreased sex drive; problems with memory and concentration; and a loss of interest in activities she had previously enjoyed. Paula's brain window was clearly fogged.

Paula did what many people do who have a fogged brain

window: she refused to get help. Millions of Americans suffer with depression; yet many remain untreated because of misperceptions and stigma.

Many problems can arise from untreated depression. Paula experienced one of these: psychosis. Paula lost touch with reality. Her brain window became so fogged that she was paranoid, believing her husband was having an affair when he was not.

Paula's paranoia was a blessing in disguise. Because of the paranoia, Tommy forced her to get help. Paula responded well to medication and counseling. The medications cleared the fog out of her brain window while the counseling helped eliminate many of her distorted thoughts about depression. Three months after Paula began treatment, she and Tommy were once again enjoying a passionately loving relationship.

You cannot live *The Seven Steps to Passionate Love* if your brain is chemically sick. You cannot ignore the fact that you have a brain window through which you experience love. Many couples try to build a relationship based on love when either one or both are walking around with a sick brain, trying to relate through fogged windows. Their attempt at love is limited. Why? Because a healthy brain is necessary for the appropriate experience of love.

Mary's father was extremely abusive. He verbally and physically assaulted both Mary and her mother. Multiple times, before the age of five, Mary watched as her raging, drunk father horribly beat her mother. At the age of six, Mary's father started to use her as a "sex toy." The sexual abuse was a daily ritual until Mary ran away at the age of 16 with her boyfriend.

Free of her abusive father, Mary decided to get help and found a "very caring, committed psychiatrist" who

prescribed her Xanax and Prozac. Within six weeks, her
emotional pain had evaporated. Mary could now talk about
her traumatic childhood without shedding a tear. Treatment
was successful and Mary moved on in life, faithfully taking
her daily medications.

I met Mary when she was 22, in her third year of marriage and the mother of an 18-month-old daughter. Her
husband, Sean, had requested that she come for an evaluation for a second opinion. Sean had been listening to my
daily radio program and had been learning about the generational curse that runs through families. When we sat first
sat down at the start of the evaluation, I asked Mary why
she had come to see me.

Sean interrupted. "Dr. Van Horn, we are here because I
have listened to your radio show for over six months. On
many shows, I have heard you say that you wouldn't give
your dog Prozac and Xanax unless you hated your dog.
Well, I don't hate my wife and I want her to be treated at
least as good as your dog."

Sean was accurate in his quote. I do believe that both Prozac
and Xanax are harmful medications, and I have expressed that
belief in many ways over the years. My biggest issue with Prozac
and Xanax is their capability to emotionally and spiritually
numb the unfortunate people who take them. A person on these
medications will experience much less emotional pain, but the
cost is a significant loss of the experience of intimacy and love.

Both are popular medications because we live in a society
that wants a "quick fix." Patients want to feel better quickly and
doctors want to oblige. Unfortunately, there is no quick fix for
years of verbal, physical and sexual abuse. There is no quick fix
for the majority of people who come from families loaded with

emotional pain that has been passed down through multiple generations. Quick fixes like Prozac and Xanax do not work.

Had Prozac and Xanax worked for Mary? At the time of our first meeting, Mary had been religiously taking Prozac and Xanax for more than six years. Mary had remained functional for the entire six years, although medication increases had been needed. Her Prozac dose had been doubled while her Xanax dose had been tripled. Past attempts to come off the medicines had been futile, resulting in Mary becoming totally incapacitated, hysterically sobbing and crying throughout the day.

Were these failed attempts to discontinue the medications proof that Mary needed them? No. Mary's failure at discontinuing the medication simply validated that she was loaded with unresolved emotional pain and that there may be a need for appropriate, non-numbing, non-addicting medications. In addition, discontinuing these medications can sometimes result in a withdrawal syndrome or a temporary worsening of the illness.

If Mary had remained functional on Prozac and Xanax, why change a good thing? The best way to answer that question is with another question, "Is functional a good thing?" Mary was not created to be functional. She was created to be a channel for God's love.

What does "being a channel for God's love" have to do with Prozac and Xanax? Prozac and Xanax both chemically numb your brain. Mary was significantly insensitive. She did not cry when it was appropriate to cry. She could function all week as a homemaker, cooking, cleaning and caring for her child, and never desire time alone with John. Mary liked being independent, rather than vulnerable and needy like many of her female friends. Her medications gave her the strength to not need anyone. With the help of her medications, Mary was independent and numb and she liked it.

Sean, however, did not like it. He knew something was wrong. Sean did not want Mary to be dependent and needy, but he did want her to be sensitive and vulnerable. When Sean was attempting to be spiritually intimate with Mary, she could not be spiritually intimate with him. When Sean wanted to grieve with Mary, she could not grieve with him. When Sean told me, "It is like something is missing," I replied, "You are right. Something is missing. The 'real Mary' is missing."

Because of her use of Prozac and Xanax, the real Mary, the sensitive spiritual being, was hidden behind a chemically numbed brain. Prozac and Xanax enabled Mary to function well in her flesh and to be insensitive to her need for true intimacy and love.

Because we have a scientific community that largely ignores the spiritual realm, research on new medicines for the brain has predominantly focused on the elimination of emotional pain. In other words, the goal is to find medications that keep people from hurting. To many people, a drug that eliminates emotional pain sounds wonderful. No hurt. No sadness. The absence of emotional pain may sound wonderful, but it truly is not.

When you medicate away your ability to hurt or to feel sad, you also lose your ability to experience the highs of life. Most importantly, you lose your ability to experience the greatest high, true love.

I am convinced that the SSRIs, the Prozac group of drugs, emotionally and spiritually numb the vast majority of people who take them. SSRI stands for Selective Serotonin Reuptake Inhibitors. This group of medications includes Prozac, Paxil, Zoloft, Luvox, and Celexa. The group is named for its biochemical ability to raise serotonin levels in the brain. The serotonin neurotransmitter is involved in the regulation of a person's mood. My belief is that if serotonin is selectively raised in a person's brain, that person will have an artificial experience of life.

Maintaining sensitivity should be a part of the treatment strategy for depression. Currently, there are no quality studies that validate which medications treat depression without inhibiting sensitivity. My belief is that medications that raise both serotonin and norepinephrine are the best anti-depressants for maintaining sensitivity while treating the depression. Several of these medications are currently available.

I also firmly believe that the benzodiazepines, the Xanax group of drugs, are effective at emotionally and spiritually numbing people. The benzodiazepines work by chemically depressing the brain and are primarily used for sleep and anxiety. Again, I am convinced that drugs like Xanax will interfere with your experience of love.

I developed my conviction concerning SSRIs and benzodiazepines over a 10-year period of assisting people in *The Seven Steps to Passionate Love*. Consistently, I found that people who were on these medications were unable to appropriately grieve and maintain intimacy. Grieving is necessary for emotional healing and spiritual growth; intimacy is necessary for love. I could tell hundreds of stories validating this position, but that is not the purpose of this book. My simple recommendation is that you and your partner avoid the use of these medications.

If you are currently taking numbing medication, you should consult your medical doctor prior to making any changes.

You should never stop a medication on your own because it may be dangerous to do so.

If you need treatment for your brain, consult a physician who believes in using medicines that do not numb.

As you have seen, the health of your brain, the clarity of your brain window, can definitely affect your love life. The following are four significant points to remember:

- Your brain is a physical organ that works off chemicals and electricity. Those chemicals and electricity need to be in the proper balance for you to experience the fullness of love.
- Your brain is like a window through which you experience love. Your brain window can be chemically fogged due to an illness of the brain or due to medications used for treating the brain.
- If you have a chemical illness of your brain, you need to get appropriate medical treatment with medications that do not numb you. You should avoid medications from the Prozac and Xanax groups.
- If you are on a medication for the brain that desensitizes you, you should seek appropriate medical care to find an alternative.

Love Factor #5: Quality of the IHR Bridge

The bridge between two people pursuing *The Seven Steps to Passionate Love* is called an intimate, healthy relationship (IHR). The fundamental characteristic of an IHR is that it is a relationship in which the Spirit of God flows. An IHR has five ingredients that function like five spans of a bridge

The five ingredients of an intimate, healthy relationship (IHR) are as follows:

- **Time.**
- **Loving Communication.**

- **Loving Commitment.**
- **Loving Touch.**
- **Loving Perception.**

Each of the five ingredients is critical to the intimate healthy relationship bridge. The strength of any bridge is determined by its weakest span. Likewise, the strength of an IHR is determined by its least present ingredient. Even if only one ingredient is significantly lacking, the flow of the Spirit of God will be lacking.

To further understand this principle, think about a bridge consisting of five spans. If four of the bridge's spans can hold up 4,000 pounds while the remaining span can only tolerate 20 pounds, what is the heaviest item that can be transported across the bridge? The obvious answer is: a 20- pound item. A bridge is only as strong as its weakest span.

An IHR bridge is only as effective
as the least present ingredient.

Mike is so committed to his wife, Dorothy, that he would gladly sacrifice his life for her. He also is a great communicator and loves to hug and caress Dorothy whenever they are together. Mike and Dorothy have talked about all of their "sins" and mistakes. There are no secrets between them. Despite knowing all the "ugly" about her flesh, Mike still has a very loving perception of Dorothy: he definitely views her as a beautiful, wonderful, precious spiritual being. The only problem in the relationship is that Mike works twelve-hour shifts, seven days per week, and is exhausted when he is home.

It appears to be a loving relationship, does it not? Mike and Dorothy communicate, lovingly touch, are committed and maintain a loving perception. But what span of the IHR bridge is missing? Time. No matter how good Mike is at all the other ingredients, without time, Dorothy will experience essentially no love from him. Remember, an IHR bridge is only as effective as the least present ingredient.

The second major concept that you need to understand concerning an IHR bridge is:

An IHR bridge is only as valuable
as the least capable lover in the relationship.

No matter how healthy the bridge between a man and a woman, if either of them is significantly lacking in their capability of flowing in the Spirit of God, the relationship will still be significantly lacking in love.

To better understand this concept, picture two hoses joined together. Assume that the connection between the two hoses is the very best possible. Now turn on the water. Will the water fully flow? Not if one or both of the hoses are partially or fully blocked. If one hose is 50-percent blocked, then the maximum water flow will be 50 percent. The quality of the connection and the opening of the other hose will not matter. You cannot simply focus on the connection between the hoses; you must also work on each hose individually.

Similarly, you should not focus exclusively on an IHR between you and your partner; each of you must work on yourself, individually, to maximize your ability to flow in love. It is extremely common for a man and a woman to be taught to work on their relationship skills while ignoring their individual capabilities of intimacy and love.

In *Men are from Mars, Women are from Venus,* John Gray perfects this approach. Not only does he fail to require personal growth, Dr. Gray actually encourages you to believe that your inadequacies are due to unchangeable, inherent, gender differences. He then outlines a plan that enables an unhealthy man and an unhealthy woman to superficially relate to each other without conflict. The end result, if you are able to live Dr. Gray's plan is that you and your partner learn to become satisfied with a lacking relationship.

Building an IHR bridge in *The Seven Steps to Passionate Love* is dramatically different. First, you and your partner are taught an emotional healing and spiritual growth process where you both learn how to individually increase your capability to flow in love. While you engage in a personal growth process, you also begin to build an IHR bridge. Building the IHR Bridge is relatively easy if both you and your lover are truly committed to a life of intimacy and love. On the other hand, two emotionally and spiritually unhealthy partners can work on an IHR bridge for years without success until both become committed to personal healing and growth.

Establishing an IHR Bridge begins with a clear understanding of each span of the bridge. I have dedicated Step 5 to the discussion of two spans of the bridge, loving communication and loving touch. I will cover the other three ingredients of an IHR in the remainder of this chapter.

IHR Span #1: Time

The importance of time in a relationship is so obvious that it almost seems unnecessary to list it as an ingredient. However, time is actually a major problem for many of the couples I work with. People have extremely busy lives and spend most of their day working, doing and entertaining. Little time is typically allotted to intimacy and love.

You have probably heard the saying, "It is not the quantity of time but the quality of time that counts." The truth to that saying is that quality of time in a relationship is very important. How you spend your time with your partner is critical to the experience of love. The lie associated with the saying is the perception that the quantity of time does not matter. **Quantity of time with your partner does matter.**

You cannot maintain the flow of love
in your relationship if you do not
spend adequate time with your partner.

How much time is necessary to maintain a passionate, loving relationship? An exact figure is impossible to state; therefore I have established a minimal acceptable standard. In other words, you may need more time than the amount I recommend, but less time definitely will not work. The minimal acceptable time that I recommend is approximately twelve hours per week of focused relationship time. In the final four steps, I give detailed directions on how to spend the twelve hours.

What if you do not have twelve hours per week to dedicate to a relationship? Then you will have a difficult time maintaining passionate love in your relationship. You will be cheated out of the purpose of your creation, the most fulfilling experience you can have.

Remember, the issue of time is never one of availability. You have twenty-four hours per day available to you. If you fail to put adequate time into your relationship, your issue is a lack of value for the relationship. The same people who do not have two hours per day available for their relationship work eight to ten hours per day. The same homemakers who do not have two hours available daily for passionate love spend sixteen hours per day caring for their home and children. The issue is never one of time; it is one of values.

If you fail to put adequate time into your relationship, your problem is not a lack of time. Rather, your issue is a lack of value for the relationship.

Why would you want to spend one to two hours per day focused on building passion in your relationship? Because it will be the best time of your day. I spend more than twelve hours per week maintaining the flow of love with my wife. Why? Because time with my wife is the highlight of my life. I look forward to my daily time of passionate love. My entire life is significantly better off because of the love that I share with my wife.

You have the time available to maintain passionate love with your partner. Establish values that place intimacy and love above everything else in your life. Change your problem from a need to find time for love because you are consumed with the responsibilities of life to a need to find time for the responsibilities of life because you are consumed with love. If you do, the quality of your life will be dramatically better.

IHR Span #3: Loving Commitment.

Loving commitment means that you are willing to do whatever is necessary to enable you and your partner to become the passionate lovers you were created to be.

A loving relationship requires emotional and spiritual healing and growth. Focused, committed effort is necessary for that
growth to occur. Unfortunately, some people are not willing to
do the necessary work. A loving commitment means that you are
willing to do the work and, subsequently, reap the benefits.

---

*Loving commitment does not mean
that you are willing to stay with your partner
no matter what choices he or she makes.*

Rather, loving commitment means leaving a relationship
when your partner clearly demonstrates a lack of commitment
to you and the relationship.

How do you know if your partner is failing to demonstrate a
true commitment? Because a detailed analysis of the process of
assessing commitment is presented in Step 6, I am going to limit
the discussion here; however, I do think it is important that I
emphasize the following two points.

- If there is any type of active abuse or addiction and unwillingness to seek appropriate help, you can be assured that
your partner is not committed. You should leave immediately.
- If your partner consistently fails to accept reasonable
boundaries or take full responsibility for his mistakes, you
can know that your partner is not demonstrating true commitment. You should leave after you spend a significant
period of time flooding him with love.

What does "flooding him with love" mean? Flooding your
partner with love means being a consistent channel of love for
him despite his failure to reciprocate. You should lovingly
affirm, touch and communicate with him on a daily basis. Your

goal is to help him experience the wonderful power of God's love, with the hope that the power of love will change him. At the same time, you should gently but directly inform him that you will not stay in the relationship forever if he fails to change his level of commitment.

How long should you stay and flood an uncommitted partner with love? I do not know. Many religious groups recommend staying forever. I do not. I know staying forever in most circumstances means a significantly lonely life for you and everyone involved including your partner, children, and future generations. In the absence of abuse, I recommend a minimum of six months of flooding with love. I do not know what the maximum period of time should be but I do believe many people stay far too long in their miserable marriages. In the vast majority of circumstances, two years of flooding your uncommitted spouse with love is more than enough time. If a change in commitment is not seen during the "flooding" stage, separation from the relationship is the next step.

The purpose of separation from an uncommitted partner is twofold: to motivate healthy change and to establish a loving home. As you have learned, people are either motivated by moving toward pleasure, away from pain or by the power of love. In an unhealthy relationship, moving toward pleasure is rarely an effective form of motivation. The good feelings have faded and you do not have much to motivate your spouse with. Motivation based on the power of love is sometimes effective; however, if you have flooded your partner with love for a significant period of time without success, you can be fairly confident that more time of love will also be ineffective.

Your last choice of motivation is movement away from pain. Your hope should be that leaving your partner would uncover him enough that the subsequent pain motivates him to change.

Most experts in addiction will tell you that movement away from pain is the only chance many addicts have. The worst thing for an addict who is active in his addiction is to have a partner who is willing to stay. The addict will very likely die in his addiction if his partner is not healthy enough to separate. On the other hand, a using addict will be much more likely to go through the pain of recovery if he knows continued use will cost him his relationship.

The same thing holds true for an uncommitted spouse. He will probably never change if you are not willing to separate. Separation is not for punishment; it is a tool to motivate your partner to work through the pain involved in becoming a lover. Your willingness to separate may be the only chance your partner has.

The second reason to separate from an uncommitted spouse is to establish a loving home. You can never maximize the flow of love in your home if your partner is not committed. The dynamics of a family system dictate that all the people who are a significant part of your home affect the flow of love in your home. An uncommitted partner will dramatically diminish the flow of love in your home. By separating from your uncommitted partner, you are making it possible to establish a loving environment for you and your children.

Separating from an uncommitted partner with the goal of healing the relationship requires the highest level of loving commitment. If more people were willing to do so, far more relationships would be flowing in love. Remember, your willingness to separate in love may be the only chance your partner has of ever overcoming his developmental emotional pain and becoming the lover God created him to be.

Loving commitment is critical to the maintenance of an IHR bridge between you and your lover. Make the decision today that you will do whatever is necessary to enable you and your partner to become the passionate lovers that you were created to be.

IHR Span#5: Loving Perception

Loving perception means knowing the "ugly" about your partner's flesh while still valuing him or her as a beautiful, wonderful, precious spiritual being based on the truth of love.

In other words, in an IHR, you view your partner as a beautiful, wonderful spiritual being despite the ugliness, mistakes, "sins" and imperfections of his flesh. Loving perception is only possible through the power of love. As you have already learned, love is the Spirit of God given to you through an intimate, personal relationship with God. It is only through God's gift of love and the sharing of that gift that you are able to view your partner as beautiful and wonderful despite his flaws. It is only by accessing the Spirit of God that you are able to move out of a flesh based perception into a loving perception.

You do not innately have the power to love or the capability to maintain a loving perception. God empowers you through His Spirit. Your capability to love determines your capability to maintain a loving perception.

"Dr. Van Horn," Jay apologetically said. "I wish I could say Lindsey is just as beautiful as when I married her. But she is not. I would be lying. She is ten years older. Her hair is thinner. Her face is more wrinkled. She is twenty pounds heavier." Jay paused, thought for a moment, then a big

*smile came to his face as he excitedly continued. "That's it,
Dr. Van Horn. I solved our problem. Lindsey needs to lose
weight. If Lindsey lost twenty pounds, I think I could do it.
I think, then, I could see her as beautiful and wonderful. It
is that twenty pounds that is getting to me."*

*"No, Jay," I replied softly be firmly. "It is your lack of
capability to love that is getting to you, not Lindsey's
weight. The real Lindsey, the precious spiritual being is just
as beautiful as she was ten years ago. You didn't see the real
Lindsey then and you don't see her now."*

Your capability to perceive your partner as his or her true
self, a beautiful spiritual being, is determined by your spiritual
maturity, your capability to access love. Loving perception has
nothing to do with the other person. Behind every flesh, no matter how nasty or ugly, is a spiritual being in need of love. In fact,
the uglier the flesh, the greater the need for love.

---

*In an IHR, you view your partner as a beautiful,
wonderful spiritual being despite the ugliness, mistakes,
"sins" and imperfections of his or her flesh.*

Does loving perception mean that you ignore your partner's
failures and mistakes? Not at all. You will learn a detailed
process in Step 7 for handling your partner's mistakes. At this
time, understand that loving perception means loving your partner as the spiritual being he or she is while making him
accountable for his mistakes. Enablers ignore their partner's
mistakes and failures. Users view their partners as their mistakes and failures.

**Lovers view their partners as beautiful
and wonderful as they make them responsible
for their mistakes and failures.**

Through the power of love, you can maintain a loving perception in your relationship. You cannot do it on your own. You must choose to pursue intimacy and love with God. You must decide that your partner is not his flesh. You must decide to flow in love despite your partner's flesh. If you make the necessary decisions and do the work to spiritually mature, you will progressively become more capable of a maintaining a truly loving perception.

It's Simpler Than It Now Appears

As you have learned, a loving relationship is a dynamic process requiring a power source, sensitivity and vulnerability, a healthy brain, a healthy mind and an IHR bridge. You may be thinking that you cannot live *The Seven Steps to Passionate Love* because it is far too complicated. At this point, the process may seem complicated, but in reality, it is quite simple.

The Seven Steps to Passionate Love predominantly consists of adopting new strategies for current behaviors. For example, you presently have established thought and feeling patterns. You are going to learn how to energize your thoughts and feelings with love. You currently communicate with your partner. You are about to learn how to do so in a manner that empowers your relationship with love. You presently spend time with your partner. You are going to learn how to insure that the time with your partner means time spent flowing in love. You currently deal with problems in your relationship. You are going to receive a process that will enable you to significantly reduce the problems in your relationship and to solve the remaining ones in love.

As you read through the rest of the book, you will be given simple daily steps to promote the opening of your shutters, the clearing of your mind and brain windows, and the development of an intimate, healthy relationship with your lover. If you follow these steps, your capability of love will grow and the quality of intimacy and love in your life will dramatically improve.

This is truly a simple process.

Step 3 Exercises

Both you and your partner independently rate the following areas of your relationship:

- **Flow of love:** 0 (no love) to 10 (100% love).
- **Clarity of mind windows [health of mind]:** 0 (very fogged) to 10 (very clear).
- **Clarity of brain windows [health of brain]:** 0 (very fogged) to 10 (very clear).
- **Openness of shutters [sensitivity]:** 0% (closed—100% (totally open).
- **Time:** 0 (severely lacking)—10 (not lacking at all).
- **Communication:** 0 (severely lacking)—10 (not lacking at all).
- **Commitment:** 0 (severely lacking)—10 (not lacking at all).
- **Loving Touch:** 0 (severely lacking)—10 (not lacking at all).
- **Loving Perception:** 0 (severely lacking)—10 (not lacking at all).

Compare and discuss your ratings.

$\mathcal{S}\,t\,e\,p\quad 4$

You must identify an environment of love where it is safe to be sensitive and vulnerable.

ESTABLISHING A FOUNDATION

*B*uilding a passionate, loving relationship is a very direct, simple process. You must first establish a firm foundation, setting the stage for love to flow. You then place on that foundation the fundamental relationship activities that are necessary for love to flow. Finally, you fine-tune the relationship by eliminating anything that is inhibiting the experience of love and promoting everything that enhances the flow of love. The purpose of Step 4 is to establish your foundation.

A strong foundation is critical to maintaining the health of a relationship. It is necessary for both you and your partner to feel safe and secure. It enables you to maintain the vulnerability and sensitivity necessary for the flow of love. A clearly established foundation leads to a reduction in conflict and the maintenance of loving communication. It gives you the base from which you can emotionally heal and spiritually mature. Without a healthy foundation, you cannot maintain a passionately loving relationship.

Establishing your relationship foundation requires the
following six steps:

I.   **Establish a time of commitment.**
II.   **Adopt foundational values.**
III. **Secure a support system.**
IV.   **Clear the table.**
V.   **Set boundaries.**
VI.   **Start regaining your sensitivity.**

I. Establish a Time of Commitment

All forms of growth and development require movement
through pain. If you desire to improve your cardiovascular conditioning, you must be willing to tolerate the pain of exercise. If your
goal is to lose excess body weight, you must be willing to endure
the pain of dieting. If you are striving to look like Mr. America, you
must be willing to deal with the pain of weight lifting.

---

*If you desire to enjoy the benefits of a passionate,
loving relationship, you must be willing to work
through the pain of emotional and spiritual growth.*

A **time of commitment** to *The Seven Steps to Passionate
Love* insures that you will remain on course despite the pain.
The failure to establish a minimum time of commitment leaves
you vulnerable to abandoning the relationship process in a
moment of pain. I will not work with a couple without at least a
four-week commitment. One of my principle goals in those four
weeks is to convince the couple to make a six-month commitment. Six months is typically sufficient time to establish a consistent flow of love. Often, tremendous benefits will be
experienced much sooner; but to solidify those benefits, more
time is needed.

"Dr. Van Horn, I'm not into this commitment stuff. Tamara knows I love her. I have no plans to go anywhere but I'm not letting any woman tie me down," John emphatically proclaimed in front of Tamara and the other fifty participants of family group.

"Tamara," I empathically asked, "Why are you accepting John's lack of commitment? Don't you realize that you deserve better?"

"I guess not," Tamara tearfully replied. "My dad left me when I was three. I never met his dad. My other grandfather died when I was five. Every man I ever dated has left me." Tamara sadly looked into my eyes as she concluded, "I guess I really don't know that I deserve better."

To emotionally and spiritually heal, Tamara needs a committed lover. She needs someone in her life that she knows is not leaving anytime soon. Does that mean John must commit to the relationship forever? No, but it does mean that John must raise his level of commitment significantly. I advised Tamara to accept nothing less than a six-month commitment. You also should request a six-month minimum time of commitment from your partner.

What does the time of commitment entail? First, you will be agreeing to adopt the principles of *The Seven Steps to Passionate Love.* I recommend that you thoroughly study the principles in this book prior to making your commitment. You cannot accept some principles while rejecting others. Every principle is critical to the outcome of this relationship process. Second, you will be committing to the daily work necessary to maintain a passionate, loving relationship. The daily work includes both personal and relationship growth exercises and consumes approximately twelve hours per week. Finally, you will be

choosing to accept the relationship as a gift with the understanding that your partner owes you nothing at the end of the
time of commitment. If, at that time, your partner chooses to
leave the relationship, you will say "good-bye" in love.

The process of establishing a time of commitment is simple.
You and your partner hold hands, look into each other's eyes
and then individually say, "I am committed to living *The Seven
Steps to Passionate Love* with you for (?) months."

Once your time of commitment is established, you can then
adopt foundational values.

II. Adopt Foundational Values

Foundational values are the following hierarchy of values
that must be adhered to if you desire to maximize your quality
of life through the passionate experience of love.

- **Value #1: Intimacy and love with God.**
  The necessity of plugging into the Power Source has
  already been extensively discussed so I will limit my comments here. I do want to emphasize that you must maintain
  a daily communion with your Creator. It is through seeking
  intimacy with the person of God in heaven and the Spirit
  of God in the people around us that we are able to stay
  connected to the Power Source. The purpose of this book
  is to teach you how to maintain and nurture intimate relationships with people. You also must daily engage in a
  process that promotes intimacy and love with God.

- **Value #2: Intimacy and love with at least two adult
  relationships, your partner being the most significant.**
  It is common to find parents, particularly mothers, who put
  much greater effort into the relationship with their
  children than with their spouse. The outcome is a lonely

parent using a child for value and fulfillment. Your capability to love your child will be directly proportional to the amount of love you are experiencing in your adult relationships. Value intimacy and love with your partner and an intimate friend second only to your relationship with God. You will then be a much more effective lover for your child.

A second point I want to make concerning this value is that you must have a second intimate, loving adult relationship in addition to the one with your spouse. This relationship will function as a channel of love for you and will be particularly beneficial when you and your spouse are upset with one another. I cannot overemphasize the significance of this second adult relationship. It is critical to the health of your primary relationship.

- **Value #3: Intimacy and love with your children.**
  If your values are in order, intimacy and love with your children will supersede your responsibility to provide for them. Love is the Spirit of God flowing from you to your child. Many parents spend all their time and energy working to provide for and take care of their children. The fruit of these homes are lonely, empty children. Be a lover first, a provider second.

- **Value #4: Providing for and taking care of your immediate family.**
  Once your life is stabilized by relationships, your focus can then shift to practical responsibilities. Because you value love more than provision, you and your family may be limited in your materialistic comforts. You will not, however, be limited in your quality of life.

- **Value #5: Maximizing your God-given talents.**
  My primary purpose for including this value is to say that

the pursuit of your dreams should never be at the expense of your relationships.

If you sacrifice intimacy and love while conquering the world, you will find the world to be an empty prize.

Once you and your partner have adopted foundational values, you can proceed to *secure a support system.*

III. Secure a Support System

Secure a support system means developing intimate, loving relationships with people other than your partner who are also committed to *The Seven Steps to Passionate Love.* Ideally, your support system should consist of a support group and, at least, one intimate friend.

Your support system will be critical to your development as a lover. The most significant value of your support system is the increased experience of love. Each person with whom you develop an intimate relationship becomes another channel of love. Ultimately, it is the love flowing from your partner and support system that enables you to emotionally and spiritually mature.

The support system also functions to assist you and your partner with problem solving. Intimacy uncovers emotional pain. Emotional pain energizes distorted thinking. Distorted thinking leads to conflict and problems in your relationship. Your support system will help you and your partner work through your emotional pain, distortions and conflicts.

The third major value of a support system is accountability. Developing a passionate, loving relationship requires regular, focused effort. The flow of love will not be maintained without daily commitment to emotional and spiritual growth and consistent work on your relationship skills. Your support system will encourage you and hold you accountable for doing the necessary work.

Securing a support system begins with identifying someone other than your partner with whom you can have an intimate, non-romantic, non-sexual relationship. In general, this person will become your "second best" friend, your best friend being your partner. The only absolute requirement of this person is that he commits to working on a relationship with you and to the principles of *The Seven Steps to Passionate Love.* The minimum time commitment that I recommend is five minutes daily by phone and two hours weekly in person. More time together is better when possible. The value of this relationship will be reciprocal, with both of you acting as channels of love as well as accountability and problem solving partners.

After you have identified an intimate friend, you should then become a member of a support group. The best support group is one consisting of couples with a trained leader. My long-term vision is to establish support groups with trained leaders available for everyone who desires to live this process. If a support group with a leader is not available to you, the second best option is a support group of committed couples without a leader. In this scenario, the authority is in the power of the group. Each person in the group works with the others as lovers, advisors and accountability partners.

Your support group can be as small as your partner and another couple or as large as six couples. A twelve-member support group is more powerful than a four member because the larger group offers a more powerful experience of love. On the other hand, if the group is too large to maintain intimacy, the benefits are dramatically limited. In my experience, a support group without a leader functions best with twelve members or less while a support group with a trained leader is effective with as many as sixteen members.

If you choose not to participate in a support group, you should at a minimum identify a spiritual authority. A spiritual authority is someone that both you and your partner know, respect and will accept advice from. Your spiritual authority should be willing to assist you in both problem solving and accountability. Having a spiritual authority as your support system is not as beneficial as a support group but it is sometimes more easily attainable.

Once you have secured a support system, both an intimate friend and a support group or spiritual authority, you are ready to *clear the table*.

IV. Clear the Table

"Clear the table" means that you and your partner must choose to forgive each other for past failures and agree not to bring up those past failures in the future.

Clear the table is critical to the flow of love in a relationship. If our past mistakes are used to measure our future potential as a lover, we will all be deemed a failure. We all have a past loaded with mistakes. Likewise, if past mistakes are used to justify the present emotional pain in our relationship, we will never get past our pain. We cannot change our own or our lover's past mistakes but we can learn to flow in love despite those mistakes. The flow of love in your relationship will be determined by you and your lover's present and future commitment, not by past failures. You must choose to clear the table with your lover.

The process I use for clearing the table is simple. Both you and your partner write letters to each other expressing your perception of how your partner has hurt and devalued you in the past. Limit the letters to three hand-written pages each as you briefly mention all past significant issues.

Read the letters to each other while sitting in chairs and in the presence of your support system with the understanding that the content cannot be challenged.

After you both have read your letters, hold hands, look into each other's eyes and individually say following:

"I am truly sorry for anyway I have hurt or devalued you. Will you please forgive me?"

If you are willing to forgive your partner for his past failures, respond by saying, "I forgive you."

At the completion of this exercise, you will have cleared the table, meaning you take full responsibility for the pain attached to past issues and you focus on present desires not past failures.

The significance of this process is covered in detail in Step 7 in the section *Forgiveness*.

V. Set Boundaries

Boundaries are critical to establishing a foundation in love. Boundaries are the framework within which you and your partner interact. Without appropriate boundaries, a relationship either crumbles with conflict or simmers along in frustration. Boundaries assist you and your partner in knowing what is appropriate behavior in different situations. Boundaries help you to know how to treat your partner, what to expect of your partner and what not to expect. It is initially a time-consuming process to establish boundaries, but over the years, the initial work of setting boundaries will save hours of pain and conflict.

Boundaries can be divided into five main categories:

1. **Values.**
2. **Preferences.**
3. **Expectations.**
4. **Responsibilities.**
5. **Consequences.**

Values *are beliefs or positions on life issues that you are not willing to change.* You perceive these beliefs as absolute. Values can be as universal as the belief that a married man should only have sex with his spouse. Most people agree with that value. On the other hand, values can be unique and limited to certain cultures. An example of a unique value is the belief among certain religious groups that women should not wear pants. Whether values are unique or universal, all are considered absolutes by someone.

A passionate, loving relationship cannot be maintained between two people who have conflicting values. We all acquire values during our life. It is critical that you and your partner identify your values, write them down and come to agreement on each of them. I strongly encourage couples dating to come to agreement on all values before marriage. A conflict in values will destroy the foundation of a marriage. Agreement on values, on the other hand, solidifies the foundation for problem-solving in love.

In contrast to values, **preferences** are not absolutes. *Preferences are choices that you make based on your feelings.* Examples of preferences include your choice of restaurants, your favorite television show, your passion for a specific football team and your selection of clothing. Preferences can vary based on how you feel. For example, whether you desire ice cream can vary with the seasons. How you cut your hair can vary every year. No matter what your preferences are, their essential feature is that you do not consider them to be absolutes and you are willing to adjust them.

A passionate, loving relationship can prosper between two people who have markedly different preferences. In fact, a contrast in preferences between two lovers can add variety and stimulation to a relationship. Each person should be allowed to enjoy his preference when possible. A conflict in preferences can be worked out through compromise and giving without damaging the strength of the relationship.

Compromising and giving are also essential to the establishment of **expectations** and **responsibilities.** *Expectations are simply what you expect of your lover in the relationship. Responsibilities are what you perceive that you are responsible for in the relationship.* You should establish expectations and responsibilities for all the significant areas of your life, including finances, employment, homemaking, sexual intimacy, children, and romance.

"Appropriate independence" is important in establishing expectations and responsibilities. *Appropriate independence simply means that you should let your partner deal with his or her responsibilities as he allows you to you deal with yours.* Unsolicited advice is destructive. For example, if your partner has the responsibility of driving the car while you are a passenger, do not assist him with advice unless it is requested. Do not "back-seat drive."

The same rules apply to occupational and household responsibilities. Obviously, it is okay to offer your help or to assist your partner when your help is requested. It is not acceptable, however, to expect your partner to do a job the way you would do it.

Agree on the final product and allow your partner to arrive there how he desires. Inappropriate interference in your partner's responsibilities will result in much unnecessary conflict while appropriate independence will make the fulfillment of expectations and responsibilities far more enjoyable.

Expectations and responsibilities should be specific, objective and simple to measure and monitor. Specific boundaries are defined in exact terms. Objective boundaries are defined in a manner that eliminates, as much as possible, subjective interpretation. Boundaries are considered simple to monitor and measure when both you and your partner have agreed upon and set in place a method for validating that the responsibilities have been fulfilled.

What should you do if you cannot come to agreement on boundaries? First, determine if there is a disagreement on a value. Remember, a value is a position that you believe is absolute on which you are unwilling to change. If a conflict in values exists, then you cannot move forward until someone changes his or her position. As I said earlier, a conflict in values will undermine a relationship. It is extremely important, therefore, that before you establish a value that you make sure you are right. Do not take a value position unless you are convinced that you are dealing with an absolute. On the other hand, never compromise on a value position or you will be cheated out of the fullness of love.

If there is no conflict in values, then you are dealing with preferences. Attempt to find a boundary where both you and your partner can have your preferences met. Be creative and generous. Write down the reasons for your position and possible compromises. Compare your list with your partner's and attempt to find some common ground. With most boundaries, there is a fair solution where everyone can be satisfied. However, if either you or your partner is selfish or narrow-minded, the process will be a struggle.

What if you go through the process of pursuing compromise but no solution is found? A spiritual authority is your answer. A spiritual authority is someone that both you and your partner know, respect and to whom you are willing to listen. Having a spiritual authority for your relationship can be tremendously helpful. I often take the role of spiritual authority for couples who come to me for help. As a spiritual authority, my goal is not to give direct answers. Rather, I want to teach my clients how to problem-solve in love, how to come to solutions as a couple.

If you choose a spiritual authority and find that his or her preferences, not your own, are dictating the solutions, you have chosen the wrong authority. On the other hand, if your spiritual authority is teaching you and your partner how to creatively and generously find solutions that meet both your preferences, you have selected the right authority. The more your spiritual authority helps you learn to problem-solve, the less you and your partner will need that person in your journey to maintain boundaries.

What happens if you cannot agree on boundaries even with a spiritual authority? You are stuck. Someone is going to have to give in. If both you and your partner remain adamant in your position, your unwillingness to compromise will erode the foundation of your relationship. A healthier approach would be to concede to your partner's wishes while expressing that your compromise is a gift of love. Hopefully, the love that your partner experiences will inspire him to also compromise in love. Over time, if both you and your partner are compromising in love, you will come to full agreement on your boundaries.

Once the boundaries are agreed upon, they should be written down. Written boundaries will assist you in avoiding future disagreements. Boundaries should not be considered established until they are agreed upon in writing. Agreement and documentation of your expectations and responsibilities initially requires many hours of dedicated effort. In the end, however, written boundaries save time by eliminating hours of conflict.

After your expectations and responsibilities are documented in writing, you should then establish **consequences.** *Consequences are future behaviors, activities or losses that you are willing to engage in or accept if you fail to meet your responsibilities.*

The purpose of consequences is to help you do what you want to do.

Consequences help you fulfill the responsibilities to which you have committed. They should be viewed as a tool to assist you, not as a punishment to hurt you.

Consequences are only as valuable as your commitment to meet your responsibilities. If you do not agree with your responsibilities, yet accept consequences anyway, it is only a matter of time before the process breaks down. Consequences are not to be used to force you to do what you do not want to do. It is, therefore, critical that you fully agree with your responsibilities prior to establishing consequences. If you and your partner cannot come to agreement on expectations and responsibilities, then consequences are of no lasting value. On the other hand, if you and your partner agree upon your boundaries in writing, consequences are a great tool to assist you in maintaining those boundaries.

Consequences can be simple, complex, minor or major. The loss of money often works well as a consequence. An example is the payment of $5 for each minute of tardiness. Being late is devaluing to your partner. The $5-per-minute charge is simply a tool to help you value your lover by being on time. It is fascinating to watch people who have a long history of arriving late become consistently punctual through the use of this consequence.

Two other consequences that I particularly like to recommend are "love slave" and "work slave." "Love slave" simply means that, for an agreed upon period of time, you will do whatever your partner asks you to do to demonstrate your romantic love for him or her. "Love slave" activities can range from a simple massage to passionate lovemaking. Being a "love slave" for your partner enables you to pay your consequence while you are also blessing your partner romantically. As a "love slave," you can both deal with your mistake and give to your lover.

"Work slave" is similar to "love slave" except, in this case, you commit to a period of time to do whatever work your partner desires for you to do. Your "work slave" time could be spent on a range of activities, such as cleaning cars, mowing the yard, or doing laundry. As a "work slave," you are at your partner's beckoning to do the work he or she chooses. Remember, the "work slave" consequence is for your benefit "to help you do what you want to do."

Mary was a wife and mother who benefited greatly from the "work slave" consequence. Mary agreed to the boundary of no screaming and yelling, either at her husband or child. Initially, her consequence was 30 minutes of "work slave" for every episode of yelling. Mary understood that the purpose of the consequence was to "help herself." Mary wanted to stop the screaming. She did not want to verbally abuse her family. Mary was attacking her problem both by working on healing the emotional pain that energized the yelling and by setting consequences. Despite her emotional healing and the acceptance of consequences, the screaming continued.

Mary decided to increase the severity of the consequence. Over several months, the consequence was steadily raised. Eventually, Mary was responsible for five hours of "hard labor" as a consequence for any verbal outburst. The yelling and screaming finally stopped. As Mary said, "It was less painful to shut up than to do five hours of hard labor." Mary is convinced that without the "work slave" consequence, she would never have won the battle with her mouth.

The "work slave" consequence worked for Mary, but what if a consequence does not achieve the desired results? What if your partner regularly fails to meet a responsibility despite written boundaries with consequences? You must then answer the following four questions.

1. Is the responsibility appropriate, well defined and agreed upon?

Make sure that your partner clearly knows what he or she has agreed to and truly desires to meet his or her responsibility. Your partner may initially agree to a boundary, not because he or she believes in it, but simply to keep you happy or shut you up. This problem is actually quite common, especially with people who avoid conflict. How do you know if this is your problem? Ask your partner.

Generally, if your partner says that he understands the responsibility and agrees to it, then assume he is being honest and move to the second question. If your partner says that he really does not agree with the boundary, then return to the process of defining boundaries. Once the boundary is agreed upon, you can proceed to the second question.

2. Is the strategy adequate?

It is common for people to accept responsibilities but then not have a strategy to fulfill them. If your partner is failing to meet a responsibility but verbalizes a desire to do so, work with him or her to find a successful strategy. Many people need help in a variety of areas, including time management, occupational training, financial planning, communication skills and relationship development.

Martha, a young mother of a 2-year-old son, was consistently failing to meet her responsibility to value her husband sexually. She agreed with the responsibility. In fact, Martha greatly enjoyed making love to her husband as long as she was rested. The problem was that by the time she spent her day chasing her child, cleaning the house and cooking three meals, Martha was exhausted. Sex was the last thing she desired. The solution was simple but required a significant contribution from her husband. He took responsibility for the household and the childcare for two hours prior to their scheduled time for romance. Martha spent those two hours resting, bathing and preparing for some great sex.

Martha needed a better strategy to meet a responsibility that she truly desired to fulfill. Make sure the reason for the failures in your relationship are not due to a faulty or inadequate strategy. Work as a team to develop strategies that help both you and your partner enjoy all the benefits that you desire from the relationship.

3. Is the consequence adequate?

If your partner has a good strategy to meet an agreed upon responsibility but is still failing, you must then ensure that the consequence is adequate. You should judge the adequacy of a consequence by its effectiveness, not its severity. A $1 consequence that maintains a desired boundary is much better than a five-hour "work slave" consequence that fails.

When a person agrees to a responsibility, he should set his own consequences. Remember, the consequence is not punishment. It is a tool to help you and your partner change behaviors that sabotage the flow of love. If an initial consequence does not result in fulfillment of the responsibility, the consequence needs to be increased until it is effective.

John knew that he had a problem with being late. He also knew that his frequent late arrivals were devaluing to his wife. Because he was committed to truly loving his wife, John agreed to the responsibility of being on time. He committed to setting a specific time of arrival for all activities involving his wife. The consequence that John chose was $1 for each minute that he was late. By the end of two weeks, he had paid his wife more than $100. Obviously, John was not meeting his responsibility for being on time.

John and his wife reviewed the boundary. They agreed that it was specific, objective, easy to monitor and appropriate. John still wanted to value his wife by being punctual. John developed a new strategy, allowing himself fifteen minutes extra when he set his arrival time. He also increased his consequence to $5 for every late minute. For the next two months, John had a perfect record of arriving on time.

The $1-per-late-minute consequence was inadequate for John. He was not achieving his goal of being punctual. John wanted to value his wife, so he chose to increase the consequence. The $5-per-late-minute helped John accomplish his goal. If a responsibility is not being met, you must ensure that the consequence is adequate.

4. Is your partner truly committed?

If you have an adequate consequence combined with a good strategy for an agreed upon responsibility, you should expect regular compliance with that boundary. If your partner still fails to reasonably meet his or her responsibility, you must question your partner's commitment. No one is going to be perfect. Do not use your partner's imperfections to prove that he or she is not committed. However, there is a big difference between imperfection and a regular failure to meet a responsibility. Many people will verbalize a commitment to love but are not willing to pay the price to live a life flowing in love. You can waste years of your life trying to maintain a loving relationship with someone who simply is not committed.

How can you know if your partner's failures are due to a lack of commitment? Committed lovers are willing to adjust strategies, work at those strategies and accept consequences until they consistently meet their responsibilities. Cons will talk about strategies and consequences but consistently fail to follow through. If you are not sure whether you are in a relationship with a committed lover or a con, develop a strategy and consequences that you know are reasonable for your partner. Cons will bail on the process. Cons will not accept reasonable consequences. If you are relating to a committed lover, you will see change.

Peter swore that he was committed. "Dr. Van Horn, I will do anything to beat my addiction. I am so tired of turning to pornography. I am hurting the people I love the most, my wife and children. Can you help me?"

"Of course, I can help you," I assured Peter. "If you are willing to pay the price to heal, you will get over your addiction."

I knew from years of working with addicts that it is one thing to say you are committed. It is another thing to live it. To test Peter's level of commitment, I asked, "Peter, are you willing to do anything?"

"Anything, Dr. Van Horn. You tell me. I will do it."

"Peter, I have a 12-week group starting next Tuesday at 5:30 P.M. It will consist of twelve men and women, all committed to healing in love. I would like you to attend that group where you can openly reveal the nastiness and ugliness of your pornography problem."

"But Dr. Van Horn, I want to work alone with you. I want one-on-one sessions."

"Peter, I don't think your approach will work. You need the group setting. It is important that you come clean and stop hiding your problem."

"It's not that I want to hide anything. I would just be more comfortable alone with you. Let me think about it, Dr. Van Horn. I will get back with you."

Peter was a con, conning himself and the people around him. In less than five minutes, he went from saying that he was willing do anything to debating about what he needed. I never expected to see Peter in my group. He never came.

My initial recommendations were designed to test his level of commitment. I knew that exposure would be painful for Peter.

He wanted to overcome his addiction without suffering much pain. Because all healing requires growth through pain, Peter had a lot of pain to grow through. His healing would require much more than the initial exposure of his problem in a 12-week group. Peter was not even willing to do that.

Peter was not committed. He was destroying the foundation of his life with his addictive use of pornography. Peter had been wasting his life for years.

Do not let an uncommitted partner waste your life. Make sure your partner is truly committed.

Boundaries are critical to maintaining a loving relationship. Commit the time and effort necessary to establish values, preferences, expectations, responsibilities and consequences. Make each boundary specific, objective, and easy to monitor as you document them in writing. The work will be extensive, but the benefit to your relationship will be far greater.

VI. Start Regaining Your Sensitivity

How do you become more sensitive? If you learned to survive well without love, how do you get rid of those survival skills? If you are partially covered, how do you become totally uncovered? If your shutters are somewhat closed, how do you get them wide open? If your hose is calcified, how do you clean it out? How do you return to that sensitive, vulnerable state of a little child where you can fully experience and share love? How do you get back to that state where you hurt more, cry more and, most importantly, experience and share love more?

All of the above questions refer to the same process: **regaining your sensitivity.**

You cannot establish a firm foundation without beginning the journey to greater sensitivity.

As you can see, I have established several different analogies to help you understand sensitivity. Why? Because sensitivity is critical to the flow of love, yet few people understand or pursue it in their lives. The vast majority of people are pursuing new and better ways to cover up. Most relationship processes teach people how to cover up. Most religious doctrines assist their followers with covering up. This section is dedicated to teaching you how to uncover, clear your pipes, open your shutters and return to the sensitive, vulnerable state where you can passionately experience love.

Having helped hundreds of people regain their sensitivity, I can assure you that there will be some resistance to the process. A part of you will be excited to become sensitive to the intimate experience of love while a part of you will want nothing to do with it. Sensitivity, initially, is painful and uncomfortable, even frightening. You will be returning to that state of vulnerability that you worked so hard to leave behind and uncovering feelings that you so effectively stuffed over the years. You will probably pause in the process to question why you are putting yourself through so much pain. At times, your survival skills will take over and you will blame, distance or find some other way to sabotage the process. In the end, if you stay the course, you will move beyond the pain and fear into the warmth, safety and healing power of love.

"Dr. Van Horn." I faintly heard Shelly's voice as she attempted to get my attention. We were finishing up the Thursday morning session, the first day, of my four-day workshop. I was explaining the proper technique for an intimate hug

when Shelly called my name. I continued with my explanation when Shelly loudly and forcefully intruded again. "Dr. Van Horn, I have a question."

I turned to Shelly and asked, "Shelly, do you mind if I finish my instructions?"

"Actually I do," Shelly emphatically stated. "What I have to say applies to what you are doing. I want to ask you something."

I smiled at Shelly as I considered telling her to wait. She looked so upset that I decided to let her voice her issue. "Go ahead, Shelly. Ask your question."

"Did you say that you were a psychiatrist, a medical doctor?" Shelly asked the question with a twisted smile, the kind you see when someone is sarcastically cutting you.

"Yes, Shelly. I prefer to be called a medical doctor who specializes in the . . ."

"Well, whatever," Shelly interrupted. "How long have you been doing this type of therapy?"

"I have been teaching people how to emotionally heal in love for about 15 years," I calmly replied.

"Well, I have been going to a psychiatrist and a psychologist since I was five." Shelly's voice was slowly increasing in volume and pitch. "That's 35 years. And you are the most ignorant doctor I have ever met. Nobody makes people hug each other after three hours of group." Shelly yelled, "Are you nuts?"

I looked at Shelly's red face, her bulging neck veins and her clenched fists as I decided how best to handle the situation. Smiling, I softly said, "Shelly, I won't make you do anything. I would appreciate it if you would lower your voice, but I certainly will not make you hug anyone."

Shelly, still obviously upset, replied in a slightly quieter voice, "I was not going to anyway. I just cannot believe you would want anyone to hug a stranger."

I turned to the workshop group of 20 people and said, "I know it is uncomfortable to hug strangers. This is a voluntary process. None of you have to do anything. You paid me to help you experience more intimacy and love. We have four days to achieve that goal. Hugging is a big part of this process. I encourage you to do it. Four days from now, the hugs will be one of your favorite parts of the workshop." I paused and, while looking around the room, stated, "If you do not want to hug, raise your hand." Only Shelly raised her hand.

The four-day workshop continued. Shelly eventually chose to hug but not until Friday afternoon. As the workshop came to an end on Sunday, each participant had the opportunity to summarize his or her experience. Shelly started crying when it was her turn. With tears streaming down her face, she said, "Dr. Van Horn, I came in here because I had nothing to lose. I am about to go through my third divorce, so I figured it couldn't hurt. I haven't trusted anyone my whole life. I have talked to doctors, pastors and counselors for the past 35 years. None of them helped. When I met you on Thursday, I thought you were an arrogant fool who was going to try to force me to trust him.

"But you didn't force me to do anything. You just asked me to stay around and experience the change. I didn't know what you meant, but I stayed. I watched the change. I experienced it. You call it the 'flow of the Spirit of God.' I don't know what it is, but I know that I like it. I am closer to you and the other people in here than I have ever been with anyone in my life. I am really saddened to be leaving. I wish I could stay here and hug everyone forever."

Shelly had become sensitized by the thought of hugging strangers. At the beginning of the workshop, her cover was to attack and blame. When her pain hit, she blamed me.

Shelly had to make the decision to trust, to become vulnerable enough to be exposed to the hurt of betrayal, a hurt she had already experienced far too many times.

Despite her fears, Shelly eventually chose to participate in the process of uncovering. Her participation not only uncovered great pain but also opened her up to the healing power of love. On Thursday, the lonely little girl was fighting to stay at a "safe" distance. On Sunday, the same lonely little girl was begging to stay close to the channels of love she had found.

Foundational Decisions

Regaining your sensitivity requires uncovering pain and moving toward love in the midst of that pain. The uncovering process begins with four foundational decisions.

1) **You must decide that you believe in *The Seven Steps to Passionate Love.***
2) **You must choose to accept the premise that intimacy and love require sensitivity and vulnerability.**
3) **You must decide that the benefits of love are worth the suffering associated with uncovering emotional pain.**
4) **You must decide to do whatever is necessary to return to the sensitive, vulnerable state in which you were created to live.**

Regaining your sensitivity begins with your foundational decisions.

Are the decisions easy to make? Not at all. One of the principle goals of my four-day workshop is to convince participants
that *The Seven Steps to Passionate Love* is the truth. In only four
days, a group of people who have been spending most of their
lives trying to avoid pain are taught to experience love through
intimately grieving, hugging and affirming each other. Each
participant dissects the relationships in their families of origin
to learn how and why love was missing. They discover that
much of what they have believed about love is not true. The ultimate goal of the workshop is to motivate the participants to
make their foundational decisions.

The validation of those decisions is the incredible flow of love
that each participant experiences. In just four days, a group of
20 strangers are transformed into a passionate, loving family.
The major transformation occurs through the revelation of emotional pain, followed by a time of grieving. As the hurts are
revealed in the midst of tears, the sensitive, vulnerable spiritual
beings begin to emerge and slowly bond in an environment of
love. Each participant's ultimate proof is the experience of love.

Your ultimate proof will also be the incredible experience of
love that you discover in *The Seven Steps to Passionate Love.*
Once you start the process of increasing your sensitivity and vulnerability, the emotional pain will come. If, in the midst of the
pain, you move toward your loving relationships, you will heal.

*Nick had not cried in 15 years. Occasionally, tears would
fill his eyes, but he never really cried. It was not due to a
lack of effort. Nick had been coming to my group for more
than two months seeking to be more sensitive. Nick wanted*

to return to the sensitive, vulnerable state he once experienced as a child. Unfortunately, he could not remember a time when he was sensitive. He chose to trust me that there was such a time.

Nick arrived at group announcing that today was his day to cry. In previous groups, he had read multiple letters describing how his father verbally and physically abused him. The abuse was horrible. The letters were extremely sad, but Nick still did not cry. As painful as the memories were, they were not breaking through his covers.

Today, Nick sounded different as he read his letter. His voice quivered as small tears rolled down his cheeks. Nick was describing one of the many times that he had seen his father beating his mother. On this particular occasion, Nick's father was violently choking his mother. Nick could remember where he was standing, what he was wearing and specifically how his mother looked when she was gasping for air. As Nick recalled hiding behind a chair, knowing for sure that his mother was going to die, he began sobbing and fell to his knees in the middle of the group. As I went to help him off the floor, he sobbed and begged, "Mommy, please don't die. Please, mommy, don't die."

A strong competent man was transformed into a weeping little boy. The sensitive, vulnerable, traumatized Nick had been found. Nick cried for more than 30 minutes as intimate friends lovingly touched him. After the sobbing turned to light crying, I gently asked, "Nick what are you thinking?"

Nick replied, "Dr. Van Horn, it wasn't fair. I was just a little boy. I was scared to death. I knew my mommy was going to die. It wasn't fair. "

I responded quietly, "You are right, Nick. It wasn't fair, but it is good to cry. No little boy should go through that *experience." Nick cried for another hour.*

After the cry, he told the group that he had never experienced so much pain in his chest, his back and his legs. "My heart felt so bad, it felt like someone was putting it in a vice and squeezing it. I have never felt that level of emotional pain in my life. In fact, I don't think I have ever experienced any physical pain that was more intense than the pain in my chest."

The next day, Nick returned to the group and very excitedly reported, "Dr. Van Horn, it's so wonderful. It's absolutely wonderful."

"What are you talking about Nick," I asked. "What's so wonderful? What happened?"

"I woke up this morning, looked at my wife and children, and tears came to my eyes," he replied. "I felt this rush of warmth coming out of my chest. It was so wonderful. It was unlike any experience I have ever had before in my life. It was warm and pleasant. Is that what love is Dr. Van Horn? Is that what you mean by the flow of the Spirit of God?"

"I can't say for sure Nick, but it certainly sounds like it. Your shutters are opening. Your covers are coming down. You are starting to access some of the spiritual energy that God created you to experience. It truly is wonderful Nick. There is nothing better than experiencing true love in a state of sensitivity and vulnerability."

Do you want to maximize your experience of life? The route is through greater sensitivity. Nick began the journey, not when he cried in group, but when he made his foundational decisions. You can begin the journey today. You can make your foundational decisions and then do whatever is necessary to regain the sensitivity that was stolen from you.

Environment of Love

Once you make your foundational decisions, you must identify an environment of love. Identifying an environment of love means finding a place where you can hurt, you can grieve and you can be real with a group of people. Ideally, your support system should function as your environment of love.

You must identify an environment of love where it is safe to be sensitive and vulnerable.

It is critical that your environment of love consists of people who completely accept the fundamental principles of *The Seven Steps to Passionate Love.* Why? Because the last thing you want is to return to the sensitive, vulnerable state of a little child and be traumatized again. I do not mean traumatized sexually, verbally or physically. I mean traumatized by a self-righteous individual incapable of seeing you as the beautiful, wonderful spiritual being that you are despite the flaws in your flesh.

Why would someone be incapable of seeing the real you? Self-righteous people cannot see the real you because they live in their fake flesh. They live in a facade of righteousness by denying the ugliness of their own flesh. Because they are not aware of their own ugliness, they are incapable of seeing beyond your flesh.

Self-righteous people will not traumatize you with a dirty mouth or a direct attack. They will assault you with smiles to your face and gossip behind your back. Often, their mode of attack will be to organize people to pray for you, believing that they have your best interest in mind. In truth, it all serves to protect them from an honest look at themselves.

How can you avoid getting personally caught up in the vicious web of self-righteousness? The answer is quite simple.

Become deeply aware of how little true value you have without God's love. The more you experience your value through your accomplishments or the avoidance of mistakes, the more you will judge others and the less capable you will be of love

---

The more you experience your value through the gift of love, the more you will be able to truly love others.

Can you regain your sensitivity in an environment of love that is limited to you and your partner? It is possible to regain your sensitivity in an environment of love consisting of only you and your lover, but it is very difficult. When the uncovering starts, the emotional pain emerges and distortions usually accompany the pain. A common distortion is to blame your partner for your pain. If blaming starts, the process is dead. You cannot experience much love from someone you are blaming or from someone who is blaming you. Consequently, I recommend you include at least one other person in your environment of love.

Should you pursue a perfectly safe environment, an environment with the total presence of love? The obvious answer is no. Because there are no perfectly safe environments, you need to engage in this process in an environment of people committed to becoming the best lovers that they can be. You need committed lovers not perfect lovers.

Once you have made your foundational decisions and identified your environment of love, you are ready to access the emotional pain.

Accessing the Emotional Pain

Accessing the emotional pain simply means getting in touch with the emotional pain behind your shutters and under your covers. On a practical level, you know that you are accessing your emotional pain when you begin to cry.

Crying is a sign that your shutters are open beyond your normal baseline. In other words, grieving is a sign of greater sensitivity.

Grieving is a sign of greater sensitivity.

Grieving in an environment of love does for your emotions what exercise does for your body. If you want to keep your body in the best physical condition, you have to exercise regularly. The regular exercise of your body enables you to maintain the healthiest baseline functioning of your heart, lungs and blood vessels. Likewise, if you want to keep your emotions in the best condition to experience and share love, you need to exercise them regularly by crying in an environment of love. Crying in love is the healthiest way to overcome the unhealthy emotional impact of living in a stressful, unloving world.

***Regular grieving in love enables you to maintain
your healthiest emotional state
and your highest level of spiritual sensitivity.***

Regular grieving in love is also an opportunity to move to a higher level of baseline sensitivity. Baseline sensitivity is the sensitivity level that we function at in our normal daily life. It would be wonderful if we could stay fully sensitive all the time. In our fully sensitive state, we are best able to share and experience love. However, in our fully sensitive state, we are also much more vulnerable to being hurt. Therefore, the process of increasing our baseline sensitivity is one of grieving in safe, loving environments and covering in less safe environments.

For example, a significant part of my medical practice is leading groups where I assist clients in the emotional healing process. The healing power is love. Each person in the group, including myself, who has an intimate relationship with God, is a channel for love. I have several roles in the group, of which the most significant is being a channel of love. The more sensitive I am, the more flowing I am. Therefore, I want my shutters to be as open as possible when I am leading a group. To maintain the highest level of sensitivity, I often will cry alone prior to the group or cry early in the process of leading the group. The grieving is a sign that I am attaining a higher level of sensitivity—a more sensitive, flowing state—a state in which I can be a more effective channel of love.

I wish I could stay fully sensitive in every environment in my life but I am not spiritually mature enough to do so. Remember, my spiritual maturity is reflected in my ability to access the Spirit of God in different environments. If I am more sensitive than my ability to access love, I simply hurt. My current spiritually maturity enables me to access a high level of love in the safety of my groups, in my home environment and with my intimate friends. In these environments, I regularly grieve in love and, thus, stay very sensitive and flowing. In less safe environments, I avoid grieving and stay more covered. As I have spiritually matured, I have become more able to access the Spirit of God from within and thus can stay more sensitive and flowing in less safe environments. In other words, my baseline sensitivity has steadily improved.

Your baseline sensitivity, therefore, is a function of your spiritual maturity, the frequency with which you grieve in love and the amount of love in your foundational relationships. The more spiritually mature you are and the more love there is in your home environment, the more sensitive you will remain. The process of increasing your baseline sensitivity, therefore, requires regular grieving as you spiritually mature through a foundation of loving relationships.

Sound strange? It certainly would have to me ten years ago. At that time, I perceived emotional and spiritual health as the absence of pain and the absence of sin. I perceived love as being nice, kind and caring. I avoided crying and helped the people who were crying learn how to stop. I now know that love is the flow of the Spirit of God, sensitivity is necessary for love to flow and crying in an environment of love is necessary to maintain sensitivity.

How do I know this? I have experienced the positive impact of sensitivity through grieving in my work, marriage and relationships with my children and intimate friends. I have also observed the process of sensitivity in hundreds of groups and thousands of lives. Sadly, I have also observed the damage due to a lack of sensitivity in hundreds of relationships and families. Grieving in love is critical to the maintenance of a loving relationship.

Is it possible for someone to become so spiritually mature that he no longer needs to grieve in love? The best way to answer this question is with another, "Is it possible to become so physically conditioned that you no longer need to exercise to maintain the conditioning?" The obvious answer is no. In a world so lacking in love and so full of emotional stress and pain, emotional conditioning through grieving in love will always be necessary. The more sensitive and flowing you become, the more obvious this principle will become to you.

Accessing the emotional pain means getting in touch with the emotional pain under your covers and behind your shutters. Grieving is a sign that you are accessing the emotional pain. Grieving does not heal you. The love flowing in your environment heals you. Grieving in love on a regular basis will enable you to maintain the best state of sensitivity necessary to be the lover you were created to be.

Grieving Techniques

What are some techniques for learning how to cry in love? By far, the most effective technique that I know of to assist you in regaining and maintaining your sensitivity is the writing of letters. Letters written about past painful experiences can be powerful tools in your quest to open your shutters. I have listened to thousands of letters while leading emotional healing groups and, unquestionably, reading sad letters in a group process can be a very sensitizing experience.

The content of the letter is far less significant than your response to the letter. In other words, what you write about is not nearly as important as how much you cry. If you cry, the letter is good. If you sob, the letter is great. If you do not cry, no matter how sad the story or how excellent your writing, the letter is lousy. Grieving is the goal of the letters.

Start with the content that is most likely to trigger your tears. The content that is most sensitizing varies with each person. Topics generally sensitizing include the following: the death of a loved one, an abortion, harm or injury to a child, an affair, a betrayal by a significant person, the breakup of a relationship, the death or injury of a pet, past or present abuse, and harm or injury to a close friend or family member. Finding a topic, any topic that will trigger your tears, is the most important issue during the early stages of regaining your sensitivity.

---

*It is critical that in writing the letters
you focus on grieving, not blaming.*

Grieving letters focus the on sensitive, sweet, vulnerable child inside you who is hurting. Blaming letters, on the other hand, focus on the person or event that hurt you. When writing your letters, focus on how hurt you were by the event. I am not saying to ignore the hurtful event or person; I am saying to make your focus the pain you experienced in the midst of the event. Later, I will explain in detail why blaming is so destructive. For now, simply understand that you want the letters to be grieving not blaming letters.

As you progress in your sensitivity, I suggest that you write about early childhood experiences. Remember, you were born with wide-open shutters, fully sensitive. It was during your early childhood that you were the most sensitive. Painful memories of early childhood experiences often produce the greatest sensitivity.

As you write letters about your childhood, there will be an appropriate time to write separate letters to your mother and father. The content of these letters should focus on the ways you were hurt by your parents, both passively and actively. Passive harm would include the ways your parents failed to love you by not doing what they should have done. Examples of passive harm would be your parents' physical absence, lack of communication and lack of loving touch. Active harm would include the ways your parents failed to love you by doing things that they should not have done. Examples of active harm would include any form of abuse ~ verbal, physical and sexual.

***Writing a letter about the lack of love
from your parents is often the door to full sensitivity.***

Writing a letter about the lack of love from your parents is often the door to full sensitivity. Why? Because your parents were there when you were your most vulnerable and sensitive. It was with your parents that you first started covering up. Writing about painful experiences with your parents can return you to the state of sensitivity that you experienced prior to any covers.

Writing a sad letter to your parents initially may be very difficult for you. Every child has an inherent desire to protect his or her parents. Many children maintain that protective desire into adulthood. Therefore, it may be difficult for you to see how your parents hurt you. If, at first, you have difficulty writing sensitizing letters about your parents, save the task for a later time. Focus, instead, on topics that more readily sensitize you. Return to your parents' letters later.

Often in the process of writing letters to access the emotional pain, you will get stuck. You will try one letter, a second letter, write about different things and still not feel much emotional pain. It is critical that you continue to search for a theme or a person that sensitizes you to the emotional pain. It is not unusual for a person to write multiple letters without significantly crying, and then come upon a particular person or theme that triggers intense emotional pain. Working on that trigger will be a doorway to greater sensitivity. As you write letters about one painful memory, you will become more sensitive to the pain associated with other memories.

Another important component of accessing emotional pain is being able to do it in the presence of other people. As you have learned, crying is a sign that your shutters are open. When you are crying, you are more sensitive to the healing power of the Spirit of God. Each person who has the power source, the Spirit of God, is a potential lover. A group of lovers produces a far more powerful healing environment than any single person can.

**A group of lovers produces a far more powerful
healing environment than any single person can.**

In my workshops, I find that the optimum group size is 18 to
20 people. Without a trained leader, I recommend group size be
limited to approximately 12 people. As long as the group is
small enough to maintain intimacy, the more lovers present, the
more powerful the group.

What if you cry when you are alone but shut down in front of
people? If you have problems crying in front of people, it is
because there is a part of your brain that is taking over to protect you. It is a part of your brain that developed in a childhood
where it was not safe to cry in front of other people. It may have
not been safe to cry for many reasons, including ridicule, abuse
or simply a lack of comfort. Whatever the reason for the origin
of your problem, the answer is always the same: Attend more
groups where you have a chance to cry in front of people. If you
keep writing sad letters and attending loving, sensitive groups,
you will eventually cry.

Two other points I want to mention in respect to grieving techniques are the use of sad movies and the benefit of professional
help. If you have tried letters and are not getting to your emotional
pain, watching a sad movie will often help. The best movies to
watch depend on each individual's response. Once you discover a
theme that sensitizes you, find movies with that theme.

If you still are unable to access your emotional pain despite
writing letters and watching painful movies, the next step is
professional help. In my work, I often function as a facilitator to
assist people in getting past the barriers to their emotional pain.
I know that many who have been through my workshop would
never have been able to regain their sensitivity without
professional help.

Do It Today

A critical part of your foundation is regaining your sensitivity. How you regain your sensitivity is not near as important as whether you regain it. You must regain your sensitivity or you will never enjoy the full experience of love. Sensitivity is available to everyone. Sensitivity is not a feminine trait. It is a lover's trait. If you want to be a lover, start regaining your sensitivity today.

To regain your sensitivity, start with your foundational decisions. Identify an environment of love in which to cry. Access the pain by writing letters and watching sad movies, and with professional help, if necessary. In the short run, you will hurt more, you will suffer more emotionally, and you may even wish you could go back to being numb. In the long run, you will experience a quality of life that you may not even realize is possible. You will experience the quality of life for which you were created.

Step 4 Exercises

Time of Commitment

Exercise 1: First, you and your partner agree on a time of commitment, at least four weeks, preferably six months. Then stand facing each other while holding hands, and alternately say the following:
"I am committed to working on an intimate, loving relationship with you."

Exercise 2: Establish a daily time of 1 to 1 1/2 hours where you and your partner can be alone and focus entirely on loving each other. In later steps, you will receive an exercise to do during your daily time.

Exercise 3: Establish a weekly time of a minimum of three hours for a date. You will be going on a date each week, alternating between casual and romantic dates. A romantic date consists of three hours alone together in a setting where you are entirely focused on each other and intimate conversation is possible. A casual date, on the other hand, can be spent with other couples in a setting where your focus is distracted by some form of entertainment. Examples of romantic dates include a picnic in the park, a romantic dinner and an intimate time alone in your home. Examples of casual dates include movies, plays and times of entertainment with friends. Children are not allowed on both casual and romantic dates.

Foundational Values

Exercise 1: Create a declaration of values in the following manner. List the five foundational
values. Directly beneath the list, write the
following statement:
"I agree with and commit to each of the
above values."
Both you and your partner sign the declaration of values.

Clear the Table

Exercise 1: Both you and your partner write letters to
each other expressing your perception of
how your partner has hurt and devalued
you in the past. Limit the letters to three
hand-written pages each as you briefly
mention all past significant issues.
Read the letters to each other while sitting
in chairs and in the presence of your support system with the understanding that the
content cannot be challenged.
After you both have read your letters, hold
hands, look into each other's eyes and individually say following:
"I am truly sorry for anyway I have hurt or
devalued you. Will you please forgive me?"
If you are willing to forgive your partner for
his past failures, respond by saying, "I forgive you."
At the completion of this exercise, you will
have cleared the table, meaning you take
full responsibility for the pain attached to
past issues and you focus on present
desires not past failures.

Establish a Support System

Exercise 1: You and your partner identify and agree upon a support system, either a support group, another committed couple and/or a spiritual authority.

Set Boundaries

Exercise 1: You and your partner independently write down your expectations and responsibilities. Bring your completed list together and attempt to establish agreement on each of the boundaries. Take any areas of disagreement to your support system and complete the process.

Place the completed, written list of boundaries in a notebook and establish consequences for any areas that you perceive will be difficult to maintain.

Finally, both you and you partner sign the boundary list, indicating your agreement and commitment.

Remember the purpose of setting boundaries is to eliminate conflict and enable you to focus on flowing in love. The process is initially very time consuming; but in the long run, you will spend markedly less time dealing with issues.

Exercise 2: Establish a daily issue time. You may schedule up to two-15 minute periods per day to discuss issues. Establish a consequence for any issue verbalized outside of issue time. Every time an issue comes to your mind, write it down and lovingly affirm your partner.

Start Regaining Your Sensitivity

Exercise 1: Write one sad letter per week and read it in the presence of your support system. If reading letters is not sensitizing you, then watch a sad movie while you and your partner are holding each other. Remember, the goal of this exercise is to cry in the presence of others.

S t e p   5

The ultimate value of loving communication
is a greater experience of true love
for both you and your lover.

COMMUNICATE LOVE
IN WORDS AND TOUCH

*W*ords are powerful. They can be used in very destructive ways—to destroy a relationship, to abuse a person, to deceive or to lie, to create chaos, to insult and shame, or in general, to destroy the flow of love. Words also can be powerfully positive if used to stabilize and enhance a relationship, to uplift a person, to establish the truth, to promote trust or, in general, to enhance and promote the experience of love. In this step, you will learn to powerfully energize your relationship by promoting positive communication and eliminating negative communication.

Clearly, most communication in a relationship is not determined by logic or love. It is determined by the feeling states of the people involved. If a couple is feeling good in a relationship energized by the Spirit of God, they will communicate in a way that is positive and uplifting. If a couple is feeling bad in a relationship energized by emotional pain, they will communicate in a destructive or insulting manner. The ultimate key to healthy communication is, therefore, not simply learning to communicate but learning to flow in love. The essence of this step is to teach you how to communicate in a manner that will promote, enhance and maintain the flow of the Spirit of God in your relationship.

What is the value?

The ultimate value of loving communication is a greater experience of true love for both you and your lover.

In addition to the ultimate value, there are five specific values:

1) Clarity of brain windows.

As you have learned, your brain is like a window that you experience and share love through. Eliminating arguments, blaming and other forms of negative communication, along with the regular use of positive communication, will significantly reduce the stress on your brain and reduce the risk of a fogged brain window.

2) Clarity of mind windows.

You have also learned that your mind is like a window through which you experience and share love. The mind window is often fogged in relationships because of problems in communication. Blaming, criticism, and distortions are just a few ways that your mind can get fogged. Communicate Love in Words and Touch will help you eliminate that fog by assisting you in maintaining healthy thoughts and feelings.

3) Promotion of sensitivity and vulnerability.

Probably the fastest way to destroy sensitivity and vulnerability is to use your mouth as a weapon. People frequently exposed to negative communication cover up fast while people blessed with an abundance of positive communication are more likely to live with open shutters.

4) Maintenance of four spans of the intimate, healthy relationship bridge.

Loving communication is critical to your IHR bridge. Four spans—loving communication, loving touch, commitment and loving perception—all require that you Communicate Love in Words and Touch.

5) Reinforcement of Trust

Love cannot flow consistently without trust. For love to flow, sensitivity must be present. Negative communication destroys the vulnerability that accompanies trust. Positive communication assists in eliminating the pain associated with the choice to trust. Trust cannot be maintained unless you Communicate Love in Words and Touch.

What is the process?

---

*Communicating love in words and touch
is a simple, direct process that anyone can do.*

There is nothing mystical or supernatural about loving communication. You don't have to be educated, exceptionally smart or uniquely talented to be a great communicator of love. You don't have to be a big talker, a skilled speaker or have a large vocabulary. You simply have to be willing to change, learn new skills and daily practice those skills.

I hear many excuses when I first teach couples how to communicate in love. "I'm not touchy, feely." "Men don't talk like that." "My parents didn't do that." "Where I grew up, that wasn't loving. That was sissy."

Whatever excuses come to your mind, simply discard them. What you are about to learn is not sissy, is definitely for both men and women, and has been proven to powerfully energize a relationship with love.

Discipline Your Mouth

Loving communication begins with a daily decision to discipline your mouth. **Discipline your mouth** may seem like a strange way to say it, but that is exactly what is required if you want to learn to communicate in a way that enhances the flow of love in your relationship. Most people lack loving communication skills. Growing up without an appropriate model, you learned to communicate in a manner that was appropriate for your family system. The communication patterns of your system were well programmed in your mind during your development. Changing those patterns requires discipline.

Discipline starts with daily decisions to think before you talk, to talk when it is appropriate, and to shut up when talking will interfere with the flow of love. You must learn how to positively communicate and do so even when you do not feel like it. You must avoid destructive communication even when it is very painful to do so. In the end, you willingness to discipline your mouth will determine your success.

Most of what you will learn in this step will be simple. Simple, well-defined rules are the foundation to loving communication. These rules have been tested and proven to work. At first, following the rules will be strange and uncomfortable. Loving communication is not a natural process for most people. However, moment-to-moment discipline with a conscious effort to follow the rules will over time lead to patterns of communication that are both loving and natural.

If you commit to the process with focused discipline, you will find yourself communicating love without even thinking about it. You will be lovingly touching your partner without any conscious effort. And, most importantly, you will experience and share love to an extent that very few enjoy.

Promoting Positive Communication

The essence of **positive communication** is that it enhances the flow of love. Positive communication includes four main areas of communication:

1) **Sincere Affirmations.**
2) **Regular Expression of Gratitude and Appreciation.**
3) **Healthy Discussion of Life Events.**
4) **Problem Solving In Love.**

Sincere Affirmations

Positive communication begins with simple sincere affirmations. A sincere affirmation is nothing more than saying something that enhances your lover's ability to experience how precious and wonderful he or she is as a child of God. Sincere affirmations fall into two general categories: those that reinforce your *lover's value as a spiritual being* and those that reinforce your *lover's value in the flesh*. To spontaneously inform your lover of how beautiful and wonderful he or she is would be a reinforcement of his or her value in the spiritual realm. To compliment your lover on how beautiful he or she looks today would be reinforcing his or her value in the flesh. In general, both categories have value, but reinforcement of your lover's spiritual value has longer lasting value.

The ability to sincerely affirm your lover is a skill that does not just happen naturally and is seldom taught or modeled in families. I grew up in a family in which superficial compliments were rare; sincere affirmations were essentially non-existent. I made a decision about 15 years ago that I was going to learn how to sincerely affirm people. The amazing thing about my initial experience with sincere affirmations is that when I even thought of complimenting someone, I would start experiencing bad feelings. My heart would race and my stomach would hurt. I had rarely complimented people in the past and learning to do so was an uncomfortable experience. So, how did I get past my discomfort? I practiced. That is right! I practiced affirming people and worked on reprogramming my mind. Whenever I saw something that I truly liked about a person, I would extend a compliment. No matter how bad my heart raced or my stomach hurt, I would still verbalize the affirmation. Now, I regularly affirm friends, family and even strangers without any heart racing or stomach pain.

As I was learning to sincerely affirm others, I had another strange experience. Having developed many loving friendships, I commonly received affirmations. Every time I received a sincere compliment, my stomach would hurt and my face would get hot. In fact, if someone were to compliment me, I would feel much worse than if someone were to insult or criticize me. Why was that? Why would I feel bad when someone affirmed me? The answer is simple. My mind was programmed in an emotionally painful childhood. It was programmed wrong. You are not supposed to feel bad when you receive an affirmation. But I did and many people do. How did I overcome my bad feelings? I practiced. I practiced being affirmed and worked on reprogramming my mind. Now, I am regularly affirmed by many people and feel good during the experience.

As you can see, the reprogramming of your mind is critical to your ability to sincerely affirm. A fogged mind window can severely interfere with your communication of love. If I had not understood how my feelings lie to me, my initial impulse would have been to both avoid affirming others and avoid people who affirmed me. If I had not known how to reprogram my mind, I would have had to numb or avoid sincere affirmations. Prior to understanding *The Seven Steps to Passionate Love*, I did a little of both. I numbed while giving superficial compliments. I also maintained relationships in which sincere affirmations were uncommon. Many people raised in homes with a limited amount of love pick relationships that enable them to avoid the pain associated with affirmations.

What do I mean by superficial compliments? It is important that you understand the difference. A superficial compliment is a product of your flesh, while a sincere affirmation is a product of love. Sincere affirmations will promote the flow of love; superficial compliments do not. There is a fine line between a superficial compliment and a sincere affirmation. Two people can say the exact same words, with one person sincerely affirming and the other superficially complimenting.

The essence of the difference between a sincere affirmation and a superficial compliment is the flow of love. If you are flowing in love when you compliment a person, you are extending a sincere affirmation. If you relate in your flesh while you affirm a person, you are extending a superficial complement. How can you know the difference? Only by learning the difference between flowing in love and relating in the flesh.

I frequently see people trying to practice loving communication by offering superficial complements. Superficial compliments are particularly prevalent in religious circles where everyone is trying to "love" each other. It is very common to find children from religious homes that have received thousands of superficial complements from well-intentioned parents. Although these children have consistently been told how wonderful they are, their lives and choices reflect the pain of lonely, empty spiritual beings. Everyone believes that the parents have done a great job "loving" their children when, in truth, the children have received very little love. Affirmations are only as valuable as the love that accompanies them.

To further illustrate this point, I have a brief story about two different husbands. The first husband, Paul, had a severe speech impediment; he stuttered with each word he spoke. Paul never finished high school and English was his worst subject. In practicing loving communication, Paul regularly affirmed his wife on a daily basis. The affirmations were simple and difficult to understand but given by a sensitive man flowing in love. The second husband, John, was a college English professor. He was articulate and gifted in his use of words. John could affirm his wife in many beautiful ways. Not only could he affirm her, but he did so regularly with a cheerful voice and a smile on his face. John affirmed his wife several times a day, every day of their marriage, even during the year that he had his affair. Who was more blessed by the affirmations, Paul's wife or John's wife?

Affirmations are only as valuable as the love that accompanies them.

Make sure that you do not use affirmations to cover up a spiritually empty relationship. Many couples do. Many counselors teach couples to do this. Superficial compliments bring no lasting value to relationships. Sincere affirmations, on the other hand, are a significant part of the bridge between two loving people.

Sincere affirmations are most beneficial when the focus is on your lover's value as a spiritual being and not based on performance, looks, talents or behavior. An example of an affirmation that can be given by a man to his wife is as follows:

"You're a beautiful, wonderful woman of God, and I'm very blessed to have you as my wife."

Typically, the above affirmation should be accompanied by a hug or a kiss. The goal is to reinforce the wife's value simply because she exists as a child of God. I recommend that you practice this affirmation or a similar one at least ten times per day. At first, it may seem redundant or boring, and you may find it difficult to remember to do the affirming. But as the flow of love improves in your relationship, sincerely affirming your lover will become a pleasure, not a chore.

Compliments that reinforce your value based on talents, looks or behavior also have some value but are less significant in the development of loving relationships. The problem with affirmations based on the flesh is that the flesh changes. If you are experiencing a significant amount of value due to looks, as your looks deteriorate with age, you will experience much less value. If you use performance to find value, when you perform poorly, you will hurt and experience little value. If you seek value through your talents, as your talent deteriorates, so will the value received from the talent. On the other hand, if you experience value through loving relationships, you will experience value no matter how you look or perform and no matter how talented you are. Sincere affirmations that reinforce value through love promote the experience of lasting value.

Sincere affirmations are a powerful part of communicating love in words and touch. Sincere affirmations are compliments that enhance your lover's ability to experience how wonderful he or she is as a child of God. Sincere affirmations are only as valuable as the love that accompanies them. Sincere affirmations are most powerful when they reinforce your lover's value as a spiritual being who is truly loved. Sincere affirmations should be a significant part of your daily communication.

Expression of Gratitude and Appreciation

You cannot be too thankful. You cannot express your gratitude too much. You cannot express appreciation for your lover too often. The regular expression of gratitude and appreciation is a powerful way to enhance the flow of love in your life.

If you were to monitor the content of the communication within a typical relationship during the romantic phase and compare it to the content of the communication within a relationship of five years duration, what differences do you think you would find? Many differences would exist. A major difference would be the decrease in the expression of gratitude and appreciation. During the romantic phase of a relationship, there is an appreciation for just about everything in the relationship. Gratitude is extensively and regularly expressed. Both lovers frequently verbalize their appreciation for even the simplest benefits of the relationship. At five years, communication has changed as entitlement has set in. What used to be greatly appreciated is now expected. The benefits that were so obvious five years before are overshadowed by the current inadequacies or needs. Little gratitude is now shown while expectations are voiced regularly. These typical changes in the expression of gratitude are very detrimental to the flow of love in a relationship.

A regular expression of gratitude and appreciation is exactly as it sounds. You should spend a significant amount of your time communicating and expressing thanks for what you have, the people around you and the beauty of the world in which you live. You should particularly communicate appreciation for the lover in your life. Make it clear daily that you are blessed to have such a wonderful person in your life. Let your lover know that, without a doubt, you are thankful for the relationship.

What if you are not thankful for the relationship? If you are not thankful for your partner in the relationship, either make a decision to be thankful or get a new partner. The best of those two choices is to make a decision to be thankful. You cannot heal a relationship if you do not first choose to appreciate the true person, the spiritual being, to whom you are relating. There must be a foundation of appreciation before the healing process can move forward. Staying in a relationship but not appreciating your lover is damaging to you both. **Healthy people either stay in love or leave in love.** They do not stay and blame. Make the decision to stay in love until you know it is time to leave.

Gratitude is a powerful way to enhance the flow of true love. Being thankful for your lover, your job, your daily blessings and life in general can powerfully change your experience of life. What if your thought is: "I don't have it that good"? But you do have it that good; you are simply not aware of how good you have it. It is the old half-full/half-empty paradox. Is the glass half full or is it half empty? It is all determined by perspective. You need to develop a grateful, appreciative perspective. Be thankful for the blessings you have. Does that mean you ignore the problems or issues in your life? No, it means that you appreciate and value the good and the positives in your life while you work on the solutions to the problems.

A daily expression of appreciation and gratitude is necessary to maintain a consistent flow of love in your life. I recommend that you start by making a conscientious effort to appropriately say "thank you" throughout your day. Saying "thank you" may seem insignificant to you but it is very significant to establishing an attitude of appreciation. Many people express thanks to everyone except their primary partner. The rationalization is that their partner "already knows that they are thankful." Even if your partner "knows" you are appreciative, you cannot express your gratitude too often.

Another daily exercise in appreciation that I recommend is the communication of nine simple expressions of gratitude to your lover every day:

- Three ways that God has blessed you during that day.
- Three ways that your lover has blessed you during that day.
- Three things you appreciate about your lover.

You cannot be too thankful. You cannot express your gratitude too much. You cannot express appreciation for your lover too often. Start improving your capability as a lover today by regularly expressing gratitude and appreciation.

Healthy Discussion of Life Events

A healthy discussion of life events means that you and your partner should identify and cultivate common life interests that you can enjoy talking about on a daily basis. The word "enjoy" is significant because it eliminates the discussion of issues and problems. You should maintain a sincere interest in and regular communication about each other's positive life events. You should regularly talk about the good things in life, the experiences you enjoy and the topics that you find interesting. You should spend time talking about your lover's work, friends and recreational activities. You should develop an adequate understanding of each other's interests so as to be able to carry on an enriching conversation. Regular, pleasurable conversations about life events are important to a loving relationship.

You may think that every couple regularly enjoys regular discussions concerning positive life events. In truth, many couples do not. Most established couples either talk very little or spend the majority of their communication time talking about issues and problems, particularly if they have children. Couples are also often too busy with individual responsibilities and activities to spend the time hearing about each other's lives. And in some relationships, the issue is not a lack of time; it is a lack of interest.

What if you simply have no interest in your partner's activities? Then develop an interest; cultivate an interest. Why would you want to cultivate an interest? Because it will make your relationship better. Do it as a gift to your partner. Although an activity may not be interesting to you, your lover is of interest to you. So, if you do not enjoy the topic of conversation, enjoy the communicator, your lover.

A healthy discussion about life events is critical to maintaining intimacy in your relationship. Make a commitment to focus daily time on enriching your life by learning about your lover's work, hobbies, and interests. Make your lover's passions your own and you both will be blessed.

Eliminating Destructive Communication

Destructive communication is defined as **communication that moves you away from love.** After working with and studying thousands of relationships, it is obvious that most couples have more destructive communication than positive communication. During the initial stage of the relationship when good feelings dominate, positive communication flourishes. Over time, the good feelings start to fade, the bad feelings grow, and destructive communication becomes obvious. In previous sections, you learned how to positively communicate. Now, you will learn how to eliminate the destructive communication.

Destructive communication comes in many containers and many shades. It can be subtle and it can be obvious. Destructive communication can be delivered with a sweet voice or with an explosion. It can be veiled with a smile or it can be magnified with a glare. No matter how it is delivered, destructive communication always cheats you out of the full experience of love.

You may be skilled at delivering a destructive message and not even know you have the talent. If you were raised in a family where destructive communication reigned, you are probably blind to your ability to block the flow of love with your words. It is, therefore, critical that you study the different categories of destructive communication and see what fits. Ask your lover to help you realize when and how your words dampen the flow of love. Make a commitment that you will become aware of any personal patterns of destructive communication and will be accountable for their elimination from your life.

The more effectively you eliminate your destructive communication, the more powerfully your positive communication will enhance the experience and flow of love in your relationship. The key to eliminating your unhealthy forms of communication starts with their recognition. There are many forms of destructive communication but the following eight categories are the most significant:

- **Absence of communication**
- **Sarcasm and joking**
- **Complaining and blaming**
- **Indirect and passive**
- **Deceitful or lying**
- **Screaming and yelling**
- **Gossiping and splitting**
- **Using the past to predict the future**

Study these eight forms of destructive communication well. Many of them are subtle and, like a slow disease, progressively destroy the health of your relationship.

Absence of Communication

You probably realize that abuse comes in all different forms in a relationship, the most common being physical, verbal and sexual. What you may not realize is that one of the most powerful forms of abuse is the *absence of communication*. Screaming and yelling are not required for verbal abuse to be present. Silence can be a very effective way to inflict pain upon someone.

I have worked with many adults who as children were punished with silence. Mom or dad would simply refuse to talk to them for a period of time after they broke a rule. Consistently, these adults recall that the silent treatment was terrible. Why? Because the absence of communication means the absence of love. Consequently, a parent verbally withdrawing is very painful for a child who is sensitive to his or her need for love. You can definitely hurt a child simply by failing to communicate.

The same is true for an adult who desires a relationship with love. A sensitive adult aware of his or her need for love will be emotionally and spiritually hurt in a relationship lacking in loving communication. The absence of communication is as damaging as active verbal abuse. Both significantly undermine the foundation of a loving relationship.

As a participant in a relationship, you have a responsibility to lovingly communicate to your partner. You must learn how to positively affirm your partner. You must regularly compliment your lover. You must daily express appreciation and gratitude for that person in your life. You must cultivate an interest in your lover's life and express that interest through knowledgeable conversation. You must consistently use your words to enhance the flow of love in your relationship.

What if you grew up in a family where loving communication was absent? As an adult, your skills are going to be lacking. Is that an acceptable excuse for being a poor communicator? Absolutely not. Your responsibility to be a loving communicator is the same no matter how lacking loving communication was in your family of origin. You simply have to do more work. You have to practice.

What if you are simply not much of a talker? Again, your developmental inadequacies are not an acceptable excuse to relieve you of your responsibility for loving communication. You can learn to be a good communicator. Do you need to be as articulate as Shakespeare? No. But you do need to be capable of intimately communicating to your spouse how beautiful and wonderful he or she is. You need to have the skill to passionately express your love for your partner.

Loving communication is not a genetic inheritance, a personality trait or a gift from God; it is a developed skill. If you do not have the skill, you can acquire it. No matter how lacking your communication skills currently are, you can become a sensitive, passionate communicator of love.

Joe grew up on a farm as the only child of two workaholic parents. From sunup to sundown, his father worked the farm while his mother worked around the house. Joe was shy by nature, and talking was not his thing. With two busy parents, Joe could easily play alone all day without ever speaking a word. Academically, Joe was above average and migrated toward subjects that required little verbal expression.

Paula grew up in a family where screaming was the mode of communication. Paula could not recall a single day in her childhood where her mom or dad did not scream at least once. Outgoing and verbally expressive by nature, Paula's primary form of entertainment was talking to someone. She was a member of the debate team in high school and won her class presidency after giving a stirring speech during the election.

Joe and Paula met at college. She was a communication major while he was pursuing a degree in agriculture. Joe was attracted to Paula's beauty and her "amazing wit." Joe loved to sit and listen to Paula tell stories for hours. Paula was initially attracted to Joe's soft, polite and quiet manner. Over time, she fell in love with "my handsome farmer who is a great listener." Most importantly, Joe fulfilled Paula's most important criteria; he never screamed in two years of dating. Paula and Joe knew that their marriage would be long and blessed.

After three years of marriage, perceptions had changed and they agreed to marital counseling. Paula talked first: "Joe is the most boring, numb, quiet 'moron' that I have ever met. I am so sick of listening to myself talk. Joe never says a word. Only if I throw a fit, screaming and yelling, will I get a response out of him. Dr. Van Horn, believe me, the only reason I am here is for the children."

Paula paused, looked at Joe, and then said, "Dr. Van Horn, I have spent three years with this moron who has averaged less than ten words per day of communication with me. Can you fix him?"

"But Paula, wasn't Joe quiet before you married him?" I asked, hoping to slow down Paula's blaming.

"Yes, he was quiet but not this bad," Paula responded, scowling at Joe the entire time. "At least, he focused on me while we were dating. Now, he just sits in front of the TV or works around the house. Joe acts like he is avoiding me and the children."

I looked at Joe who sat quietly, acting as if he were a little boy being scolded by his angry mother. I asked, "What are your thoughts?"

Joe hesitated, took a deep breath, and with a soft voice, replied, "Dr. Van Horn, I know I say more than ten words a day but I'm not a big talker. I have always been quiet. I like listening. Paula's a great talker and I used to love listening to her. But I got tired of listening to her complain and blame. I was afraid to tell her to stop so I just learned to stay busy. Her complaining became screaming so I got busier. Now Paula screams and yells every day. I am sure that if I open my mouth, she will just use hers to rip me apart."

What happened between Joe and Paula was sad but simple. By marrying Joe, Paula was escaping a loud, verbally abusive family. She mistook Joe's quiet and calm demeanor for love. Initially, Paula was thrilled to simply have a man who would listen and not fight. Joe was satisfied to have a pretty wife who dominated the relationship. Neither Joe nor Paula had any reasonable perspective of a truly loving relationship.

As the romantic feelings faded, Joe continued in his quiet, "numb" manner while Paula started hurting, longing for more intimacy in her marriage. Tired of doing all the talking, Paula pushed Joe to be more active, more romantic, more "loving." Joe dealt with Paula's pressure in the same manner that he had always responded to stress: He withdrew. He became even more quiet and reserved. Paula was devastated. Joe's response convinced her that she had been duped. After three years of marriage and two children, the "real" Joe was becoming evident: a quiet, boring "moron."

And Paula let the "moron" know that "those who dupe Paula, pay for it." She screamed, yelled and threw things. Her emotional fits were daily and intense. Paula decided that divorce was "too good" for Joe. If he was going to ruin her life, she was going to ruin his. Marital therapy was Paula's ultimate dagger. With the help of a professional, she was going to prove that Joe was worthless and the cause of all their problems.

Paula was initially pleased with therapy as she and Joe learned about "loving communication." Joe had obviously failed because of his almost total absence of communication. Joe learned about his responsibility to develop the skills of a loving communicator. He learned that he had a choice and that he had been choosing to be a sorry lover by shutting up and staying numb. Joe made a commitment to become a truly sensitive, loving communicator and he backed his commitment up with work.

Paula "knew" that she had little or no work to do when she entered therapy. She saw herself as a "great" communicator, a wonderful lover. When asked about her verbal outbursts, Paula defended her behavior with the excuse that Joe needed motivation. When confronted with the reality that yelling and screaming are abusive forms of motivation, Paula initially argued but quickly broke into tears. She admitted that her verbal assaults were abusive and that she herself was abused this way in her childhood. Paula committed to ending all forms of verbal abuse and she backed up her commitment with some severe consequences.

Both Joe and Paula committed to *The Seven Steps to Passionate Love*. Paula turned her talented mouth that she had been using as a weapon into a powerful tool for sharing love. Joe actively worked on his sensitivity as he daily affirmed, thanked and verbally showed interest in Paula. After one year of living *The Seven Steps to Passionate Love*, Paula announced to me, "I am living with the most stimulating, wonderful loving communicator that I know."

The absence of communication was destroying the foundation of Joe and Paula's relationship. Communication is a necessary component of a loving relationship. Loving communication is possible for anyone who is willing to make the commitment and do the work. Make the decision today that you are going to develop the skills to be a consistent communicator of love.

Sarcasm and Joking

Ann and John were traveling home after attending an office party when Ann said, "John, your personal secretary, Cathy, sure is cute. I bet it is hard to keep your hands off of her."

John was surprised by what he perceived as Ann's jealousy and replied, "Actually, Ann, it is not hard as long as Cathy and I maintain our weekly appointment at the Hilton."

"John, you are so mean. I was just kidding when I commented about Cathy," Ann said tearfully.

"Obviously, I am kidding, too," he replied. "I have no personal or sexual interest in Cathy. She's a very good secretary, and I am thankful for that."

Vicki had just burned the spaghetti sauce. The smell permeated the kitchen. Tim walked in and said, "Now, I know why McDonalds stays in business."

Vicki, red faced with frustration, responded, "If it wasn't for Tim Jr. doing 'what daddy does' by taking food to his bedroom, I would not need McDonalds. I was in Tim's room cleaning the food out of the carpet when the sauce burned."

Tim laughed, "Here Vicki, let me help you with dinner." Vicki was not laughing.

Sarcasm and joking are commonly used forms of destructive communication. Ann was obviously having some jealous feelings. Rather than approach John in a healthy way and ask for reassurance of his fidelity, she made a sarcastic remark. John, sensing Ann's jealousy, fueled the feelings by joking in return. An opportunity to strengthen the safety of the relationship and assist Ann in healing was turned into a painful joke. Why? Because neither Ann nor John knew how to appropriately deal with Ann's insecurities.

Tim used Vicki's mistake as an opportunity to "be funny." Unfortunately, the joke was only funny to Tim. Vicki was already overwhelmed by the situation. She did not need a comedian for a husband. Vicki needed a lover. Tim took an opportunity to support his wife emotionally in love and used it for his comical pleasure. Tim's sarcasm only made the situation worse.

When are sarcasm and joking inappropriate in a loving relationship? The following are four rules to follow:

1. Do not use your lover as the "butt" of a joke.
2. Do not joke about your partner's inadequacies, insecurities or mistakes.
3. Do not use joking or sarcasm in relation to issues that you have with your lover.
4. Do not tell jokes that are devaluing to your partner, another individual or a group of people.

Many people claim that being the butt of a joke does not trigger pain but I have yet to meet someone with good sensitivity who would make that claim. People learn to numb to the sting of cutting humor and, in the process, lose some of their sensitivity to love. Remember, you are supposed to be the safest person in the world for your lover. That is not possible if he or she is the butt of your jokes.

Inappropriate humor also fogs the mind window. Devaluing humor triggers bad feelings in sensitive people. Bad feelings fog the mind window and energize distorted thoughts. The bad feelings and distorted thoughts undermine the experience of a truly loving perception. It is very difficult to experience how beautiful and wonderful you are while relating to someone who devalues you with humor.

What if you are simply trying to be entertaining? Using your lover as the butt of a joke is not loving entertainment. There is no situation where making fun of your partner will add to the flow of love. Remember, your primary purpose in your relationship is to be a lover, not an entertainer. As a lover, your goal is to assist your partner in experiencing how wonderful and beautiful he or she truly is. There is no way that being the butt of a joke will enhance your lover's experience of true value. You may be entertained by the joke. Even your lover may find the humor entertaining. But in the end, you and your lover will be cheated out of the full experience of love.

Many people resort to humor when confronted with their own or their partner's inadequacies. Sarcasm is an easy escape from the discomfort of failures. Unfortunately, humor is only a temporary escape, not a long-term solution. It is through the healing power of love that we overcome our deficits. It is through the flow of love that we come to know that we are not our mistakes. You are the primary channel of love in your partner's life. Take advantage of the opportunity for healing by being a lover, not a comedian, when failures and deficits are revealed.

An opportunity for healing also exists when you and your lover have issues. If you are someone who avoids appropriate confrontation, you very likely use sarcasm or joking to inappropriately address issues. The use of humor to raise issues only sabotages the process of problem-solving. No true healing can take place. Sarcastic remarks concerning issues may give you some temporary relief from the pain associated with the issue, but in the end, the pain is worse.

Sarcasm is also a way to blame or ridicule your partner's positions on issues. Again, you are only making the situation worse. Avoid sarcasm and joking when dealing with issues. Instead, pursue lasting healing and resolution of those issues through problem-solving in love.

When are jokes and sarcasm not devaluing to a loving relationship? There are no absolutes to this answer. In general, if you are laughing with someone and not at someone, the humor is most likely appropriate. If the humor is helping you and your lover clear your mind windows, move toward greater spiritual intimacy, or simply relax without devaluing anyone, it is probably beneficial. You determine the ultimate answer. If the jokes and sarcasm enhance the flow of love in your life, they are good.

If they diminish the flow of love, the jokes should be eliminated.

Eliminating destructive jokes and sarcasm from your communication is critical to the health of your relationship. If you have always been a "comedian," then maintain the healthy comedy and eliminate the unhealthy. If you only resort to sarcasm when you are hurting, then move toward love instead. If you are afraid life will be "boring" without your humor, then replace the devaluing humor with positive communication and watch how exciting life can really be. Ultimately, you have a choice: the temporary pleasure of sarcasm and joking or the lasting fulfillment of love. Choose love. It truly is better.

Issues and Blaming

The elimination of issues and blaming from your relationship is a powerful change. The elimination of issues does not mean that you do not have issues in your relationship. It simply means that you limit the discussion of issues to a very specific, limited period of time called **issue time**. You should set aside one or two specific times each day where you deal with all of your personal, professional and familial issues. You will then be free to spend the rest of your communication time on positive communication. If you limit issues to issue time, you will see a dramatic improvement in the flow of love.

To limit issues to issue time requires that you know what an issue is. I have chosen to define an issue based on what it is not because I find it is an easier way for people to eliminate the inappropriate discussion of issues.

An issue is anything that <u>is not</u> a positive affirmation, an expression of gratitude, a positive interest or a positive invitation.

In other words, if you are communicating with your partner and it is not positive communication, then you are discussing an issue.

The purpose of issue time is not only to eliminate issues from your normal conversation but also to ensure that the majority of your communication is positive. You cannot positively communicate too much, but you can definitely spend too much time dealing with issues. If you have a history of worrying, complaining or bringing up issues, use your automatic sick thoughts to your advantage. Every time a worry, complaint or issue comes to your mind, use it to remind yourself to affirm your lover. You will quickly become a great positive communicator.

Issue time will be discussed again in more detail in Step 7. For now, the most important thing to remember about issue time is that it works.

Blaming is attributing your pain to anyone or anything outside of you. The elimination of blaming means that you take full responsibility for your pain and move toward love when you are hurting.

Blaming is discussed in detail in Step 6; therefore, I will simply emphasize two points at this time.

- Blaming is an effective way to kill the flow of love. Don't blame. Don't let your blaming mouth cheat you out of the fullness of love. All blamers have miserable lives. You don't have to participate in that misery.
- The most destructive form of blaming is blaming God or your partner. Behind all blaming is emotional pain. The answer to your emotional pain is love. God is your source of love and your partner is the most significant channel of love in your life. God and your partner are part of the answer. Only fools blame their answer. Don't be a fool.

Issues and blaming dominate many unhealthy relationships. The inappropriate discussion of issues and the presence of blaming undermine the flow of love. Limit your issues to issue time and eliminate blaming from your communication. If you do so, you will be one step closer to the full benefits of *The Seven Steps to Passionate Love.*

Indirect Passive Communication

The hallmark of indirect, passive communication is the failure to communicate negatives appropriately and honestly. People who indirectly and passively communicate rarely directly address issues and problems. Rather, many mixed messages are communicated, allowing the communicator to deny any negative intent and leave the recipient to decipher the message. The verbalized intent of indirect, passive communication is to be nice and to avoid "hurting anyone's feelings." The true intent is the avoidance of the pain associated with honest, appropriate confrontation and criticism.

A foundational belief among those who indirectly and passively communicate is the following cliché: "If you can't say something nice, do not say anything at all." There are two significant distortions underlying this belief:

- The idea that verbalizing criticism is destructive.
- The belief that the failure to appropriately verbalize criticism is not destructive.

Appropriately communicating criticism is **not** destructive. Rather, it is critical to the flow of love in a relationship. Honest, objective criticism is necessary for personal and relational growth. It is important to be critiqued and assessed and to receive input on what needs to be improved and changed.

Without appropriate criticism, growth and maturation are impossible.

> *I once had a friend, Joe, tell me, "I didn't confront you about your problem because I wanted God to show you. I just prayed and waited." My response was as follows: "Joe, starting today, if you are not willing to appropriately criticize me, we can no longer be friends. You are here to be used by God to help me see my faults. If you do not tell me what you perceive is wrong with me, you are not much of a friend."*
>
> *Joe agreed to lovingly critique me once per week. We moved on in our relationship with a greater experience of love.*

Communicating negatives is a value that must be met for a relationship to flow in love. As you lovingly critique your intimate friend, make sure you maintain a loving perception, knowing that you are dealing with a beautiful, wonderful person. If you support your criticism with a loving perception, you will see wonderful changes in your relationships and the life of your intimate friend.

The key to communicating criticism is doing it in a way that promotes love. You can accomplish this goal through problem-solving in love, which is discussed thoroughly in Step 7. For now, I simply want to emphasize that there is an appropriate way to express your criticism.

People who passively and indirectly communicate do express their criticisms; they simply do it in a destructive way. An honest, objective communicator who desires to knife you will do so to your face. An indirect, passive communicator who desires to knife you will hug you first and stab you in the back. When you fail to appropriately communicate your criticism, you are choosing to be a "back-stabber."

Make the decision to eliminate indirect, passive communication from your life. Choose to deal with issues through open, honest objective communication by problem-solving in love. If you do so, you will be one step closer to the full benefits of *The Seven Steps to Passionate Love.*

Deceit and Lying

You cannot have a loving relationship if you are not willing to be honest. Because honesty is so critical to the flow of love, I have included a discussion here and a more thorough one in Step 7.

Why do people lie? To avoid the pain associated with being honest. Most people who lie grew up in homes where it was not safe to be honest. Liars come from all types of family systems, but no system is more effective at producing liars than a righteous, performance-based home. Parents in these homes often have unreasonable expectations of their children and become very upset when the child does not meet these expectations. The child quickly learns that lying is less painful than being honest. Hiding mistakes and "sins" becomes a way of life. Typically, once the patterns of dishonesty are established in childhood, they continue in adult relationships.

Not all lying is equal in severity or destructiveness, but *all lying is destructive.* Lying destroys the safety and trust necessary for love to flow. Lying demonstrates a lack of true commitment while sabotaging communication and loving perception in a relationship. Any degree of lying significantly undermines the flow of love in a relationship.

If you have a pattern of lying, how can you change? Tell the truth. Tell the truth in all situations at any cost. Make honesty a critical priority in your life. Lying is a choice; being honest is also a choice. Make the decision today, that you will be honest in every area of your life. If you do so, you will be one step closer to the full benefits of *The Seven Steps to Passionate Love.*

Screaming and Yelling

Imagine that you have a beautiful, large German shepherd that is the most wonderful dog in the world 24 hours a day, seven days a week except for one five-minute period each month. During that period, the dog aggressively chews on your leg, removing as much of your flesh as is possible. You never know when to expect his chewing assault but you know that it will happen for five minutes each month.

What would you do if that were your dog? The assault is only once a month for five minutes. The remainder of the time you have the most wonderful dog in the world. Obviously, despite having the best dog 99 percent of the time, you would have to get rid of him. What if you could not get rid of the dog? The next obvious solution would be to protect yourself, either by avoiding the dog or establishing an impenetrable barrier between you and the dog.

Remember the "dog story" the next time you scream or yell. Screaming and yelling destroy the environment for intimacy and love. Even limited, intermittent verbal outbursts damage the sensitivity necessary for the flow of love. People who relate to a screamer either distance or build emotional barriers so the verbal assaults do not hurt. The distancing protects them from pain as it undermines the flow of love.

Why do you scream and yell? Verbal outbursts give you some

immediate relief from emotional pain. To put it simply, you feel better in the short run if you yell or scream. Someone or something triggers your brain, unresolved emotional pain explodes into your conscious experience and you obtain some temporary relief by screaming. If you doubt that this is true, try a simple experiment. The next time you ride a roller coaster scream the whole time. You will not experience near as many bad feelings. Your bad feelings are temporarily relieved with screaming and yelling, but the underlying emotional pain is unchanged.

Remember, every time you hurt, you have an opportunity to heal. The decisions you make in the midst of your hurt determine whether you heal. Screaming and yelling are destructive decisions. You cannot heal if you choose to verbally explode.

How much screaming and yelling is acceptable? None! You must stop the verbal outbursts. What if you cannot stop? You can! Don't lie to yourself that you can't stop. I have helped hundreds of people stop their verbal assaults. Stopping is definitely possible.

Ending the verbal assaults is a matter of will and value. Are you willing to do what is necessary to win the battle with your mouth? Do you value yourself and the people around you enough to stop the yelling? Do you value love enough to stop your sabotage? If the answer to these questions is "yes," then you can stop.

Stopping verbal outbursts entails two fundamental processes: short-term control of the outbursts with a variety of techniques and long-term emotional healing in love. The simplest technique to stop the yelling is to bite your tongue. Place your tongue between your teeth and bite down. Many people prefer to place their tongue between the teeth on the side of their mouth. Placing your tongue between your teeth enables you to make the choice not to explode.

It is essentially impossible to scream or yell while biting your tongue. If you have a severe problem with verbal outbursts, you need to keep your tongue between your teeth throughout the day or, at least, when you are around the people at whom you scream. Biting your tongue will be effective unless you fail to do it quick enough or to maintain it.

If you prefer a technique of control that requires less personal responsibility at the moment of decision, both the use of tape and a mouthpiece are effective. You can place a band-aide or tape to the side of you mouth or over the corner of your mouth. The tape and band-aide act to remind you to either bite your tongue or shut up. A mouthpiece is an extremely beneficial tool if you have a difficult time controlling your outbursts. You simply wear the mouthpiece whenever you are in a situation where you perceive you might lose control of your mouth. The mouthpiece gives you time to make a healthy decision when your emotional pain hits.

These techniques may seem extreme but they are a small price to pay to keep from destroying your life. I have worked with many people who were destroying their relationships with outbursts and were saved with these techniques. If you can stop your screaming and yelling with a decision, then do so. If you need to bite your tongue, wear tape or use a mouthpiece, then do it. Do whatever is necessary to control your mouth, or you will never move past your emotional pain.

Moving past your emotional pain also requires engaging in an active process of emotional healing in love. In Step 6, you will learn the emotional healing process. At this time, I want you to know for sure that you cannot experience the love you were created to enjoy if you continue your yelling and screaming. Make the decision today that you will do whatever is necessary to ensure that you do not yell or scream. You will be one step closer to the full benefits of *The Seven Steps to Passionate Love.*

Gossip and Splitting

Gossip is talking negatively about people when they are not present.

Splitting is a specific form of gossip where the outcome is division within a relationship or system of relationships.

The rule about gossip and splitting is:

"DON'T DO THEM."

The definition of gossip is easy for most people to understand. If you are talking about or listening to something negative about a person or group of people—a problem, a mistake, a sin, an inadequacy, an illness, a failure—and they are not present, you are participating in gossip. The only exceptions to this rule are if you have permission from the person or the person is a public personality and not a part of your relationship system.

Splitting is slightly more difficult to understand. Splitting is a form of gossip where a person is creating division within a relationship or a system of relationship. A simple example of splitting occurs with a group of three people. John, Joy and Mary are all friends. John and Mary are dating and Joy is jealous. Joy tells Mary that John told her that he couldn't stand the way she kissed. Joy tells John that Mary thinks he is kind of stupid. Mary gets mad at John. John gets mad at Mary. They break up and Joy steps in to date John. The end result is that Joy has used gossip to divide John and Mary and temporarily benefit herself.

Splitting is often undertaken purposely. Other times, people split and do not realize that they are doing so. The key to ending splitting is the elimination of gossip combined with open, honest communication. If John and Mary had not participated in gossip with Joy, their conflict would never have occurred. If you never participate in gossip, you will never be involved in splitting.

Gossip and splitting are powerful destroyers of trust and safety in relationships. You cannot maintain an environment of love if gossip and splitting occur. You cannot maintain honest communication if gossip and splitting occur. You cannot maintain a loving perception if gossip and splitting occur. You cannot live *The Seven Steps to Passionate Love* if you or your intimate friends engage in gossip and splitting.

How common are gossip and splitting? Extremely! Sadly, gossip and splitting are common is most arenas of life. Businesses, churches, civic organizations and families all suffer with the negative influence of these two forms of destructive communication. There is probably no more prevalent or destructive form of communication in most systems.

Gossip and splitting come in many forms. **"Will you please pray for Bill. He . . ."** **"It is so sad what happened to Jane . . ."** **"I don't know what to do for poor Sally who . . ."** Many people gossip out of concern or sympathy. Others do it viciously. In either case, it is destructive.

What if you are asked for advice by one person concerning someone else? Both people should be present when you give the advice. If you are giving relationship advice, you should have both partners present. If it is not possible to have both people present, the person who does not attend should be informed of the meeting prior to its occurrence. If the discussion is to be about issues concerning someone who is part of your intimate relationship base, insist that your intimate friend be present. Under no circumstance, should you talk about issues concerning an intimate friend without their permission or presence. Even well meaning gossip is destructive.

If you do end up giving advice concerning someone who is not present, realize that you received a biased version of the problem. I have advised couples where both people were intelligent and honest, yet their perceptions of the same experience were dramatically different. Who was describing reality? Maybe, the man. Maybe, the woman. Or maybe neither. I did not and still do not know. Your advice and counsel is limited by the biased information you have.

Gossip and splitting are prevalent in almost all relationship systems. Do not participate. Choose to value the people around you. Develop relationships with people who will also honor this boundary.

Using the Past to Predict the Future

Using the past to predict the future means **looking at past failures to validate future failure.** Everyone is doomed to fail if the past is used as a predictor. Who has not failed in the past? If you are trying to move to a more mature experience of love, your past will always look worse than your future goal. Future success as a lover is determined by what happens today and tomorrow, not yesterday.

This concept sounds so simple that you may be wondering why I mention it all. I mention it because people use the past to predict the future of their relationship all the time.

Paul and Jane were committed to The Seven Steps to Passionate Love. *It had been one year since they left the intimacy and love workshop. Prior to the workshop, their relationship was in shambles. Paul had tried everything to make up for his affair but nothing worked. The workshop changed everything. Their commitment to true love combined with hard work had resulted in progressive growth. Three weeks ago, they both reported that love was flowing better than ever.*

Today, Jane wanted out. "If Paul goes to Hawaii, I will leave him."

"Jane, why would you leave him?" I asked.

"Because he will have an affair in Hawaii!" Jane screamed at me.

"An affair?" I was confused. "What makes you think that?"

Crying but much calmer, Jane replied, "He did it before. He will do it again."

"But Jane, Paul's affair was the fruit of a lonely marriage and a lonely life." I gently challenged her distortions. "He is now passionately in love with you and is accountable to many loving friends. Why would he want the cheap thrill of empty sex when he can have the tremendous experience of true love with you?"

Jane was experiencing life through the fogged mind window of a lonely little girl who had been raised by an adulterous father and a lonely woman who was married to an adulterous man. She was not experiencing the reality of a beautiful woman who was married to a passionately loving, faithful husband. Paul had changed but Jane was relating to him based on the mistakes of his past. Jane was using the past to predict the future. By doing so, she was sabotaging the flow of love in her marriage.

Should Paul's past affair simply be ignored? No. Paul had agreed to be open and honest about his sexual feelings and be accountable for controlling his thoughts and behavior. If Paul found his thoughts moving in the wrong direction, he was committed to immediately informing his accountability partners. With their help, Paul had been consistently making good decisions. Paul's new foundation of love and accountability combined with personal commitment insured that he would never again betray Jane.

Past mistakes, including affairs, do not happen in a vacuum. Looking at a person's past to judge their capability of making healthy decisions while living *The Seven Steps to Passionate Love* is a waste of time. Men and women who have made many bad decisions while living lonely lives often can make consistently good decisions when they are involved in relationships based on love.

Remember, it is the power of love that enables a person to make healthy choices. Rarely will a person choose dog food when they can have steak. True love is steak. Steak was not available in Paul's past. He chose poop. Once he feasted on real meat, the odds of him returning to poop were slim.

Do not use the past to predict your relationship's future. Commit to true love with your partner. Savor in the steak. Focus on what needs to be done today to enhance the flow of love in your relationship. If you do so, you will have no concern for the past as you enjoy the wonderful experience of love in the present.

It's not easy, but it's worth it!

What is necessary to eliminate destructive communication from your relationship? Decisions and Discipline. Daily decisions and discipline. Study this chapter until you truly understand the different ways destructive communication can sabotage your relationship. Make the decision to discipline your tongue and your mind so that no destructive communication comes out of your mouth. When your emotional pain hits, stop, bite your tongue and think before you fall back into destructive communication.

You were created to be a lover. Lovers control their mouths. Lovers promote the flow of love with positive communication. Lovers eliminate destructive communication from their lives. Live, think and talk like the lover you were meant to be.

Loving Touch

"But Dr. Van Horn, I am just not a 'touchy, feely' person. I cannot be what I am not," John adamantly proclaimed as he and his wife, June, sat in my office. "That is one of the main problems with my marriage. June wants to make me into someone I am not."

John was a big man, handsome by most standards, and still muscular despite being in his mid-fifties. He was sitting with his arms folded over his chest, clearly informing me that he was not here for change. John had told me both verbally and nonverbally on many occasions that he was happy with the way he was and that June had the problem, not him. I looked into John's soft, big, brown eyes, smiled and said, "John, when you say that you are not a 'touchy, feely' person, what do you mean?"

"I mean that my father did not spend his day hugging and kissing my mom," John confidently defended his position. "My grandfather did not hug and kiss my grandma all day. Men in my family don't do those kinds of things. I will be glad to kiss June 'good morning' and 'good night,' but all this other touching is not for me. Why can't June be happy with what I have done for the last thirty years?"

"John, that is a good question," I softly answered as I turned to June. "June, why don't you answer John's question."

"I will be glad to Dr. Van Horn," June said. She was an extremely attractive woman who looked much younger than her recorded age of fifty-four. Her pretty eyes sparkled as she spoke. "John, you are right about some things," she said. "Your grandma and grandpa did not touch much when they were alive. Your dad does not touch your mom much. And you have not been a 'touchy, feely' person since I met you 32 years ago. If I had never come to Dr. Van Horn's intimacy and love workshop, I probably would never have realized what you and I have missed. But I did go through the workshop and I received more intimate hugs. . . ." June paused as she started to cry. "John, I received more intimate hugs from those 'strangers' in four days than I received from you in 32 years." June bowed her head to her hands and sobbed into her tissue.

I looked at John, who had tears in his eyes, as he watched his wife cry. I asked, "What are your thoughts, John?"

John took a deep breath, steadied his emotions, and replied, "Dr. Van Horn, no one loves his wife more than I love June. It kills me to see her hurt. I wish I was that 'touchy, feely' person she wants, but I am not."

"John, who told you that you were not?" I persisted. "Who told you that you were not capable of hugging, kissing and gently caressing your wife when you are around her?"

"No one told me, Dr. Van Horn," John answered in a much less defiant tone. "I have never been like that. No one had to tell me."

"But John, there was a time when you were 'touchy, feely.' There was a time when all you wanted to do was

cuddle. A time when kissing, hugging and caressing were natural and wonderful for you."

"I don't remember that time," John responded.

"Of course, you do not remember. " I looked directly into John's eyes as I replied. " It was when you were a very little baby. All babies are comfortable with loving touch. Many of those babies are taught to stop touching, learn to be uncomfortable with touch, and turn out like you." I paused briefly, smiled at John and then continued, "That is the bad news, John. The good news is that you can change. You can learn to act like the 'touchy, feely' person you were created to be. You can learn to enjoy being touched as you lovingly touch June. Or you can stay as you are and be cheated out of the love that you were created to experience."

Loving touch is critical to the experience of love. Loving touch is one of the five ingredients of an intimate healthy relationship and must be present for the Spirit of God to flow in your relationship. You cannot be a good lover if you are not comfortable with loving touch.

What if you are like John and are the offspring of generations of men who were not "touchy, feely?" You can overcome the curse of your family. And believe me, it is a curse to not be a "touchy, feely" person. You were created to be touched intimately and to touch others intimately throughout your life. You were created to enjoy loving touch, to savor in the experience of a warm hug and experience love as you gently touch the people around you.

Learning about touch requires that we explore three fundamental areas:

- **The significance of touch in a loving relationship.**
- **How to lovingly touch your partner throughout your normal day.**

- **How to energize your sex life with the Spirit of God by incorporating the four essential features of a heavenly sex life into your relationship.**

After you finish this section, you will be ready to pursue a life as a "touchy, feely" person.

Why touch?

A thirteenth century emperor wanted to know what language children would "naturally" speak if they never heard anyone speak. He designed an experiment where he developed a nursery of newborn babies who were cared for by attendants. The attendants were allowed to do whatever was necessary to care for the children except touch or speak to them.

The emperor patiently waited to hear what language "naturally" developed for these children. He never found out. All of the children died. It was concluded that their deaths were caused by the lack of physical touch.

How important is touch? Touch is critical to the sustenance of life. A baby cannot survive without touch. Children cannot thrive without touch. Adults cannot love without touch.

If touch is so important, why do many adults get by with very little touch? Because many adults have lost their sensitivity to the spiritual realm and are surviving only in the flesh. Without touch, adults can survive physically but not spiritually. The flow of love is necessary for spiritual survival and touch is absolutely essential to the flow of love.

Touch may not be critical to the survival of the adult flesh, but it appears to be beneficial. Studies are currently being conducted throughout the country to determine the health benefits of massage. There appear to be a variety of health benefits for adults, including some in the areas of heart disease, hypertension, anxiety disorders and depression.

The health benefits have been demonstrated most clearly with premature babies in the intensive care unit. Daily massage of the premature babies produced statistically significant benefits in many areas. Babies who were massaged had a more rapid weight gain, decreased apneic episodes and earlier hospital discharge. The touch was clearly beneficial to the baby's physical health.

Touch is also beneficial to your emotional health, particularly your feeling states. Loving touch can produce dramatic changes in your feeling states. The emotional healing process is dependent on the experience of love through physical touch. I am convinced that a person cannot emotionally heal without loving touch. I have long believed that a "holding" center, where people come to cry while they are being held, would be more beneficial for most people than the typical counseling center. Unfortunately, in a society that sexualizes the majority of touch, a "holding" center is not feasible. It is feasible, however, for you to be intimately held by your partner when you are emotionally hurting.

You cannot maintain your sensitivity without loving touch. Your shutters close automatically if you are not appropriately touched. The lack of touch partly explains the sensitivity difference between men and women. As compared to females, most males are touched more infrequently and less intimately throughout their lives. Compare the physical interaction of parents with their male children and female children. You will easily see that females are more intimately touched, particularly as the children age. Compare the touch between adult males to that between adult females. Again, you will quickly observe a much greater amount of intimate touch among females. The lack of appropriate intimate touch for males has definitely contributed to their decrease in sensitivity.

Even if appropriate sensitivity could be maintained without loving touch, love still would not flow. Loving touch is one of the five spans of the IHR bridge. Remember, the IHR bridge is the connection that is necessary for love to flow between two partners. A bridge is only as good as its weakest span. Without adequate loving touch, the IHR bridge will not be capable of maintaining the flow of love.

Loving touch is clearly critical to your physical, mental and spiritual health.

Do not believe the lie that you can have a high quality life without appropriate touch. You cannot. Do not believe the lie that you can be a good lover if you are not a "touchy, feely" person. You cannot. You were born a "touchy, feely" person. If you have numbed to your need to touch and be touched, you can change. You can learn to live as the passionate, "touchy, feely" lover that you were created to be.

Daily Touch

Daily touch is the consistent loving touch that should occur throughout your normal day.

Daily touch consists of spontaneous and planned hugs, kisses and caresses. You can never hug, kiss and caress your lover too much, but you can certainly touch too little.

Spontaneous hugs, kisses and caresses may not be natural for you. If you were raised in a home that lacked appropriate touch, then you will have to learn how to lovingly touch your partner. The education process should start with communication. Ask your partner how he or she likes to be touched. Ask him or her to demonstrate the type of touch that results in the greatest experience of love. At the same time, you want to be communicating how you would like to be touched. It is always valuable to document the preferences in writing so that both of you can periodically remind yourself of your partner's preferences.

It is important to be aware of a very significant weakness to the above process of establishing preferences in the area of touch. If you and your partner both have limited experience in the area of loving touch, you may not be aware of all the wonderful ways that you can touch each other. You may also initially feel bad when you are appropriately touched and, therefore, conclude that certain types of touch are wrong.

How do you overcome these potential problems? First, it is important to understand some general guidelines concerning loving touch. Loving touch should never be painful or harmful and should always be consensual and system appropriate. The recipient of the touch should determine what is considered painful. What is viewed as harmful should be determined by medical facts. Your environment determines system appropriateness. For example, a man gently caressing his wife's breast is appropriate at home alone but not while walking through the mall. The term "consensual" means your partner must consent to the type of touch.

"Planned touch" simply means that you establish a boundary for a certain number of hugs, kisses and caresses that you will accomplish daily. Why would you want to plan your loving touch? The main purpose of planning the touch is to ensure

that you do it. As I said earlier, loving touch does not come naturally if you were raised in a family that was lacking in touch. The process of learning to touch your partner initially can be difficult and painful. It is often necessary to set goals and be accountable daily for meeting those goals. After you consistently meet your planned goals for several months, you will find that your loving touch becomes spontaneous and enjoyable.

Many people attempt to sabotage the learning process of planned goals by saying that the touch does not mean as much if it is planned. That is a destructive and erroneous perception. If you require that you and your partner engage only in spontaneous physical intimacy, the chances are slim that you will have enough touch. Everyone has deficits. Overcoming deficits always requires a willingness to change and be accountable for the change. Daily goals and monitoring of your loving touch are simply tools to help you maintain the flow of love.

How much daily touch is necessary to maintain the flow of love? Obviously, there is no set amount. As I said earlier, there cannot be too much loving touch, but there can be too little. I have developed minimal acceptable standards to enable you to have a starting point. Those standards will be covered in the exercises at the end of this step.

As you and your partner consistently meet your goals for daily touch, you will experience a consistent increase in the flow of love. As you experience more love, you will enjoy the daily touch even more. The end result will be a relationship dominated by passionate love and intimacy.

Heavenly Sex

Sex is much more than a biological act. Sex is the door to the greatest experience of intimacy and love possible. That door can only be opened if there is a foundation of true love prior to the sex. Sex in a superficial relationship, energized by the lust of the flesh, is a devaluing experience. It moves you away from love. Whereas, sex in a spiritually intimate relationship, established with true commitment and energized by the Spirit of God, is an extremely enriching experience. It results in the ultimate experience of passionate intimacy and love. The purpose of this section is to provide you with a foundational understanding of a sex life empowered by true love. It is not to give you a manual on sex. There is no way to appropriately cover the entire subject in this section. The focus, therefore, will be on providing you with a clear understanding of the essential features of a heavenly sex life.

Lifelong Commitment

The first essential feature of a heavenly sex life is a lifelong commitment to love.

A lifelong commitment to love means that you value intimacy and love with your partner more than everything else in your life except intimacy and love with God and that you will not leave the relationship unless your partner breaks his or her commitment.

Heavenly sex cannot be found in one-night-stands. Sex outside of a lifelong commitment may result in temporary pleasure, but it is a devaluing experience. The pleasure will never last. If you are sensitive to the spiritual realm, you will hurt once the pleasure is over.

Heavenly sex also cannot be found in an empty, supposedly committed relationship. If you and your partner truly value intimacy and love with God first and each other second, then you will be doing your daily homework and maintaining the flow of love outside of your bedroom. If you are not doing the work to flow in love, then you are not truly committed. Your sex life will reflect the emptiness.

Sex should be like a cherry on top of a soda—the soda being an intimate, loving relationship.

The cherry takes the soda to a higher level of experience. Likewise, sex takes a loving relationship to a higher level of experience.

If your relationship is lacking a reasonable flow of God's love then you should refrain from sex until the flow is restored. Sex, in an empty relationship, is like a cherry on top of a pile of poop. Both the sex and the cherry end up stinking. Sex should, therefore, be avoided in an empty relationship.

A lifelong commitment to love also means that you will stay in the relationship as long as your partner remains committed to *The Seven Steps to Passionate Love.* Lovers do not leave their partners because of inadequacies, failures or a change in feelings, all of which can be overcome through the power of love. Neither do lovers stay with unhealthy partners who are demonstrating their lack of commitment by consistently making destructive life choices. Lovers stay with committed partners and leave those who lack true commitment.

Engaging in sex with a partner who is not sure of his commitment is a devaluing experience. Do not use sex to keep your partner around. For sex to result in a greater experience of value and love, the commitment must be established first. If your partner does not want to be with you—a wonderful, spiritual being—and is just staying for sex, both you and he are being cheated. End the sex until the commitment is there.

A lifelong commitment to love validated by the daily flow of love is an essential feature of a heavenly sex life. If you do not have the commitment, the sexual experience cannot be maintained. On the other hand, if the sexual experience is surrounded by the daily experience of intimacy and love, you will consistently enjoy great sex.

A Gift

A second essential feature of a heavenly sex life is a total commitment to giving. Sexual intimacy is a gift to your partner that only you can give. Sexual intimacy is also a gift to you from your partner that only he or she can give to you.

If two lovers approach sex as a gift to each other, the experience will be wonderful every time.

A frequent complaint among couples is that one partner wants sex more than the other. Although the common explanation is that one person has a stronger sex drive than the other, the real problem is that the couple does not treat sexual intimacy as a gift. If you approach your sex life as an opportunity to give to your partner in a powerful and personal way, then how could your sexual experience not be wonderful? You do not need a strong sex drive to have a wonderful time giving.

What about the reality of a lacking sex drive? Am I saying just to ignore the problem? No, you should seek appropriate help for any physiological sexual dysfunction. I do not want you to ignore your lack of sexual energy. Rather, I want you to focus on the truth that sexual intimacy is far more than a biological act.

Sexual intimacy is an opportunity for you and your lover to experience and share love in a way that separates you from everyone else in his or her life. Sex is the ultimate gift. When your lover wants to make love with you, he is offering the ultimate gift. When you give sexually to your lover, you are giving a gift. Value your sex life as the most intimate, wonderful gift you can give or receive.

If you desire to experience the full benefits of love, become a great sexual giver. Make your time of sexual intimacy a highlight of your life. Strive to give of yourself sexually to the most wonderful person in your life. If both of you and your lover choose to use sexual intimacy as a passionate gift of love to each other, you will quickly see your relationship move to a much higher level of intimacy and love.

Consistent Communication

A third essential feature of a heavenly sex life is consistent communication. Your goal as a passionate, sexual giver is to please your partner as he or she pleases you. You and your partner want each other to be touched and aroused in the manner that each most desires. You cannot touch, arouse or please each other in the most valuing manner if the two of you have not communicated.

Many adults avoid sexual discussion because they still have the feelings of a child that has done something naughty. I have seen successful, competent adults who could talk eloquently about almost any subject become mute at the mention of sex. The best way to conquer this inhibition is to talk about sex frequently with your partner and intimate friends. People more comfortable with their sexuality can help the group advance.

When having sexual discussions, the content of the conversation should always support a healthy perspective of sex. Devaluing sexual jokes should be avoided. Sexual suggestions or innuendoes that undermine monogamy or fidelity also should not be allowed. Personal sexual details are acceptable in the conversation as long as the participants are healthy and mature enough to maintain appropriate personal and psychological boundaries. In other words, if a participant in the group cannot listen to another person's sexual information without engaging in a fantasy relationship, that person should not be a part of the conversation.

Many religious groups ban sexual conversations, believing that it helps maintain sexual purity. This perception is grossly incorrect and often leads to increased sexual perversion and misconduct. When I work with sex addicts from repressed religious homes, a significant part of the treatment involves open discussions about sexual issues in groups of both men and women.

The defense for avoidance of sexual conversations is that people are not healthy enough to handle the material. In general, this perception is not true. Having participated in and worked with many different relationship groups, I can assure you that with appropriate leadership, most people not only can handle intimate, sexual discussions but also, in fact, will benefit from them.

Although sexual conversations in groups have their place, the discussions that you have with your lover are much more important. To assist you in maintaining consistent sexual communication, I have developed a sexual communication questionnaire. Every week, you and your partner should fill out the questionnaire alone and then discuss the information together. It is important to fill out the questionnaire alone because you are more likely to be completely honest. Without honesty, this communication process is of little value.

It is important to realize you have a right to enjoy sex and to have your own sexual preferences. You do not have a right, however, to engage in activities that are devaluing or harmful to you, your partner or the flow of love in the relationship. In communicating your preferences, you want to establish boundaries that enable you to maximize the quality of your sexual experience without harming you, your partner or the relationship.

How do you know where to draw the line? Start by defining the areas of your sex life that you and your partner agree upon. When it is time to deal with areas of disagreement, each of you should be willing to give wherever it is possible to do so without devaluing each other or the relationship. If you cannot agree on an issue, you should seek counseling with a spiritual authority that you both respect. He or she should be experienced in the area of sexual advice because many spiritual authorities are uncomfortable with sexual discussions. After seeking advice, complete the communication process by documenting your sexual boundaries in writing.

Consistent communication is a necessary feature of a heavenly sex life. Learn to be comfortable communicating about your desires, your partner's desires and your perception of the sexual experience. If you and your partner truly desire a passionate sex life, you can achieve it with appropriate communication.

Sexual Time

The fourth and final essential feature of a heavenly sex life is sexual time. Sexual time is the time that you specifically set apart to sexually interact with your partner. You should schedule a minimum of three one-hour sexual encounters per week. You cannot schedule too many sexual encounters as long as there is mutual agreement.

Scheduling a sexual encounter includes more than simply setting a time to meet with your lover. You are also responsible for ensuring that you are prepared for the rendezvous by showering, perfuming and appropriately dressing. You and your partner should alternate the responsibility of preparing the room with music, candles, ointments, toys and anything else that would be appropriate.

The most significant resistance to sexual time comes from people who believe that sex must be spontaneous. My response to that perception is that those people must not live in the same world that I live in. In my world, spontaneous sex typically means two tired people having a "quickie" right before falling asleep. I do not discourage spontaneous sex or "quickies." I do, however, recommend that they be in addition to your minimum of three sexual times per week.

What if you simply do not have enough time to schedule three sexual times each week? **Change your values.** You have enough time. You are just using it up elsewhere.

If you do not have enough value for your relationship to set aside three hours per week for sexual intimacy, then you will never experience anywhere near the quality of life for which you were created. Change your values. Schedule the time and watch the quality of your life improve.

Start Today

Loving Touch is for you. You were created to be a "touchy, feely" person. Maximize your capability of experiencing and sharing love through touch. **Daily Touch** your partner with hugs, kisses and caresses. Commit time to **Heavenly Sex** and enjoy the passionate experience of making love in a relationship energized by the Spirit of God. Start today. Make **Loving**

Touch a priority in your life and you will experience another
wonderful benefit of *The Seven Steps to Passionate Love.*

Step 5 Exercises

Exercise 1: Both you and your partner each initiate
a minimum of two kisses with affirma-
tions per day. Gently and passionately
kiss your partner, hold the kiss for at
least five seconds, then stand back, hold
hands and affirm with the following:
"You are a beautiful, wonderful, precious man/woman of God and I am
blessed to have you as my wife/
husband/lover."

Exercise 2: Both you and your partner each initiate
a minimum of two hugs with affirmations
per day. Gently and firmly hug your
partner (a loving hug is full body with no
patting). Hold the hug for at least five
seconds, then stand back, hold hands
and affirm with the following:
"You are a beautiful, wonderful, precious man/woman of God and I am
blessed to have you as my wife/
husband/lover."

Exercise 3: Lovingly touch and briefly affirm your partner a minimum of ten times per day. Loving touches include the following: gentle stroking or massage of arm, back, hair or other body part. Ask your partner what he or she enjoys the most. A brief affirmation includes the following statements: "I love you." You are wonderful." I am really blessed to have you in my life." "Thank you for being my lover." "You are really special to me."

Monitor: For each of the above exercises, you need to have a small notebook where you monitor your affirmations and touch. Monitoring may seem unnecessary. However, it is very important to insure that you are changing behavior patterns. A simple check on notebook paper is sufficient for monitoring. After affirmations and touch have become second nature for you, the monitoring will not be necessary.

In Step 4, you established a daily time of 1-1½ hours to focus on your relationship. The following exercises should be completed during that time.

Exercise 4:   Find a comfortable setting in which to intimately hold each other (typically, this exercise is done in bed or on a sofa). You and your partner are to hold each other in the cradle position, meaning that the person being held lies sideways and places his/her head and chest against the chest of the other person. The person doing the holding should warmly wrap his/her arms around his partner and gently but firmly hold him close. You maintain this position for ten minutes and then change roles; the person doing the holding becomes the person being held. Whether you being held or in the position of holding, your focus should be on experiencing and sharing love with your partner not on daily activities or responsibilities.

The following are several ways you can promote the experience of love during this exercise:

- Performing the holding in the nude promotes more intimate (not sexual) touch.
- Background music that you and your partner perceive enhances your intimacy with each other and God can be very powerful. If there is a difference in preferences for music, simply rotate the music choices on an every other day basis.
- Visualizing God holding you while you are in the cradle position can also enhance your experience of love.
- Crying during this exercise will increase sensitivity and promote intimacy.

- When you are the person doing the holding, efforts to visualize and experience the Spirit of God flowing from you to your partner can be very rewarding.
- Proceeding from this exercise directly into making love often results in a very passionate experience.

Important Note: Initial attempts at this exercise can be "very boring," particularly if your shutters are significantly closed. As with all the exercises, the daily true commitment to sensitivity will enhance the experience. If you are struggling with your sensitivity, crying during this exercise will definitely help.

Exercise 5: Spend approximately fifteen minutes to discuss your positive life experiences. Included in this discussion should be the following:

- Three ways your partner blessed you in the previous twenty-four hours. This is an opportunity to help your partner understand your preferences and desires.
- Three things you like about your partner. This is an opportunity to demonstrate appreciation for your partner and reinforce the value of his/her talents and attributes.
- Three ways God blessed you that day. This is an opportunity to reinforce an attitude of appreciation and gratitude.

Exercise 6: Spend approximately thirty minutes 4 times per week doing something fun with your partner. Fun activities should be agreed upon and either require mutual interaction or allow close physical touch (i.e. Cuddling with each other as you watch a television show). Examples include card or board games, audio and video entertainment and athletic activities.

Exercise 7: Schedule a minimum of three one-hour periods for sexual intimacy. You and your partner are both responsible for personal preparation (i.e. bathed, perfumed and rested) while you should alternate responsibility for room preparation (i.e. candles, music and lotions).

Exercise 8: Both you and your partner independently fill out the Sexual Intimacy Assessment once every week. Meet together, exchange forms and discuss the answers. View criticism as a blessing to improve your sex life, not as an insult. Be objective and specific when expressing your sexual desires.

SEXUAL INTIMACY ASSESSMENT

We made love _____ **times this week. I desire** _____ **times per week.**

I really like it when you:

- Wear _____
- Smell like _____
- Prepare room with _____
- Prepare yourself with _____
- Say to me _____
- Touch me with _____
- Touch me on (location) _____
- Kiss me on (location) _____
- Suck on _____
- Lick my _____
- Bathe with me _____
- Shower with me _____
- Make love in (position) _____
- Comments _____

I really dislike it when you:

- Wear _____
- Smell like _____
- Prepare room with _____
- Prepare yourself with _____
- Say to me _____
- Touch me with _____
- Touch me on (location) _____
- Kiss me on (location) _____
- Suck on _____
- Lick my _____
- Bathe with me _____
- Shower with me _____
- Make love in (position) _____
- Comments _____

SEXUAL RATING SYSTEM:

1—Very poor.   4—Good to very good.
2—Fair to poor.   5—"The best."
3—Good but could much better.

I would rate the quality of our sex life over the past week: _____

Because I did not rate it 5, I recommend that we make the following

changes:_____

I rate your attitude of "giving" sexually: _____

You can be more giving by: _____

I rate your sexual passion this week: _____

You can be more passionate by:_____

I would rate your preparation for our sexual time:_____

I would like you to prepare by: _____

I would rate your sexual communication: _____

You can improve your sexual communication by: _____

I would like to schedule the following times to sexually give to you:
(Schedule at least three one-hour periods.)

Date	Time	Date	Time
1._____	_____.	3._____	_____.
2._____	_____	4._____	_____

$Step$ 6

*The power of love is great enough
to overcome the hurt of any situation.*

HEAL YOUR EMOTIONS

The phone was ringing. I searched in the dark, knocking items off my bedside table as I slowly opened my eyes.

"Hello, this is Dr. Van Horn," I grumbled in my half-awake state. I was on psychiatric call, and it was 2 A.M. "Dr. Van Horn. This is Mary in the emergency room. We have a 19-year-old female college student in Room 3. Dr. Jones ordered a psychiatric consult."

"Thank you. I will be down shortly," I answered politely, wanting to scream. I was tired of going to the emergency room in the middle of the night to see young college girls who were having problems. I was confident of Lisa's diagnosis prior to even meeting her. Young college girl + ER + middle of night = overdose.

Sure enough, Lisa could not respond when the nurse introduced me. She had tubes in her nose and mouth and both arms strapped to the bedside. Her face, hands, arms and chest were covered with a black residue from the use of a charcoal lavage, used to clear toxins from the digestive tract of a person who has overdosed. Lisa had overdosed on her mother's antidepressant medication.

Why would a young, healthy, female college student try to kill herself? In most cases, the answer is sad but simple: boyfriend problems. As her chart indicated, Lisa had overdosed shortly after a fight with her boyfriend. The pain of romantic relationships is responsible for many of female college-student overdoses. The initial treatment is medical stabilization. The real treatment is emotional healing. Lisa was stabilized in the medical intensive care unit, then transferred to the behavioral medicine unit. After writing orders, I returned to bed.

"Good morning, Lisa. I am Dr. Van Horn," I spoke softly as I walked into Lisa's hospital room. I will be your primary doctor while you are here in the hospital."

"Dr. Van Horn. Great! I am so glad you are here. I want out! Now!" Lisa adamantly demanded, as she rose from her bed.

"Lisa, sit down for a minute," I gently directed her to the bed where we both sat down. "Why do you think you are here?"

"Because you people think I am crazy," Lisa answered with an anxious laugh.

"You people? Who is that?"

"You and the nurses, Dr. Van Horn. Crazy people are in this hospital. I am afraid to leave my room."

"Lisa, I cannot speak for the nurses, but I know you are not crazy," I replied while touching her shoulder for reassurance. "This hospital is not for crazy people but for hurting people. Clearly, Lisa, you have been hurting a lot or you would not have tried to end your life."

"I was feeling great until I saw Pat, my boyfriend, with another girl. Then I was feeling horrible. The pills were for relief."

"Relief from what?" I questioned. "The emotional pain or your life?"

Lisa paused, started crying, then replied, "I just wanted to stop hurting. Death was OK with me. Pat and I are in love. If I can't have Pat, I don't want to live."

I took Lisa's hand and said, "It is really sad that you were hurting so bad, especially over Pat."

"What do you mean 'especially over Pat?' Pat is a great guy. I love him. I want to be with him. I cannot live without him," Lisa sobbed

"It is really sad you are hurting, Lisa," I spoke quietly. Lisa laid her head on my shoulder and cried.

After about five minutes, Lisa stopped crying and asked, "What did you mean when you said 'especially over Pat'?"

"What I meant is that it is really sad that you have such a distorted perspective of love. That you believe what you and Pat have is love."

"If it is not love, why do I hurt so much when I think I will lose him?"

"Lisa, imagine that you are 20 years older and have a 19-year-old daughter." Lisa was intently listening as I spoke. "Your daughter comes home from college and tells you that she found her steady boyfriend, the 'love of her life,' kissing another girl. What would be your advice?"

Lisa hesitated then answered, "I want to say 'dump him hard,' but I know what that means for me and Pat."

"Why would you want your daughter to dump her boyfriend?"

"Because he is a jerk, an unfaithful bum. My daughter deserves far better than that."

"Why don't you deserve 'far better than that'?"

"But it is different with Pat and I. We are really in love."

"So in love that he lies to you and sees other women behind your back?"

Lisa paused and tearfully replied, "Then why do I hurt so bad? I know he is a bum. This is not the first time that Pat has cheated on me. He has been with many other girls. I want to dump him. But when I think of being without him, I hurt so bad that I want to die."

Why did Lisa "hurt so bad" when she perceived that she was losing Pat? Was it because Pat really loved her? Obviously not. Pat was a user, not a lover. Two of the spans of the IHR bridge in a loving relationship are commitment and honest communication. Pat was dramatically lacking in commitment and he was flagrantly dishonest. Pat was not even close to being a lover.

Was Lisa's emotional pain an indication of her love for Pat? No. Lisa's emotional pain was an indication of her "need" for Pat, her dependency on him, not her love for him. Remember, love refers to your ability to access and share the Spirit of God with another person. Lisa had so little ability to access love that she attempted suicide. Lisa did not love Pat. She used him. Lisa used Pat as a cover.

As her cover, Pat gave Lisa temporary relief from her spiritual emptiness and emotional pain. Only true love, the Spirit of God flowing, could ultimately heal Lisa's spiritual emptiness and emotional pain. No emotional or spiritual healing took place in her relationship with Pat because no true love was in the relationship. Her lonely relationship with Pat only prolonged her agony. When Pat was around, Lisa felt somewhat better by numbing to the emptiness and pain inside. When Pat was gone, Lisa's ability to cover up her emotional pain was also gone. A devastated, spiritually empty little girl was left behind.

Where did Lisa's spiritual emptiness come from? The

spiritual emptiness was with Lisa from birth. Like all of us, Lisa was born spiritually empty, needing to be filled with love. Lisa did not get filled with love growing up. Instead of receiving love, she experienced the pain and emptiness of an alcoholic father who abandoned her at three years of age. Growing up without a father, Lisa never received the love that she needed to spiritually mature. Her flesh became a young woman, but her spiritual self remained a baby. The spiritually empty little girl that entered the world at birth was the same lonely little girl who overdosed.

The ultimate result of the overdose was that Lisa received an opportunity to spiritually and emotionally heal. Spiritual healing required that Lisa change her distorted perception of love and develop a foundation of loving relationships. Emotional healing required that Lisa learn how to reprogram her emotional computer.

You also have an emotional computer that needs to be reprogrammed. *Your emotional computer consists of your brain and mind and is the storage facility for your emotional pain.* You, like everyone else, have some amount of unresolved emotional pain in storage. Stored-up emotional pain reduces your capacity for intimacy and love in many ways: the greater the pain, the more negative the impact on your relationships. The purpose of this step is to teach you how to resolve your emotional pain by reprogramming your emotional computer.

Storage of Emotional Pain

Emotional pain is stored in your emotional computer like a ball of bad energy waiting to come out. The pain is stored in your brain and comes out in your mind. If you picture your brain to be like a window through which you experience and share love, then your stored-up emotional pain is like a dark fog on that window: the greater your unresolved emotional pain, the bigger the fog in your brain window and the more negative the impact on your relationship.

The stored-up emotional pain alternates between being covered up and experienced. When the pain is covered up, your shutters are somewhat closed, you are less sensitive than you were created to be and you do not experience the emotional pain. The emotional pain is localized to a part of your brain and the fog is limited to a part of your brain window. The remainder of your brain window and the entirety of your mind window remain clear.

On the other hand, when the emotional pain is uncovered, your shutters are open, you are more sensitive, and you consciously experience the emotional pain. The uncovered emotional pain floods your brain and mind energizing bad feelings and distorted thoughts. The dark fog that was limited to a part of your brain window becomes a diffuse light fog that is spread throughout both your brain and mind windows.

Whether the emotional pain is flooding your mind and brain windows or simply being covered up, it is still interfering with your capability of love. When your pain is covered, the closed shutters and smudged brain window decrease your capacity for intimacy and love. When you are hurting, the fogged brain and mind windows interfere with the flow of love in your life. So, whether you are numb or hurting, unresolved emotional pain cheats you out of love. It is, therefore, critical that you learn how to resolve your emotional pain.

To better understand how emotional pain decreases your capacity for love, imagine that a large white house is given to you at birth. The purpose of the house is to enable you to experience the fullness of life. Now compare that house to your brain and the freshness of the air in the house to your mind. Breathing fresh air in the house is equivalent to experiencing love. How much love you experience is determined by how many rooms you have in which to breathe and the freshness of the air. The more clean air you breathe, the more love you experience and the more fulfilling your life is.

At birth, your house is clean and your parents provide the air. Your parents share both fresh air and emotional pollution with you. By the time you are an adult, a significant portion of your house is filled with the emotional pollution that you inherited from your parents. When you are not feeling your emotional pain, the emotionally polluted rooms are closed off to the rest of the house. You can still breathe fresh air in the open part of your house, but there are fewer rooms in which to breathe. In other words, your brain is partly occupied with the storage of emotional pain, and your mind is clear. You can experience some love but not the full experience that is available.

When you are feeling your emotional pain, the doors to your emotionally polluted rooms are open and the air in the rest of your house is somewhat impure. You have more rooms in which to breathe, but the air is less pure. In other words, you have more brain available, but both your brain and mind are somewhat fogged. Again, you can experience some love but not the full experience that God created you for.

The process of emotional healing consists of opening the doors to the emotionally polluted rooms, clearing out some of the pollution and then closing the doors again. That entails: Uncovering the emotional pain in your brain, experiencing it through your mind, resolving some of the pain and then covering it back up again. After each time you engage in emotional healing, a little more of your house and a little more of your brain are free to experience love: the more of your house and brain that are available, the greater your experience of love. The ultimate goal is to regain the full use of your house with clean air throughout and the full use of clear brain and mind windows.

From a more practical perspective, emotional healing means grieving in an environment of love and then following the steps to reprogram your emotional computer. *Grieving in an environment of love means having intimate relationships with people with whom you can cry and experience love in the midst of your tears.* The grieving does not heal the emotional pain; the love you experience does. The grieving is a sign that you are accessing the stored pain. You must access the pain to eventually resolve it.

As you access the emotional pain, you must also reprogram your bad feelings and distorted thoughts. As you learned earlier, you store memory circuits for thoughts and feelings in your mind and brain. By reprogramming your emotional computer, you can actually change the electrical recordings for your thoughts and feelings. By changing the stored up recordings, you can clear the fog from your brain and mind.

If you simply grieve but do not reprogram your computer, you will never get past your pain. On the other hand, if you do not access the sick recordings through grieving, you cannot have the opportunity to change them. Both accessing the pain and reprogramming the circuits are necessary for emotional healing.

Understanding the process of emotional healing requires that you first learn a series of definitions followed by five principles and four steps. I recommend that you acquire a basic understanding of the definitions prior to reading about the principles and steps.

Definitions

Feelings—*Bodily Sensations.*

We experience feelings as bodily sensations. Examples of bodily sensations are as follows: neck pain, muscle tension, nausea, stomach pain, chest tightness, chest pain, increased body temperature, body heaviness, and headache.

Feelings can be any body sensation. The way I demonstrate an experience of feelings in a group is by asking everyone to close their eyes. They are then instructed to pay attention to the sensations in their bodies. As they are relaxing, I scream at the top of my voice, "Open your eyes." I then instruct them to observe the differences in body sensations before and after the scream.

Feelings arise from electrical circuits in your brain. The exact location of their origin is not fully determined; however, for the purpose of this process, I want you to think of feelings as arising from right brain circuits.

Your right brain starts storing electrical programs for feelings early in development, possibly as early as the fetal stage. The programs for feelings sit in your head like old records waiting to be played. Many people spend their adult lives being directed by these old records.

In general, you cannot immediately control your right brain, the feeling part of your brain. For example, if a woman who had been molested as a child were to see her molester for the first time as an adult, she would instantly have a change in her bodily sensations. Her heart might race, her stomach might churn, or her chest might hurt. She would not have the ability to immediately stop the feelings, but she would have control over her behavior and thinking. Through emotional healing in love, she could eventually gain control over her feelings as well.

For now, understand: *Feelings are bodily sensations arising from electrical memory circuits stored in your right brain, over which you have limited immediate control.*

Thoughts—*Visual and verbal mental representations of previous experiences.*

All words and mental pictures are thoughts. For practical application, think of thoughts as arising from electrical memory circuits in your *left* brain. When you remember a name, you are obtaining your information from left brain circuits. Reading stimulates left brain circuits. Remembering how someone or something looks requires left brain circuits to fire. Your left brain stores the circuitry for thoughts.

In general, you have immediate control over your thoughts. If you have a thought in your mind, you can instantly replace it with another. You can choose your thoughts despite your feelings. A critical component of emotional healing is maintaining control over your thoughts.

When the woman who was sexually abused as a child sees her molester as an adult, she would immediately experience many bodily sensations, accompanied by thoughts. Her thoughts may include visual memories of the abuse and/or negative thoughts about herself. Although her feelings may not quickly change, she could change both her visual and verbal thoughts. Controlling her thoughts despite the feelings would be necessary for emotional healing.

Because you do have direct access to your left brain, your thoughts are the key to reprogramming your mind. Your mind contains the programming for your thoughts and feelings. Your mind does not care about reality; it responds based on programming. Likewise, your thoughts and feelings are not determined by reality. They are determined by how your mind is programmed. And your mind is programmed by your thoughts. By consistently controlling your thoughts, you change the programming of your mind.

Thoughts do not appear in your mind out of nowhere. Thoughts are programmed in your mind through visual and verbal input throughout your life. You begin programming verbal thoughts shortly after you begin speaking words. Visual thoughts are programmed at about the same time. The most important point to realize is that the programming of your thoughts is an active process that you can and must control if you desire to live *The Seven Steps To Passionate Love.*

Emotions—*The dynamic interaction of your thoughts and feelings.*

Emotions are your feelings and thoughts together. In the process of reprogramming your emotional computer, it is important to separate your emotions into thoughts and feelings. Why? Because you can immediately change your thoughts but not your feelings. The thoughts you choose in the midst of your feelings will affect the intensity and duration of your feelings. Thinking based on the power of love despite your bad feelings will enable you to progressively eliminate many of your bad feelings.

Labeling your bad feelings with previously learned labels reinforces the intensity of those feelings. For example, many people will say that they "feel lonely" when they have a heavy, hollow sensation in their chest. Have two of these people with the same intensity of chest pain sit in separate rooms alone. While one repeats the statement, "I'm lonely," have the other repeat the phrase, "I am loved." After 30 minutes of repetition, ask both to describe their chest sensations. The person labeling his feelings lonely will have much more chest pain than the one with thoughts of love.

Because labeling your feelings reinforces their intensity, it is important that you learn how to change your labels. To do so, you have to first separate your emotions into thoughts and feelings. Remember, feelings are physical sensations in your body while thoughts include all visual and verbal memories. Examples of emotions being reduced to thoughts and feelings include the following:

Emotion	Feeling (body sensations)	Thoughts
Fear	heart racing, hands sweaty, muscle tension, shallow breathing, chest tightness.	"I'm afraid." "I'll be hurt."
Anger	muscle tension, hot face, flushing, heart racing, fast breathing	"I'm angry.." "I hate . . ."
Guilt	gnawing stomach pain, body heaviness.	"I am sorry." "I feel guilty."
Lonely	hollow chest pain.	"No one loves me." "I am lonely."

Trigger—*anything that turns on a brain circuit.*

Triggers can turn on right brain circuits resulting in feelings and left brain circuits resulting in thoughts. In general, when your right brain is triggered, the emotional energy stored in your right brain sends electricity to your body, energizing feelings, and to your left brain, energizing thoughts. For example, if you see your favorite ice cream, the visual input triggers your right brain, which sends electrical signals to your body, resulting in your mouth watering and stomach churning. At the same time, electrical signals are also sent to your left brain, resulting in the thought, "I want some ice cream."

The left brain can also be initially triggered, resulting in both automatic thoughts and the production of new electrical signals. The new electrical signals trigger the right brain, resulting in emotional energy being sent to the body, producing feelings, and to the left brain, energizing thoughts. For example, someone offers you a piece of chocolate cake. You immediately get a visual picture of chocolate cake while your mouth starts to water, your stomach churns and you think, "I want some cake." The visual and verbal thoughts result from the left brain being triggered while the physical sensations arise when the right brain is triggered. The emotional energy of the right brain energizes the entire experience.

What if someone were to offer you dog food? Your left brain would fire when you hear the offer and thoughts would be triggered. If the offer were disgusting enough to you, your right brain would also be triggered, producing emotional energy. Signals would be sent to your stomach, producing feelings, and to your left brain, reinforcing thoughts. On an experiential level, you would become nauseous as you verbalize the thought, "No."

You have now been introduced to an extremely simple model for understanding the way thoughts and feelings are electrically programmed in your brain. The actual neurology is much more complicated; however, this model will enable you to change the way your emotional computer has been programmed.

A trigger is anything that initiates electrical flow in the brain by turning on a circuit.

Triggers can turn on circuits in both the left and right brain. By learning how to reprogram your emotional computer, you can learn to control your feelings instead of triggers controlling you.

Solidify Your Understanding

You must solidify your understanding definitions prior to moving on to the next section. Study this section thoroughly. Discuss the definitions with your partner. Make sure you clearly understand the definitions. You will then have a much easier time learning the principles, steps and concepts of reprogramming your emotional computer.

The process of reprogramming your emotional computer is a powerful one. If you learn and apply the process to your life, your experience of love will dramatically change. You may find the process difficult to understand and apply at first. Not because it is particularly difficult. Rather the process appears difficult because it is so different from the way you have approached life in the past. If you stay committed despite the difficulties, reprogramming your emotional computer will eventually become a very comfortable and natural process.

Fundamental Principles for Reprogramming Your Emotional Computer

Principle #1

When you hurt, you hurt because your brain is firing and you are experiencing your spiritual emptiness.

Have you ever wondered why you emotionally hurt? Is it because of problems outside of you? Is it because of what happened to you as a child? Is it because of the way your partner is treating you? What is it that determines when and how we feel emotional pain?

Emotional pain comes from inside you. You hurt because of something happening inside of you, not because of an external event. The easiest way to validate that emotional pain arises from an internal source is through the use of prescription medication. No matter how bad you are hurting, how upset you are or how distraught you feel, I can eliminate your feelings with medication. I have done so with patients for years. How? Simply by giving medications that dampen the brain's electrical firing.

What does this prove? That emotional pain comes from inside of you. External events and life's problems are simply triggers for the pain already inside of you. You cannot hurt if your brain does not fire. It doesn't matter how horrible the situation is. If your brain does not fire with electricity, you cannot emotionally or physically hurt.

If you are still struggling with this concept, then go to the stroke unit at your local hospital. Find someone who is "brain dead." See if you can make them hurt. Of course, you cannot. The family members around will be hurting but not the "brain-dead" patient. Why? Because you cannot hurt if your brain will not fire.

Let me give you another example to validate this concept. If you were to convince me that my child was dead when in fact my child was alive, how would I feel? I would feel terrible. I would cry and be just as upset as if my child were actually dead. On the other hand, what if my child was dead, but I did not know it? For example, if my child died shortly after I left for work and no one was able to contact me. Would I experience the sadness of a child being dead? Not at that time. Why not? Because I would believe that my child was alive. My emotional experience would not be determined by the reality of my child's life or death but by my perception.

> *Our emotional state is determined by our brain's response to external experiences, not by the experiences themselves.*

Why is this an important concept? Because you can learn to determine your emotional response to experiences instead of the experiences dictating your feelings for you. You can learn to control your feelings. You can learn to experience the benefits of love in very difficult situations. You can learn to flow in love despite problems and pain around you. You can learn to love your partner even when your partner is acting unlovable.

To gain control over your feelings, you first must adopt Principle #1: "When you hurt, you hurt because your brain is firing and you are experiencing your spiritual emptiness."

What about the second half of that statement, which says that when you hurt, you are experiencing your spiritual emptiness? Spiritual emptiness simply refers to the inherent spiritual void that you were born with that can only be relieved with love. Your spiritual emptiness is an indication of your inability to experience the benefits of love. The benefits of love are the opposite of emotional pain. The benefits of love are not a mental experience. They are a spiritual experience. They are the experience of lasting value, safety, acceptance, and fulfillment. On a feeling level, the experience of love is a warm, energized and soothing state. The best way to understand the benefits of love is to experience love. Anytime you are not experiencing the benefits of love, by definition, you are experiencing your spiritual emptiness.

You may experience your spiritual emptiness in many different ways. You may complain of chest pain, almost like a deep hole settling in the center of your chest. If you are consumed with anger and bitterness, you may have tension throughout your body. Stomach discomfort, neck pain, back pain, headaches and many other physical discomforts can all be due to the experience of your spiritual emptiness.

The easiest way to understand the concept of spiritual emptiness is to recognize that any experience that is not energized by love is, by definition, spiritual emptiness.

The power of love is great enough to overcome the hurt of any situation.

If you can access love in the midst of problems, you will be able to experientially rise above those problems. Even if the problems do not go away, your empowerment with love will maintain you.

Who has spiritual emptiness? Everyone. It is human to have spiritual emptiness. Only love can move us beyond our humanity to a higher level of experience, a level that is energized in the spiritual realm. The fact that you experience your spiritual emptiness is not a failure. It is an opportunity for spiritual growth—an opportunity to move to a greater level of spiritual maturity. If, in the midst of your pain, you move toward love, you will spiritually mature. You will move beyond your humanity into a life in the spiritual realm, energized by the Spirit of God.

Where does emotional pain come from? Your emotional pain comes from inside of you, your brain firing and your spiritual emptiness. No matter what you have learned in this past, adopt this principle, and open yourself up to the healing power of love.

Principle #2

You are totally responsible for all your feelings.

No one can make you feel anything. A person can trigger the unhealthy part of your brain or expose your lack of ability to access love, but you are responsible for those feelings. A fundamental principle of living *The Seven Steps to Passionate Love* is accepting full responsibility for your feelings.

Blaming is the opposite of taking responsibility for your feelings.

Blaming means that you are giving responsibility for how you feel to someone or something outside of you.

Blaming will keep you from ever being a consistent lover. Blaming will prevent you from accessing the fullness of love. Blaming will ensure that you never have a relationship of true value and quality. You have to stop blaming and take responsibility for your feelings.

> *"He makes me so mad I can't stand it. I can't stand the way he looks, the way he smells, the way he acts, the way he talks. In fact, Dr. Van Horn I can't stand anything about him," Paulette was red faced and tense as she verbally attacked Randy.*
>
> *"When did you start thinking this way, Paulette?" I asked, as we sat in my office.*
>
> *"I have always thought that only the 'scum of the earth' would cheat on his wife and now I'm stuck being married to the scum."*

"*Do you realize that you are blaming Matthew for your pain, Paulette.*"

"*Of course, I'm blaming Matthew for my pain. He is responsible for my pain.*" Even when she was angry, Paulette looked beautiful with her big blue eyes and dark brown hair. She continued, "*I didn't feel like this before I found out about the affair. I didn't hurt this bad before he decided to 'screw' that other woman. It's not me that went out and spent all that money on another woman. It was Matthew. It was that 'dog' that I am married to.*"

Matthew and Paulette were in their third day of the intimacy and love workshop. Paulette had been blaming Matthew, making him the entire problem. I decided the blaming needed to stop. Paulette needed to heal and it was not going to happen with all the blaming that she was doing. I continued with the conversation, "*Paulette? If we define healthy as 'the ability to flow in love in relationships,' then how healthy do you think you were before you found out about Matthew's affair?*"

"*A lot healthier than I am now, Dr. Van Horn,*" Paulette replied.

"*Do you really think so?*" I asked. "*How healthy is a woman who is married to a man who cheats on her?*"

"*Well, I didn't know he was cheating on me,*" Paulette quickly defended herself.

"*Why didn't you know he was cheating on you, Paulette? You were married to him. You were with him every day,*" I strongly responded. "*How could you be with Matthew every day and think everything was fine when, at the same time, he was out having sex with another woman.*"

"*I thought everything was fine because he was nice when he was at home,*" Paulette was tearing up as she recalled her times with Matthew. "He smiled at me, treated me nice, bought me presents and regularly had sex with me."

"Regularly had sex with you. Now, that was special," I said sarcastically. "He was using you sexually while he used his girlfriend at the same time. You couldn't even tell you were getting seconds?"

Paulette started to cry. "Dr. Van Horn, that was mean. He was conning me. Can't you see that? Was that my fault?"

"I am not trying to be mean, Paulette, but I do want you to stop lying to yourself. It is not an accident that you were married to a 'whoredog' who conned you. There is a reason that you thought you had love when in fact you were being used in the worst way."

"What's the reason?" Paulette screamed. "What is it that enables a woman to know something is wrong when her husband is cheating?"

"It is sensitivity to the spiritual realm, Paulette," I quietly explained. "It is having the capability to be sensitive and vulnerable in a relationship. You were very good at living a 'numb' relationship of the flesh. You didn't have a sensitive vulnerable relationship with Matthew. You just played your role. He played his role. Both of you related in your flesh. There was no true intimacy and love."

I paused as Paulette found a tissue for her tears. I then continued, "You were very contented with your lonely marriage. You used Matthew to provide for you, to provide for your children, to give you a nice home and a nice car. And occasionally you used him for sex. You were a user just like Matthew."

Paulette interrupted, "But I didn't outright lie to him like he lied to me."

"No, you didn't lie to him, Paulette," I responded. "You

just lived a lie with him. You lived the lie of a lonely marriage and a lonely life with a smile on your face. That wasn't because of him, Paulette. That was your choice."

"But Dr. Van Horn, I did not know that I was living a lie," Paulette softly and remorsefully replied.

"I realize that you did not know. That is why we are having this conversation, so you can start knowing the difference between a lonely life and true love." I paused, smiled at Paulette and continued, "Think back to your life as a little girl. How much time did your dad spend with you? How much did your dad value you? How much did he hold you? How much did he cuddle with you?"

"He didn't do any of those things. My dad was always at work."

"You were a lonely little girl way before you met Matthew, Paulette. You grew up with a 'numb' father and learned how to survive well without true intimacy and love. Matthew just continued the tradition: Using you while you used him."

"Okay, Dr. Van Horn. I agree. I was a lousy lover when I married Matthew. But I was not a liar and 'whoredog' like him. I will never forgive him for that."

"Paulette, forgiveness means you give up your right to blame Matthew for your pain. Forgiveness is necessary for you to heal. Do not forgive Matthew for his benefit. Forgive Matthew for your benefit. No matter how bad Matthew hurt you, you have to forgive. You have to take responsibility for the pain. The only thing that is going to get rid of your hurt is love. And you cannot access love as long as you are blaming.

Healthy people either stay in love or leave in love. Forgive and leave in love if you believe God wants you to. Divorce is an appropriate consequence for adultery. Not mandatory but appropriate. On the other hand, Matthew is here. If you want a truly loving relationship with Matthew, then forgive and commit with him."

You are responsible for your pain. The answer to your emotional pain is love. You cannot access love if you do not take responsibility for your emotional pain. If someone has hurt you, forgive him or her. Open your self up to the healing power of love.

You also cannot reprogram your emotional computer if you fail to take full responsibility for your pain. Your computer does not care about reality. It responds based on programming. If you program your emotional computer with the perspective that you are hurting because of memories, events or people outside of you, your computer will make sure that you hurt in all those situations. On the other hand, if you program your computer from the perspective that the love inside of you is powerful enough to overcome any emotional pain, you computer will respond accordingly.

Take full responsibility for your pain. Give love a real chance in your life.

Principle #3

You must be capable of feeling your feelings.

It was the second hour of group when Zack finally said something. It was obvious from the beginning that Zack did not want to be part of the group. He wanted nothing to do with this 'touchy, feely' stuff. Zack only came to group because his wife, Sheila, gave him an ultimatum: "workshop or divorce."

The subject of crying came up in the group. Zack raised his hand to talk. I was surprised. It was the second day of the workshop, and he had been speechless until now. Zack stood to talk and in an arrogant, bold tone said, " Sheila does all the crying in our family; I haven't cried in forty years."

"Is that something to be proud of, Zack?" I asked.

Zack smiled and responded, "Of course, that is something to be proud of. If I cried, then Sheila would probably never stop crying. I don't see any value in crying. I have a good life. I care about my family. I work hard and tears aren't for me."

"When is the last time you cried Zack?"

"The last time I cried? I remember very clearly, Dr. Van Horn." Zack was more pensive now. "It was when I was 17 years old and my father hit me for the last time. I looked at him and said, "Dad, if you hit me again, I'll kill you. You'll never see me cry again. And you know, Dr. Van Horn, he never hit me again and I never cried another tear. Forty years and no tears."

"Do you realize, Zack, that your inability to cry is killing the intimacy and love in your relationship with your wife?" I challenged him.

"Blame it all on me, Dr. Van Horn." Zack was angry now. "You're not at my house. You don't watch Sheila blame and complain. She cries all the time. How can I be the one that's ruining our relationship?"

"I didn't say that you were the only one hurting the relationship, Zack. What I did say is that your insensitivity, your lack of ability to cry, is killing the intimacy in the relationship. Sheila does have to take responsibility for her feelings. She does have to stop criticizing. She does need to get

love in her life so she can emotionally heal. And right now, she can't get love from you, Zack, because you are a very insensitive man who is very incapable of love."

"Feeling the feelings" means returning to that sensitive, vul- nerable state where you can experience on a spiritual level. It means coming in touch with the unhealthy parts of your brain. and opening yourself up to the emotional pain that you experi- enced as a child.

Why would anyone want to experience pain after they had effectively covered it up? Because you cannot regain your sen- sitivity, heal your emotional pain or reprogram your emotional computer without feeling your feelings.

Many people become experts at avoiding their emotional pain. Consequently, they never heal from that emotional pain. Zack learned to survive an abusive home by losing his capabil- ity of feeling his feelings. He lived 40 years without crying. Zack was functional in life, but he was not a lover. To be a lover, you have to get your shutters open, your covers down and learn how to feel your feelings.

Zack was emotionally numb when he started the workshop. By the fourth day, he still had not cried, but his perception of crying had changed. Zack left the workshop committed to feel- ing his feelings. Over a six-month period of attending outpatient groups, Zack transformed from a very emotionally distant and hard man to a sensitive, vulnerable person who cried easily. The changes were obvious in many areas of Zack's life, particularly in his marriage, where he became a sensitive, intimate lover.

Like Zack, you must become capable of feeling your feelings. Your must open your shutters, uncover your spiritual emptiness and access the emotional pain you have been stuffing. The pain may be great but the benefits are greater.

Principle #4

You must think and behave
based on the power of love.

"Dr. Van Horn, how dare you! How dare you tell me how to feel!" Elizabeth screamed as she stood up from her chair. "You have never been raped. You have never been used sexually by your father."

I quietly watched as Elizabeth sat back down, put her head down to her hands and started sobbing. I then said, "Elizabeth, you are right. You have been hurt terribly. It was not your fault that your dad raped you. It is really sad that he used you as a sex toy. It definitely wasn't fair. But I still believe what I said. You have to change your thinking and your behavior." I paused and then stated emphatically, "The power of love is great enough to heal your pain. If you access love today, the pain will slowly go away. If you continue to think and act like a traumatized little girl, you will never get over your pain."

Elizabeth looked up and, with tears running down her face, said, "I am traumatized. My life has been horrible. How else can I think."

I quietly but firmly replied, "You can think based on the power of love. You can think like the beautiful, wonderful precious woman you are."

"But Dr. Van Horn," Elizabeth argued. "When I try to make love with John, I feel so nasty and dirty. I feel just like I did when my dad was raping me. I hate for John to touch me."

Elizabeth, look at me," I lovingly commanded. "You are not a nasty, dirty little girl. You are a precious, pure woman *of God. John sees you as your real self, the beautiful spiritual being. Making love uncovers the pain programmed in your brain. When you start hurting, you think and behave like an abused little girl. You have to think and behave based on love, despite the emotional pain. If you do, the pain will slowly go away."*

Elizabeth's mind was programmed with the thinking of a traumatized little girl. For 20 years, she had hidden her abuse, afraid that people would reject her if she revealed the truth. Until she started having sex with her husband, John, Elizabeth had avoided her feelings. Sex uncovered the pain, triggered her right brain. When she did feel her pain, Elizabeth's automatic thoughts were the lies programmed in her mind as a child. To emotionally heal, Elizabeth had to change her thinking and behavior to fit the spiritual truth based on love.

You also must choose to think and behave based on the power of love, not based on the unhealthy programs in your mind. Avoiding the unresolved emotional pain guarantees that the pain will always hurt you. You must feel the feelings to heal. You also must control your thinking and behavior while you are feeling the emotional pain. Your thoughts and behavior will either reinforce or inhibit the bad feelings. If you consistently respond based on the power of love, you will slowly eliminate the painful memory circuits. If, on the other hand, you think and behave based on the emotional pain, you will never get over your pain.

The difference between people who heal in love and those who never get past their emotional pain is found in the decisions that they make when they are hurting. Healing comes through thinking and behaving based on the power of love even though you are hurting.

---

*It is only when you are hurting
that you have an opportunity to heal.
Lovers make healthy decisions
in the midst of their emotional pain.
Lovers think and behave based on the power of love.*

Let's return to the example of Elizabeth and apply the principles that you have learned so far. Principle #1 is: "When you hurt, you hurt because your brain is firing and you are experiencing your spiritual emptiness." Was Elizabeth applying Principle #1? No, she was not. She was blaming her pain on the past sexual abuse. Her pain was programmed in her mind and brain at the time of the abuse, but the immediate experience of the pain had nothing to do with the abuse. Elizabeth's pain was due to her brain firing and her spiritual emptiness.

If Elizabeth continued to believe that her pain was because of the abuse, she would never get over the pain. You cannot change the past. You cannot eliminate past abuse or losses. However, through the power of love, you can heal the pain of those abuses and losses. The healing starts with your decision to realize where the pain is coming from: your brain and your spiritual emptiness.

Was Elizabeth following Principle #2: "You are totally responsible for your feelings"? No, again, she was not. Elizabeth was blaming her pain on the past abuse and the trigger. Making love to her husband was the trigger, and her form of blaming was distancing. She distanced from her husband sexually because she said that it made her feel bad.

Distancing is a commonly used form of blaming. People distance from their partners emotionally, sexually and physically to avoid pain in the relationship. Distancing brings temporary relief while guaranteeing that healing will not occur. You cannot use distancing in your relationship if you want to maintain love in your life. If there is a problem, you must resolve it in love. Lovers either stay in a relationship in love or leave in love. Lovers do not stay in a relationship and blame by distancing.

Elizabeth needed to make the decision to forgive her father, take full responsibility for the pain, engage in the healing process and move toward her husband sexually. You will never get over your pain if you blame. The pain you feel comes from inside of you, not from past events or triggers outside of you. If you respond based on the triggers or the past, you will be burdened with you emotional baggage forever.

Did Elizabeth apply Principle #3: "You must be capable of feeling your feelings"? Yes, Elizabeth felt a tremendous amount of emotional pain. Feeling your emotional pain without applying the other principles of emotional healing results in a miserable life. You are better off numbing if you do not plan on doing the work to heal. Many people are sensitive to their feelings but do not understand true healing. So they spend a large part of their life either emotionally hurting or making bad decisions motivated by the pain. Elizabeth had to learn how to heal in her sensitivity instead of hurting and blaming.

Did Elizabeth apply principle #4: "You must think and behave based on the power of love." Obviously not. The bottom line for Elizabeth was that she was both emotionally hurting and making decisions based on her pain—a guaranteed approach to a life of emotional pain. How common is Elizabeth's approach to emotional pain? Her approach is extremely common among sensitive people. Support groups are loaded with sensitive people who are not taking the necessary steps to heal.

The bad news is that Elizabeth was stuck in her pain when I met her. The good news is that through living *The Seven Steps to Passionate Love,* she healed.

Principle #5

You must trigger the emotional pain as frequently as possible and respond to it appropriately.

Why would anyone want to trigger his or her emotional pain as frequently as possible? Because you can only heal when you are feeling your emotional pain. Consequently, it is important to trigger the pain regularly. Think back to the analogy of the big white house that you were given to experience love in. By the time, you are an adult, your house is half full of emotional pollution. When the doors to the polluted rooms are closed, it means you are numbing to your emotional pain. When the doors are open, you are triggering your emotional pain.

You can keep your doors closed and stay numb, but you lose half your house and the quality of your love life is limited. You need to clear the pollution from the rooms. The only way you can do so is to open the doors to the pollution, which means you will be hurting. If you open the doors, emotionally hurt, and then respond appropriately, you will gradually clear the emotional pollution out of your house. The more often you open the doors and respond appropriately, the more quickly you clear the rooms. Likewise, the more frequently you trigger the emotional pain and respond appropriately, the faster you emotionally heal.

Is it possible to trigger the emotional pain too frequently? Yes. Every time you trigger your emotional pain, you want to work the process of healing until you are feeling good again. With Elizabeth, I wanted her to trigger her emotional pain through writing letters about her abuse and by sexually interacting with her husband. After she starting hurting, she was to cry in her husband's arms and then go through the steps of healing. I did not want her to return to the trigger until she was recovered from the previous experience and was once again feeling good.

Reprogramming your emotional computer may seem like a strange process at this point. But I assure you, the process is powerful and effective. It will make more sense after you have learned the four steps and receive more examples of the process being applied. I encourage you to thoroughly study and understand the information in this section prior to moving on in the book. If you solidify your understanding of the material you have received to this point, the remainder of the material will make much more sense.

Reprogramming Your Emotional Computer: General Concepts

Concept #1

What you know and believe is determined by decisions. Lovers make those decisions based on love not feelings.

What do you think determines what you know and believe? Is it education, experience, reality or perception? Having presented those questions to many different groups, I have received a variety of answers but rarely the correct one. Many factors influence what you know and believe, including the ones listed above. In the end, however, what you know and believe is determined by decisions.

Consider, for example, the fourteenth century perception of the shape of the earth. The smartest scientists of the time knew that the earth was flat. Today, most second-graders know the earth is round. How could very intelligent people come to such an erroneous conclusion? They considered their information, experience and education and then made a decision. They happened to make the wrong decision.

Decisions determine what you know and believe. You have been making decisions "to know" since your early childhood. You know what your name is, who your parents are and how old you are—all of which were determined by decisions. You have developed a perception of yourself by making decisions. You may think you are smart, beautiful or funny. On the other hand, you may see yourself as stupid, ugly and boring. However you perceive yourself, decisions determined what you believe.

You may be thinking that truth, not decisions, determine what you know. But how do you know what truth is? How do you know who your parents are? What if you learned today that you were adopted and that your birth certificate listed a different name and year of birth? I have worked with people who discovered their adoption as adults. Clearly, truth does not determine what you know. Decisions ultimately determine what you know.

You can immediately change what you know and believe by making different decisions.

You can eliminate old, unhealthy beliefs and establish new, empowering beliefs instantaneously with decisions. You can quickly input new and healthy data into your emotional computer by using decisions to line your thinking up with the power of love. Decisions based on love enable you to reprogram your emotional computer and empower your life with healthy, uplifting perceptions.

John and Mary had been married for 10 years when they arrived at the workshop. John's recent revelation of a past affair had precipitated a crisis in their lives. Mary did not want to loose the many good things she had with John, but she also could see no way to ever trust him again. Mary believed that John's past affair proved that he was not trustworthy.

Trust is critical to The Seven Steps to Passionate Love. Trust means opening yourself up to being hurt by someone. You cannot have sensitivity and vulnerability without trust. Unless Mary trusted John, the process would fail.

Why would Mary want to trust John after what he had done? If Mary chose to forgive John and stay with him, trust was critical. Mary could not build a relationship of love with John without trusting him. Mary had the right to leave John because of his infidelity. She could have a wonderful life of love with someone else. But she could not have a life of love if she stayed with John and failed to trust him. You cannot maintain the flow of love without trust. I advised Mary to either separate from John until she was willing to trust him or stay and make the decision to trust him.

How could Mary trust John after his infidelity? By making a decision. Mary could choose to believe that John was trustworthy. She could know that John was trustworthy simply by making a decision. Would Mary's decision to trust John make him trustworthy? Obviously not. John's trustworthiness would be determined by his future decisions not Mary's. Mary's choice to trust John could ultimately prove to be a mistake.

How could Mary know whether trusting John was the right decision? That is a more difficult question to answer.

Mary could look at John's changes, listen to advice and seek spiritual guidance. She could analyze all the facts. In the end, however, only Mary could make the decision if John was trustworthy because she would suffer the consequences if he were not.

Mary watched John change as he experienced love in the workshop. She listened to him sob as he apologized for his betrayal. She listened to his childhood memories of sitting in the car as his father "visited" neighborhood women. Mary heard John request help with his problem and agree to future accountability. At the end of the workshop, Mary decided to trust John.

Mary's decision was rewarded with a wonderful experience of love with a changed man. The positive outcome was only possible because Mary was able to change her beliefs with a decision. She had all the past evidence she needed to know that John was not trustworthy, but based on the power of love, she chose to believe he had changed.

You can immediately change your beliefs by making decisions. Most people make their decisions based on feelings or past evidence. People who prosper in *The Seven Steps to Passionate Love* make their decisions based on the power of love. If you want to experience the benefits of love, you can change what you know and believe by making decisions based on love.

CONCEPT #2:

What you like, want and desire are determined by decisions. Lovers make those decisions based on love, not feelings.

Most people's desires are dictated by their feelings. If they get good feelings with fatty foods, they like fatty foods. If they get good feelings with skinny women, they like skinny women. If blue eyes trigger good feelings, they like blue eyes. If brown hair triggers bad feelings while blond hair triggers good feelings, they like blond hair. Sounds reasonable. Determining what you like based on feelings may be reasonable, but it is not conducive to *The Seven Steps to Passionate Love*.

Lovers determine what they like by making decisions based on love, not feelings. If you consistently make decisions based on love and change your thinking to match those decisions, your feelings will change also.

I met Paul and Tara in their fourth year of marriage. When they married, Tara weighed approximately 110 pounds. Paul remembered experiencing many good feelings when he looked at Tara's thin, 110-pound body and liking it very much. In the third year of their marriage, Tara was required to take steroids for an illness. Because of the steroids, she ballooned to 140 pounds. Her weight loss efforts had been futile.

I asked Paul to look at Tara's body and to tell me what he felt and thought. Paul described his feelings as being very bad, consisting mostly of a strong discomfort in his stomach. He indicated that his main thought was, "Tara looks ugly. I have no desire for her."

Why did Paul feel bad when he looked at Tara's body?

Most people would answer "because Tara's body was fat." That is not why Paul felt bad. Paul's bad feelings were a product of his brain firing and his spiritual emptiness. Tara's fat body was simply the trigger for Paul's pain. If Paul was spiritually mature enough to flow in love when he looked at Tara's fat, would he have felt bad? No. Paul would have experienced and shared love as he encouraged Tara to regain her shapely body.

Were Paul's bad feelings doing any harm to his relationship? Definitely. Bad feelings fog the mind and brain windows, decreasing the flow of love. Any feelings that do not line up with the power of love are to some degree sabotaging the experience of love in the relationship. Paul's bad feelings, triggered by Tara's fat, dampened the flow of love in their relationship.

Tara also felt bad when she looked at her fat. When she looked in a mirror, Tara did not see a beautiful, wonderful woman. Rather, Tara described herself as "ugly and fat."

Was Tara any less beautiful with a heavier flesh? Not in the true sense of beauty. Tara's true beauty was derived from her spiritual beauty.

To experience her spiritual beauty, Tara needed channels of love. She needed lovers who were able to maintain a loving perception no matter what she weighed—who were able to see a beautiful, wonderful woman despite her fat flesh. Tara needed people who would maintain a loving perception as they held her accountable for losing weight. Through the experience of love and decisions to change her thinking, Tara would be able to know and experience how beautiful and wonderful she was even when she looked in a mirror.

Paul did not maintain a loving perception. He did not see a beautiful woman when he looked at Tara; he saw a fat *flesh. Paul's thinking had changed based on his feelings. Paul did not like, want or desire Tara physically because of the feelings he experienced when he looked her fat flesh.*

For Paul to change his desires, what was necessary? A decision. For Paul to want to make love to Tara, what was necessary? A decision. For Paul to like Tara's body, what was necessary? A decision. Paul could decide to desire Tara, to want to make love to her and to like her body no matter how fat her body was.

Does that mean that Paul should not talk to Tara about losing weight? No. Liking her body means changing his thinking based on love so that his feelings would follow. Liking her body does not mean pretending it is perfect. At the same time Paul was choosing to like Tara's body, he could be helping her lose weight. Why would Paul want to choose to like Tara's body? Because not liking her body would be reinforcing his bad feelings and sabotaging the flow of love in the relationship.

On my advice and based on his desire to better flow in love, Paul made the decisions to desire Tara, to want to make love to her and to like her fat body. By making the decisions to line his thinking up with the power of love, Paul soon started experiencing good feelings when he looked at Tara's body. At the same time he enjoyed passionately making love to Tara, Paul assisted her in a weight loss program. After Tara had lost about half of her weight gain, Paul announced, "Tara, I really like your full, feminine body. Making love is great. I don't want you to get too skinny like you used to be."

Decisions determine likes, wants and desires. Lovers make their decisions based on the power of love, not feelings. If you want to be a flowing lover, you will determine your desires by making decisions based on love. If your decisions are truly based on love and you engage in the process to reprogram your emotional computer, your feelings will follow. In time, your feelings will match your loving desires.

CONCEPT #3:

The thoughts and feelings programmed
in your mind are not determined by reality.
The programming of your mind
is determined by your conscious thinking patterns.

A computer does not care about reality. If you program a computer to compute two plus two equals ten, it will do so even though the equation is wrong. Why? Because a computer's output is simply a reflection of its programming.

Likewise, your mind does not care about reality. Your mind is programmed by your conscious thinking patterns. As a child, you had limited control over the programming in your mind. You were at the mercy of the family in which you were raised. If you were raised in a family where your mind was programmed with bad feeling states and distorted thinking patterns, those patterns will be revealed in your adult life.

Intimacy will uncover the unhealthy circuits programmed in your early childhood. If you reinforce the bad programming with unhealthy thinking patterns, you mind will remain fogged. *If, on the other hand, you line your conscious thoughts up with the truth based on love, you will gradually replace the old, unhealthy patterns with new empowering programming.*

Many people sabotage their relationships with the irrational thoughts that are triggered by sensitivity and vulnerability. As you have learned, sensitivity means returning to the state of a sensitive, vulnerable child where you are most capable of intimately experiencing and sharing love. Returning to a sensitive state also means returning to the programming of your childhood. Often the programming of your childhood will be irrational and sabotage your experience of love.

> *Tim and Sally were both excited about their honeymoon. The setting was wonderful at the Marriott in Honolulu in the most exquisite honeymoon suite. Sally and Tim had refrained from intercourse prior to marriage, believing that they were validating the highest level of respect and value for each other.*
>
> *Tim was nude in the bed when Sally crawled in wearing her beautiful, new nightgown. As Tim passionately kissed Sally, he gently touched her breast. Sally began to cry. Tim immediately stopped his activity, sat up in the bed and sweetly asked Sally what was wrong. Sally did not want to say, but with Tom's persuasion and after several minutes of crying, she finally responded, "Tim, why do you want to use me like a piece of meat?"*
>
> *Tom was insulted. His immediate thought was to attack with an insult. He bit his tongue, took a deep breadth and then kindly replied, "Sally, what is wrong? I know you would never have said what you did unless something was really bothering you."*
>
> *Sally cried even more. Tom put his arms around her and said, "Whatever it is we can work through it. I love you so much that I am willing to help you through anything."*
>
> *After 15 minutes of crying, Sally finally talked, revealing to Tom that her uncle had sexually molested her for several years as a young teenager. Tom started to cry with Sally as*

they fell asleep holding each other. They spent the remainder of their honeymoon finding ways to be intimate without sex.

Tom and Sally came for help immediately after the honeymoon. It was very evident that Sally had the mental programming of an abused, little girl. She had effectively covered it up by avoiding sex. When she and Tom attempted to interact sexually, she did not experience the reality of an adult woman making love to a compassionate, loving man. Rather, she experienced the programming of a teenage girl being raped by a disgusting man. By applying the process of reprogramming her emotional computer and with the love of Tom and friends, Sally matured into a loving wife who enjoyed passionately loving her husband through sex.

Sally's thoughts concerning sex were initially irrational. If she had maintained her irrational thinking, the flow of love in her marriage would have been severely inhibited. Everyone has irrational thoughts as they become more intimate. It is critical that you identify the irrational thoughts that are sabotaging the flow of love in your relationship.

How do you know if your thinking is irrational? *The most effective way to identify irrational thinking is through revealing your thoughts to your partner and intimate friends.* Ask them to help you identify any thinking patterns that are moving you away from love. What if there is disagreement? Seek help from a spiritual authority who understands the truth about love. Trust the wisdom of your spiritual authority as he or she assists you in eradicating irrational thoughts.

No matter from whom you seek advice, ultimately you determine your mental programming. Reality will not determine the programming in your mind. Friends, family and therapists cannot change your mental programming. You are the only one who can make the necessary decisions to reprogram your own mind. The decisions you make in your conscious thoughts will ultimately determine the patterns in your mind. Make those decisions based on love.

Your mind, like Sally's, does not respond based upon reality. It responds based on how it has been programmed. Your unhealthy mental programming will interfere with the flow of love your relationships. Your conscious thoughts are the key to reprogramming your mind. You can replace old, unhealthy circuits with new empowering programming by choosing to consistently think based on the power of love.

Concept #4:

When your brain is firing, focus on the power of love. Do not focus on the trigger or the automatic thoughts.

The essence of *The Seven Steps to Passionate Love* is learning how to flow in love, how to access and experience the power source that resides within you and share it with someone else. A key to being a lover is programming your mind to turn to love in the midst of pain instead of turning to a solution outside of you.

Growing up in a home that was somewhat lacking in love forced you to turn to solutions other than love. By the time you read this book, you may already be an expert at fixing your feelings by fixing the trigger or by solving problems outside of you. To the extent that you are a fixer, it is going to be difficult for you to focus internally on love. If you desire to be a lover, it is essential that you learn to access love in the midst of problems instead of fixing your feelings by fixing the problems.

Some of the most caring people who make sure everything is perfectly taken care of for their partners are some of the worst lovers. Not because they don't try. Rather they are sorry lovers because their focus is on fixing the problem instead of loving the person. The fruit of all their effort is a lonely life with very few problems.

Other people choose to blame the trigger in the midst of their pain. They experience some temporary relief by having someone or something to blame. Blaming is simply another destructive way to deal with pain. Being a lover is the opposite of blaming. Lovers take full responsibility for their pain, knowing that accessing love is the answer.

A critical key to accessing love is focusing on the power of love instead of the problem or trigger. *In the midst of your brain firing with pain, realize that the flow of love is powerful enough to make you feel good if you are able to access it. Every time you learn to access love in a difficult situation, you mature as a lover.* The more mature lover you are, the better the quality of your life.

Concept #5:

The foundation for reprogramming your mind is a foundation of decisions.

When your brain starts firing and you start hurting, the thoughts that you choose will determine the programming in your brain. Your conscious thoughts either reinforce your emotional pain or move you toward the healing power of love. The key to maintaining thoughts that are moving you toward love is having a foundation of decisions to fall back on.

Write down your foundational decisions and make them readily accessible. If you are in the midst of your emotional pain and are not sure of the truth, you then can refer to your foundational decisions. All of the thoughts that do not line up with your foundational decisions should be discarded and replaced with appropriate thoughts that support your decisions.

The following are a list of decisions that you should adopt as you establish a foundation upon which to reprogram your mind:

- My primary purpose in life is to experience and share love.
- I have been created to be loved.
- I have been created to love others.
- Love is a capability; I must actively make choices that enable me to grow in my capability to love.
- The power of love is more powerful than any hurt or problem in my life.
- It is more important to flow in love than to win an argument.
- It is more important to flow in love than to make money.
- It is more important to flow in love than to be right.
- It is more important to flow in love than to be successful.
- It is more important to flow in love than to fix the problem.
- It is more important to flow in love than to fix the trigger.
- It is more important to flow in love than to do anything.
- Because of the power of love, I am a beautiful, wonderful person.
- True worth comes through love not through successes, accomplishments or talents.
- I am not my failures or mistakes but I am responsible for them.
- Love can overcome the pain and damage of my mistakes as long as I accept responsibility for them.
- If I prove myself right when I am wrong, both my partner and I lose.

- The power of love is great enough to enable me to feel good in any situation.
- The power of love is great enough to enable me to flow with my enemies.
- If I access the power of love, I can love my partner no matter what he does wrong or how he fails me.
- I am responsible for my emotional pain.
- I am responsible for my bad feelings.
- No one can make me feel anything; feelings come from inside me not outside me.
- When my partner does something to wrong me and I feel bad, I am responsible for the bad feelings while he is responsible for his behavior.
- People do not hurt my feelings; they uncover the pain inside of me.
- When I hurt, I hurt because my brain is firing and I am experiencing my spiritual emptiness.
- When I hurt, I have an opportunity to mature in my capability of flowing in love.
- The answer to my emotional pain is reprogramming my mind and moving toward love.
- It is better to access love than to prove I am right.
- I can trust my partner.
- I can trust the power of God and his love.
- Through the power of love, I have no fear.
- Through the power of love, I have no frustration.
- Through the power of love, I have no anxiety.
- Through the power of love, I have no anger.
- Through the power of love, I have no disappointment.
- Through the power of love, I have no embarrassment.
- Through the power of love, I have no hate.
- Through the power of love, I have no shame.

- Through the power of love, I have no annoyance.
- Through the power of love, I have no hurt.
- I forgive so that I can be free to experience love.
- I will not blame my pain on anyone or anything.
- Blaming blocks the flow of love in my life.
- Lovers either stay in love or leave in love.
- Lovers do not stay in blame.

You should expand on your foundation of decisions as you further your understanding of the truth and power of love. I want to emphasize that the purpose of these decisions is to assist you in maintaining thought patterns that move you toward love.

- You should daily read your list of foundational decisions until they become an active part of your conscious thoughts.
- Anytime you are having thoughts that do not agree with your foundational decisions, you can know that you are moving away from love.
- By changing your thoughts to ones that reinforce the truth and power of love, you will be empowering your life with a greater experience of love.

Another excellent tool that can be used to reprogram your mind is an affirmation card. *Affirmation cards are brief, written statements that support healthy thinking and reinforce your foundational decisions.*

You should develop affirmation cards for any area of your life where it is difficult for you to maintain appropriate, healthy thoughts. For example, if you have a problem with trust, you should develop a card that reinforces your decision to trust your partner. Reading an affirmation card 25 to 50 times per day is part of the daily passion builders.

The following are examples of affirmation cards that you can use to reprogram your mind.

GENERAL

I AM A BEAUTIFUL, WONDERFUL MAN (WOMAN) OF GOD. MY BAD THOUGHTS AND FEELINGS ARE LIES FROM MY BRAIN. AS I FLOW IN LOVE, I WILL EXPERIENCE THE WARMTH AND ENERGY OF LOVE DESPITE THE PAIN AND PROBLEMS AROUND ME. THE ANSWER TO MY PAIN IS ACCESSING LOVE, NOT FIXING MY PARTNER OR PROBLEMS. THANK YOU GOD FOR THE WONDERFUL POWER OF YOUR LOVE.

GENERAL

MY REALITY IS MY SPIRITUAL REALITY. MY REALITY IS NOT MY PROBLEMS, NOT MY PAIN AND NOT MY MISTAKES. MY SPIRITUAL REALITY IS THAT I AM BEAUTIFUL AND WONDERFUL AND THROUGH THE POWER OF LOVE, I CAN HAVE A GREAT LIFE. THANK YOU GOD FOR YOUR LOVE AND THE LOVE OF MY PARTNER AND FRIENDS.

OVERCOMING PHOBIA/FEAR

I AM A BEAUTIFUL, WONDERFUL CHILD OF GOD. THROUGH THE POWER OF LOVE, I HAVE NO FEAR. I AM NOT HURTING BECAUSE OF SNAKES (PHOBIA). I AM HURTING BECAUSE MY SICK BRAIN IS LYING TO ME. AS I ACCESS AND FLOW IN LOVE, I WILL EXPERIENCE THE WARMTH AND ENERGY OF LOVE, EVEN AROUND SNAKES. THANK YOU GOD FOR THE HEALING POWER OF YOUR LOVE.

AFFIRMATION OF PARTNER

JOHN (PARTNER) IS A BEAUTIFUL, WONDERFUL MAN OF GOD. I AM NOT HURTING BECAUSE OF JOHN. I AM HURTING BECAUSE MY SICK BRAIN IS LYING TO ME. AS I ACCESS AND FLOW IN LOVE, I WILL EXPERIENCE THE WARMTH AND ENERGY OF LOVE NO MATTER WHAT JOHN DOES. I AM BLESSED TO HAVE JOHN IN MY LIFE. THANK YOU GOD FOR YOUR LOVE AND MY WONDERFUL LOVER JOHN.

Decisions determine destiny. Decisions determine the programming in your mind. Make decisions that guarantee your destiny and your mind will be energized by the power of LOVE.

Four Steps For Reprogramming Your Emotional Computer

Step #1:
Feel the Feeling.

Step #2:
Tell Yourself the Bad Feeling is a Lie from your Right Brain.

Step #3:
Tell Yourself the Automatic Distorted Thoughts are Lies from your Left Brain.

Step #4:
Think and Behave Based on the Power of Love.

Feel the feeling means to feel your physical sensations. A bad feeling is one that does not line up with the experience of love. You need to learn what the flow of love feels like—what kind of body sensations that you experience when you are experiencing love. The best way to experience the flow of love is to participate in a sensitivity and intimacy process with people who are familiar with an intimate experience of love. One of the primary purposes of my intimacy and love workshops is to enable people to enjoy a true experience of love. Sadly, many people live their entire lives without ever experiencing the full depth of true love. As you become more aware of the experience of love, you will also become more aware of your bad feelings.

A bad feeling is one that does not line up with the experience of love.

Any time your right brain fires energizing bad feelings, you want to be aware that it is happening. You may be thinking that you are always aware of your bad feelings. I can assure you that most people react automatically without ever knowing that they are feeling bad. Feel the feeling means being sensitive to each time your right brain fires.

A significant role I play as a therapist is assisting clients in knowing when their feeling state has changed or when their right brain is firing. I simply watch my clients as they talk about different topics. When I observe a feeling state change, I ask, "Can you tell that you are feeling bad? That you are more tense? That your face is turning red?" Often, my clients will be unaware of their bad feelings. They will have simply changed their thinking or behavior based on the feelings. Their bad feelings will be energizing their thought patterns.

Before I started reprogramming my brain, I would have argued that I rarely had bad feelings. I worked hard to feel good and I did most of the time. When I began to pay close attention to my body sensations, I was amazed to discover that I experienced bad feelings, typically consisting of stomach pain, more than 50 times each day. Any time I made a mistake or perceived the possibility of a mistake, my stomach hurt. My automatic thoughts were to defend myself and create a solution. Because I am very verbal, I could quickly articulate a defense or solution. As soon as I started talking, my stomach pain went away. Consequently, only a very brief part of my day was spent hurting, while much of the day was spent talking.

Through this process, I realized that my emotional pain was significantly influencing my thinking and behavior. I made the decision to "bite my tongue" and feel my feelings. Rather than automatically react to my stomach pain, I felt the feeling, bit my tongue and then considered my choices. I did not speak or act until I believed I was being motivated by love instead of my emotional pain.

Dr. Jones was one of my psychiatric professors with whom I had serious philosophical differences. Prior to my commitment to reprogram my emotional computer, I either avoided Dr. Jones' classes or attended them and argued with him. After learning this process, I purposely went to his class, bit my tongue and listened to him teach what I perceived to be psychological nonsense. As I sat there, I felt my feelings. First, my stomach would start hurting, followed by tension throughout my body. If I stayed committed to shutting up, my whole body would eventually be consumed with intense bad feelings and my thoughts would be flooded with arguments to rebut his ludicrous positions. If I verbalized my arguments, my bad feelings would immediately go away. I would obtain relief from my pain by attacking something outside of me.

I made the decision that I wanted to obtain relief from my pain by accessing an internal source, love. I knew that love produced true healing while arguing was a temporary fix. I, therefore, attended the class, bit my tongue, felt the feeling and consistently applied Steps Two through Four. Within four weeks, I could attend the professor's class, listen to his psychological baloney and flow in love.

Feel the feeling also applies to crying. Crying is an indication that you are truly sensitive to the pain inside of you, that you are truly feeling your feelings. If you are in an environment where

crying is acceptable and where other channels of love are present, then you should take advantage of the opportunity to
grieve. Remember grieving in love is to your emotions what
exercise is to your heart and lungs. Grieving in love opens your
shutters and keeps your mind in the best state to flow in love.

While you are grieving in love, it is important that you line
your thinking up with the truth about love. Healthy thoughts in
the midst of crying would include thoughts such as the following:

"Thank you God that you are healing me."
"Crying is good for me."
**"It is wonderful to have friends to love me when I am
hurting."**
**"I am a wonderful person and I am in the process of
healing."**
"Thank you God for your love."

If you are holding someone who is crying, it is important to
affirm his right to hurt. Most teenagers and adults perceive crying as a sign of weakness. It is important to reinforce the realty
that crying is healing and beneficial. It is also valuable to gently encourage the person to cry. In general, it is good to limit
your talking to a small percentage of the crying experience.
Comments that will enhance the healing when you are with
someone who is crying include the following:

"You are wonderful and it is good you are crying."
**"It is really sad that . . . (whatever the triggering
memory)."**
"It is wonderful that you are crying."
"I love you and I am glad that I am here to love you."
"It is great to see you healing."

Once it is time for the crying or hurting to stop, you should
move to Step Two by telling yourself that the bad feelings are a

lie. The purpose of telling yourself that the bad feelings are a lie is not to deny their presence or their physical reality. The purpose is to tell your mind that the feelings do not line up with the power of love. The power of love is so great that if you are fully flowing in love, your bad feelings will be replaced by the warm, energizing experience of love. If you consistently remind your mind of this truth, your mind will be reprogrammed.

Moving to Step Two is appropriate whenever you want to move out of the painful circuitry in your brain. In general, I recommend that anytime you hurt, moving toward grieving in love is your first choice. If that is not possible, moving to Step Two is the second choice. For example, if your boss triggers you at work, it probably would not be appropriate or safe enough to cry; therefore, you would want to move to Step Two. By moving to Step Two, you are telling the programming for the emotional pain to get lost.

As you tell the programming for the emotional pain to get lost, you also want to move to Step Three by telling yourself that the automatic distorted thoughts are a lie. Step Three starts the process of controlling your conscious thought. Remember, your mind is programmed with your conscious thoughts. If you are having distorted thoughts at the same time as you are hurting, you will be reinforcing the sick programming in your brain.

While Step Three keeps you from reinforcing the lies in your brain, Step Four enables you to reinforce the truth. By thinking and behaving based on the power of love, you are conditioning in your mind the reality that the experience of love is powerful enough to overcome any outside influences. The ultimate goal is to have the reality of your life determined by the internal experience of love, not the external experience of life.

In other words, if your experience of life is determined by the power of love, you will have a wonderful experience of life no matter what problems or difficulties you encounter. If you were able to maintain a perfect experience of love, you would experience and share the warmth and energy of love at all times in every situation with everyone. Obviously, that is not possible. What is possible, though, is programming your mind to move in that direction.

For example, if you believe that getting stuck in traffic is what makes you feel bad, you will always feel bad when you are stuck in traffic. If, on the other hand, when you get stuck in traffic, you first feel your bad feelings. Second, you tell yourself the bad feelings are a lie. You realize that you are feeling bad in traffic because a sick part of your right brain is firing and you are experiencing your spiritual emptiness. Third, you tell yourself that the automatic thoughts to blame the traffic are lies. Finally, you think and behave based on the truth of love realizing that the power of love is great enough to enable you to feel good while you are stuck in traffic. If you follow these four steps consistently, you will be able to access the Spirit of God in bad traffic, and you will find yourself having a great time flowing in love while everyone else is miserable and cussing.

Another simple example involves your partner arriving late. If you feel bad when he is late and blame your bad feelings on his tardiness, you will always feel bad when he is late. On the other hand, if you are aware that you are feeling bad because his being late is triggering a sick part of your brain and uncovering your spiritual emptiness, you can then learn to reprogram your brain and access love while he is late. If you do so, your partner will arrive home late and you will be feeling good flowing in love.

Does flowing in love when he arrives late mean that you ignore his tardiness? No. As you will learn in the next step, Problem Solving In Love, your first goal when your partner has failed to meet a responsibility is to flow in love. Your second goal is to hold him responsible for his failure—to apply consequences.

Your partner should pay a price for being late, but the price should not be a blaming lover. Your partner should be loved when he arrives late and loved when he pays his consequence. You love the person as you make him accountable for his mistakes. To love him, you have to be able to reprogram your mind.

If you are sensitive to your bad feelings, you will have the opportunity to reprogram your mind many times every day. Every time you feel bad you have an opportunity to spiritual grow and increase your capability to access love. The true test of your capability to love occurs when your partner is making a mistake or failing you in some way. Most everyone can flow to some degree with someone who is treating him or her nice. Lovers flow when they are being treated poorly.

Do you want to become a better lover? Your opportunity to do so is when you are hurting.

Maturing as a lover always requires moving through bad feelings.

In other words, your experience of emotional pain is an indication of increased sensitivity and is an opportunity to move into a greater experience of love. The movement through bad feelings and toward love only occurs if you think and act based on the power of love. If, in the midst of your emotional pain, you think or act based on the pain, you only reinforce your sick programming.

A classic opportunity to apply the four steps is when your lover does something that you have asked him not to do a thousand times. All of us know something about our partner that triggers us. Maybe it is his fat belly, her cellulite legs, his tossing of his clothes on the floor or her complaints about your driving. Whatever the trigger is, it is an opportunity to reprogram your mind.

When your lover triggers you, immediately feel the bad feelings. Tell yourself that the feelings are a lie. Tell yourself that
the automatic thoughts of blaming your partner are a lie.
Realize that you are not feeling bad because of your lover's
behavior. Rather, you are feeling bad because your brain is firing and you are experiencing your spiritual emptiness. Tell
yourself that the flow of love is powerful enough that if you
access love you will feel good no matter what your partner does.
Tell yourself that when your partner is doing something inappropriate, he or she needs love more than anything else. Finally,
through problem solving in love, eliminate your partner's inappropriate behavior.

Emotional healing in love applies to daily triggers as well as
deep-rooted emotional pain. To end this chapter, I am going to
tell a story about someone who healed some intense emotional
pain by applying the process you are now learning. The trigger
is bizarre but the process of healing is the same one you must
learn if you desire to live a life flowing in love.

"*Dr. Van Horn, can you help a woman get over a fear of
coke bottles?*" *Jenny, my secretary, asked me as I walked by.*

"*You are kidding, right, Jenny?*" *I laughed as I moved
past her, knowing this was a joke.*

"*No, Dr. Van Horn,*" *Jenny replied. "Her husband is on
the phone now. She won't even leave her house because she
is afraid to go around coke bottles.*"

"*I can help anyone with any phobia if they are willing to
do the work,*" *I responded. "Tell her husband to bring her to
the hospital for an evaluation.*"

*What started out appearing funny was actually a very
sad story of a 10-year-old girl, named Loni, who had
been sexually abused with a coke bottle and was now a*

40-year-old woman with an irrational fear of coke bottles. Loni had suppressed the memories of the abuse until the abuser re-entered her life when she was 32 years old. For the eight years prior to seeking treatment from me, Loni had progressively reduced the activities in her life. She now became hysterical if she went down any road where she knew there was a coke machine or a building with a coke machine. Loni essentially did not leave home.

Loni was admitted to the hospital so that she could be more aggressively helped. During the first group she attended, I told her that before she left the hospital she would drink out of a coke bottle. Loni immediately put her hands to her face and started sobbing. You would have thought that I had informed her of the death of her child. She cried uncontrollably for the next 30 minutes while other group members gently touched her.

I asked Loni how her body felt. She described physical sensations of intense nausea, deep throbbing chest pain, tightness in her chest, restricted breathing and tension throughout her shoulders, back and pelvis.

I asked Loni about her thoughts. She described thoughts of fear, anxiety, guilt, embarrassment and anger. Her angry thoughts were predominantly directed toward the abuser and me. Loni's embarrassed thoughts centered on the lie that if people knew about the abuse, they would think less of her. Her guilty thoughts consisted of the distorted perception that she had done something to deserve the abuse. Her anxious thoughts were energized by the thought of having to drink out of a coke bottle. Finally, Loni's fearful thoughts were the most persistent and consisted of the belief that she could not handle being around a coke bottle.

Loni's trigger was an unusual one but her problem was not. Not many people are triggered by or experience their spiritual emptiness around coke bottles. But all of us are triggered by and experience our spiritual emptiness around something. The process of reprogramming your emotional computer is the same for all people and with all triggers. The reason I picked Loni with her bizarre trigger is to re-enforce your understanding that the trigger has nothing to do with the pain.

It is probably easy for you to see that the coke bottle is not responsible for Loni's pain. It is most likely much more difficult for you to see that your trigger is equally not responsible for your pain. But people, events and things outside of us do not cause our pain. They uncover the pain within us by triggering our brain and exposing our spiritual emptiness. This is a critical concept that you must accept if you are to grow in love. Loni also had to accept this concept.

Loni made the decision to know that she was hurting because her brain was firing and she was experiencing her spiritual emptiness. She decided that the coke bottles were only the trigger for her pain. Loni made the decision to take full responsibility for her pain. Loni had no problem feeling her feelings, but controlling her thinking was another issue. Although it required a tremendous effort, Loni chose to line her thinking up with the power of love. She established a foundation of decisions and several affirmation cards to assist her in changing her thinking. Loni then decided to expose herself to the trigger on a consistent basis.

The first exposure was verbal. We regularly talked about coke bottles within the hospital groups. At first, Loni cried every time her trigger was mentioned. As she cried within the loving environment of the group, Loni also lined her thinking up with the truth and power of love by reading her cards. She felt the feeling, told herself the feelings were a lie, told herself that the automatic distorted thoughts were a lie and then changed her thinking and behavior to match the truth and power of love.

Loni also had the opportunity to appropriately cry while remembering her childhood abuse and neglect. Throughout her entire grieving process, Loni consistently experienced love through an abundance of loving hugs and affirmations from fellow group members who knew all her dirtiest secrets. She also received help with her thinking from staff and group members.

Loni chose to replace her distorted thoughts with the truth. Her angry thoughts were replaced with the decision to forgive. Loni's guilty and embarrassed thoughts were replaced with the belief that through the power of love, she was beautiful, wonderful and innocent despite her present and past mistakes and abuse. Her fearful and anxious thoughts were replaced by the decision to know that love is powerful enough to eliminate all fear and anxiety. Loni daily made the decision to read cards and choose thoughts that validated the truth and power of love.

Progressive levels of exposure were then possible as Loni rapidly healed. Pictures of coke bottles advanced to miniature, key chain models. Empty bottles were then placed within Loni's sight and eventually in her hands. Each exposure required that Loni actively control her conscious thoughts and move toward love. Within three weeks of entering the hospital, Loni drank out of a coke bottle while talking and laughing with the group.

Loni reprogrammed her emotional computer by learning and

applying these concepts, principles and steps. You, too, can reprogram your emotional computer if you are willing to do the work. You can get rid of emotional baggage that you have carried for years. You can learn to think and feel like the beautiful, wonderful person you are. You can move past the emotional pain and distorted thinking that is uncovered by intimacy and love. If you make the commitment and do the work to reprogram your emotional computer, you will open your life to the full benefits of *The Seven Steps to Passionate Love.*

It Is Easy to Be Confused

You have just been introduced to a very unique way to view feelings and thoughts. Most people blame their pain on someone or something and deal with their bad feelings by fixing something outside of them. When you first start learning to take full responsibility for your emotional pain and to fix your pain by accessing love, it is easy to become confused.

To overcome the confusion, study this step thoroughly until you clearly understand each principle, definition, concept and step. Once you understand the process, apply it to your life on a consistent basis and watch your experience of life change. I guarantee you that it will. Accessing love to deal with pain is a revolutionary concept for most people. It can be a life-changing concept for you.

Step 6 Exercises

Principle: When you hurt . . .

Exercise 1: Make a list of ten times in your life that you were significantly hurt. Start with the first incident and, with your eyes closed, picture yourself in that situation. Pay close attention to your feelings, the physical sensations in your body. Pay close attention to the automatic thoughts that enter your conscious mind.

As you do this drill, be aware that you are accessing stored memory circuits in your brain. The emotional pain is not because of the past event. The memories were circuited during the event; but the immediate experience of pain is result of electrical circuits firing in your brain. Remember, you cannot eliminate the past events but you can eliminate the painful memory circuits.

Exercise 2: Emotional Brain Mapping
Take a sheet of paper or index card and create four columns with the following headings:

Feeling—Trigger—Automatic Thoughts—Truth Based on Love

Under the "feeling" heading, record any feelings that do not line up with the experience of love. i.e. stomach sensations, chest pain, tension, etc. The key to this part of the exercise is the awareness of what it feels like to experience the Spirit of God. You can practice experiencing the Spirit of God during your personal time with God, the relationship time with your partner and the assembly time with your support system. Any feeling that moves you away from the experience of love is a bad feeling and should be noted. Many people, particularly businessmen, are in a constant state of tension throughout their day; consequently they experience very little love while working and notice very few feeling state changes. If you can identify with this problem, the answer is to work on flowing outside of the office and gradually incorporate greater sensitivity into your daily experience.

Exercise 2: *(cont'd)*

- Under the "trigger" heading, briefly note the person, event or experience that triggered the feeling state change.
- Under the "automatic thought" heading, briefly note the thoughts attached to the feelings.
- Under the "truth based on love" heading, briefly note what truths about love would apply.

For example, when I first charted my emotional brain mapping, I discovered that all authority figures triggered an uncomfortable sensation in my stomach. My automatic thoughts were that I might have made a mistake or done something wrong. In this scenario, the feeling is "stomach discomfort," the trigger is authority figures, the automatic thoughts were as described above, and the truth of love was that "I am a beautiful, wonderful man of God even when I make a mistake."

Other examples are as follows:

Feeling	Trigger	Auto Thoughts	Truth Based on Love
Stomach and Chest pain	Partner late for date.	What a jerk! He doesn't care about me.	The bad thoughts and feelings are lies.

Positive affirmation: I can flow in love even when my partner is late. I will deal with the issue at issue time.

Exercise 2: *(cont'd)*

Feeling	Trigger	Auto Thoughts	Truth Based on Love
Body tension Heart racing	Partner refuses to have sex.	What a selfish jerk (blaming thoughts)	The bad thoughts and feelings are lies.

Positive affirmation: I can flow in love even if my partner refuses sex. I will flow now and deal with the issue at issue time.

If you regularly spend time mapping your emotional brain, you will quickly see unhealthy patterns and have an opportunity to change them.

Exercise 3: List your ten most significant triggers in order of priority. i.e. phobias, traumatic experiences, past mistakes, current problems, worries, etc.

Start with your most significant trigger and apply the healing process.

- If someone hurt you and you have not forgiven them, do so.
- Write a letter about the sadness of the experience with the goal to cry. Focus on the emotional pain of the experience. Do not blame in the letter by verbally attacking the offender.
- Read the letter in the presence of your support system and your partner. Have your partner hold you as you cry.
- Make a card that supports the truth in love-read the card 25 times daily.

Once you can recall the incident with appropriate sensitivity and maintain healthy thinking, move on to number two on your list.

Step 7

*Flowing in love is more important
than anything in the problem-solving process.*

PROBLEM SOLVING IN LOVE

*W*hen people think of positive communication, they typically do not think of issues and problems. But **Problem Solving in Love** truly is a form of positive communication. More often, couples see issues as something to avoid at all costs. Often when couples face and discuss issues together, the time is spent fighting as opposed to resolving problems. In healthy, loving relationships, problem solving is an opportunity to enhance the flow of love. By learning how to solve conflicts and issues effectively and efficiently, you will have more time to flow in love.

To solve problems in love effectively, you must understand eight fundamental principles:

1. **Love first.**
2. **Issue time.**
3. **Personal honesty.**
4. **Assumption of honesty.**
5. **Assumption of value.**
6. **Process of Forgiveness**

7. Boundaries

8. Focus on desired outcome, not past failure.

1. Love First

Love is the spiritual energy that enables us to make the right decisions consistently æ the decisions that result in the highest quality of experience. When you see people making destructive, devaluing decisions, lowering the quality of their lives, you can be sure that they do not have enough love in their lives. It is the experience of love that ultimately changes people and enables them to make choices that bring value to their lives and the lives of the people around them. This principle applies to everyone, including you and your partner.

As you problem-solve in love, remember the most important and powerful aspect of the process is **flowing in love**. Flowing in love is more important than being right. Flowing in love is more important than accurately articulating your position. Flowing in love is more important than understanding the problem. Flowing in love is more important than solving the problem.

Flowing in love is more important than anything in the problem-solving process.

If you and your partner can learn to flow in love while you problem-solve together, the process will be a wonderful experience. By far the most common problem that I handle while teaching couples how to problem-solve is the emotional pain attached to their issues. If your brain is firing and your mind window is fogged with emotional pain, you can still problem-solve. It is simply a much more difficult process. The process you are about to learn is designed to enable you to problem-solve in spite of your emotional pain; however, the more you flow, the easier the process will be.

You are the most important channel of love for your partner. Your love is the key to your partner making and maintaining healthy changes. Your capability to flow in love while you problem-solve will ultimately determine the long-term success of the process. Flow in love first, problem-solve second.

2. Issue Time

Consider the content of communication between two people in the first year of a romantic relationship. Compare the amount of time spent talking about positive themes to that spent communicating about issues. You will find that the vast majority of communication during the early romantic phase of a relationship is about positive themes.

Do the same comparison of communication in a relationship between a couple married for five years with two children. You will quickly discover that most of the communication is about issues, problems that need to be solved, and people or things that need to be fixed. Very little time is spent positively communicating. What has happened in the relationship? The focus has changed from two people romantically enjoying each other to two people solving problems together.

The purpose of your relationship should be to experience love together, not solve issues together. The difference between experiencing love with your lover and dealing with issues is like the difference between eating steak and eating dog food. Most people end up eating dog food, thinking it is steak because they do not know that there something better out there. Others pretend the dog food is wonderful to avoid confronting pain. Most couples spend most of their time communicating about issues. You were created to eat steak, to be a lover in your relationships, not a problem-solver.

Does this mean that you should ignore the issues in your life? No. You should make passionate intimacy and love the focus of your relationship while you set aside time to deal with your issues. The time that you set aside is called **issue time.**

Issue time should consist of approximately 15–30 minutes per day in which you specifically deal with the problems and issues in your life. During issue time, you deal with practical problems, parental responsibilities, financial matters, relationship problems and anything else that is an issue. In other words, you only talk about issues during issue time. During the rest of your day, you focus on positive communication.

An issue is defined as anything that is not a positive affirmation, an expression of gratitude, a positive interest or a positive invitation.

I defined an issue based on what it is not so that you can clearly know what the majority of your communication should be. Anytime that you are talking with your lover outside of issue time, you should be positively communicating. You should not be talking about issues.

- If an issue comes to your mind during the day, instead of talking about it, positively affirm your lover.
- Write the issue down and deal with it during issue time.
- Focus your communication on letting your partner know how wonderful he or she is and what he or she means to you, how thankful you are for your blessings, and other positive topics of interest.

If you adopt an issue-time policy for your relationship, it will dramatically change the dynamics of your communication. You and your lover will consistently promote the flow of love through your communication. You will not deal with problems throughout your day. Your partner will become a bearer of good news instead of problems and issues. You will find yourself excited to talk to your lover.

Issue time is a powerful tool. It requires a change in focus and discipline. The results are immediate and significant in most relationships. Adopt an issue-time policy for your relationship. The benefits will be obvious.

3. Personal Honesty

What does personal communication really mean? If personal honesty is defined as "telling the truth in every situation," it then becomes necessary to define what is meant by "telling the truth." Does "telling the truth" mean that your communications must line up with reality, or are you just required to communicate your perception of reality? Obviously, "telling the truth" must be defined as a commitment to communicate your "perception of reality." Why? Because it is impossible for anyone to truly know reality. We are all limited to our perception of reality, what we perceive to be the truth. If we are being honest, the best we can do is communicate our perception of reality.

Personal honesty is, therefore, defined as "a commitment to openly and honestly communicate what you perceive to be the truth, your perception of reality, in all appropriate situations.

Now that personal honesty has been defined, it is easy to establish a definition for "lying." The definition of lying would simply be the failure to openly and honestly communicate what you perceive to be the truth, your perception of reality, in all appropriate situations. Lying can be either active or passive. Active lying means that you tell what you know to be a mistruth. Passive lying is the failure to tell what you know to be the truth when it would be appropriate to do so.

Personal honesty is absolutely necessary if you desire to live *The Seven Steps to Passionate Love.* No matter how bad your mistakes or weaknesses, if you are honest about them, you can overcome their damage through the power of love. On the other hand, no matter how minor your mistakes or weaknesses, if you hide or lie about them, you can never enjoy the full benefits of love. Why? Because the benefits of a loving relationship are not determined by our perfection or our imperfections. The benefits of love are determined by the quality of our relationships. You will never have intimate, healthy relationships in which you experience the benefits of love if you are not totally committed to personal honesty. Lack of honesty in a relationship destroys the sensitivity and vulnerability necessary for the relationship to be empowered by love. No one can be sensitive and vulnerable with a person who lies, and love cannot flow without sensitivity and vulnerability.

Not only is personal honesty critical to a relationship, but the definition of personal honesty is also critical to a relationship. Individual perceptions of reality can vary dramatically among people who have been through the exact same experience. I have worked with each individual partner. After hearing both perceptions of the same experiences, I had no idea what had actually happened. The two perceptions were dramatically different. Was someone lying? I cannot know for sure; however, in most cases, I believe both partners were expressing their honest perception of the situation. If I were to define personal honesty as communicating the truth about a situation and insisted that the truth must line up with reality, both partners would be lying. Neither I nor anyone else can ever know what reality is.

Fortunately, it is not necessary to know what reality is. To empower a relationship with love, it is simply necessary that both individuals are committed to being honest about their perception of reality in every appropriate setting.

The issue of the *appropriate setting* is very important. You do not have to—nor is it appropriate—to give your honest opinion in every situation. You are not lying if you withhold your opinion when you perceive that it would not be appropriate. In superficial relationships, it is often appropriate to withhold your opinion. In intimate, loving relationships it is appropriate to withhold your honest opinion temporarily until the timing and setting is right.

***It is never appropriate to permanently withhold a
perception or thought from your lover
if you desire to maximize the love in your relationship.***

I am often asked, "Should I tell my partner . . ." If you are asking that question, the answer is always "yes." The issue is not "Should you tell," the issue is "When should you tell." Your lover should be your best friend, your safest confidant. If you cannot tell your lover "everything," you do not have much love in the relationship.

What if you cheated on your spouse in the past and the affair was never revealed? I have addressed this situation on multiple occasions for many years. The answer is simple but painful: You must tell your partner if you want to maximize the love in your life. If you had an affair, it would be safe to conclude that the

affair was one of the worst sins of your life. It would also be safe
to conclude that your affair would be one of the most significant
issues for your spouse? If one of the ugliest sins of your life and
one of the most significant issues in your spouse's life are kept
a secret, how much honesty and love do you really have? Not
much. As painful as the decision is, you must choose to tell the
whole truth to the most significant lover in your life or there will
not be much true love in the relationship.

What if you reveal the ugly secret and your spouse decides to
dump you? If your partner decides to leave, it is her choice. You
cannot make her stay. Her departure would be a sad consequence of your sin, but it would not be the end of your life. In
fact, if you choose to pursue love, you can still have a wonderful life of love, a much better life than the one you had with your
partner. You do not need a specific lover to have a wonderful life
of love, but you do need honest, open communication.

What if you tell your spouse and she decides to stay with you,
will she ever get over the affair? I have helped dozens of couples deal with infidelity and every one of them overcame the
pain of the affair if they were willing to do the work necessary
to live *The Seven Steps to Passionate Love*. Competent professional help is almost always necessary for a couple to overcome
an affair, but healing is definitely possible.

Whether you are dealing with a personal failure such as an
affair or simply dealing with daily life, personal honesty is
absolutely necessary. You must commit to open and honest communication of what you perceive to be the truth in all appropriate situations. You must be willing to reveal all significant
thoughts and perceptions at the appropriate time. If you and
your partner choose to commit to a relationship with personal
honesty, you will open yourself up to a much greater experience
of love.

4. Assumption of honesty

You must assume in all communication that your partner is being honest. As indicated earlier, a relationship cannot flow in love unless both partners are committed to personal honesty. A relationship also cannot flow in love unless each partner believes the other one is being honest. Even if both partners are being honest, if both do not assume that the other is being honest, the relationship will be seriously lacking in sensitivity.

People falsely accused will not stay sensitive with partners who do not trust them, while accusers will not stay sensitive with partners they perceive to be liars. Without the assumption of honesty, the result is minimal sensitivity and, therefore, a significant lack of love. What if your partner has lied in the past? Past lying does not necessarily predict future lying. Many people who have lied extensively in the past are capable of personal honesty when they participate in *The Seven Steps to Passionate Love*. Most people who lie, do so to avoid the pain of admitting the truth. Often, the pain of admitting the truth is associated with a mistake or failure. When people are in relationships in which their value is dependent on true love—not on performance—they often are much more willing to be honest. If your partner has lied in the past, offer him or her a chance to start over with a commitment to honesty.

What if your partner is not willing to commit to personal honesty, or what if you do not believe he or she will live up to the commitment? In both cases, do not waste your time in the relationship. Without honesty, a relationship based on true love would be out of the question. You need to separate from the relationship until your partner commits to personal honesty and you decide to believe in his or her commitment. You cannot have a loving relationship with someone choosing to lie or whom you do not trust. If you cannot trust your partner to be honest, separate from the relationship until you can.

How do you begin the process of restoring a relationship with someone who has lied to you in the past? The answer is simple, yet painful: You must make the decision to trust. When you trust a person, you put yourself in the position of being hurt by the potential betrayal of your trust. *Trust is not a feeling state; it is a decision.* You can choose to trust a person no matter how much they have hurt you in the past.

Am I saying that you should automatically choose to trust anyone who has hurt you in the past? Absolutely not. I am not telling you whom you should trust. I am saying that after you and your partner make a decision to pursue a loving relationship, then you must choose to trust, even if your partner has hurt you in the past. You cannot have a loving relationship without the decision to trust. Therefore, do not return to a relationship until you are prepared to make the decision to trust. The question, then, is not whether you should trust but whom you should trust. If you want to restore a relationship with someone who has lied to you in the past, you must make a decision to trust and assume honesty in the present.

If you are not ready to choose to trust, do not try to restore the relationship. It is useless to work on a relationship with the goal of finding out if your partner can be trusted. If I am working with a couple and one of them will not make the decision to assume that the other person is being honest, I stop the therapy immediately. I know the relationship will go nowhere if one partner is doubting the truthfulness of the other. I often encounter this situation when there has been an affair. For example, a wife will stay in a marriage with her previously adulterous husband and use his past affair to justify her right not to trust him. If that woman wants to heal the relationship, she must decide to trust, to assume that her husband is being honest. If she is not willing to make the decision to trust, the relationship cannot heal.

What if you choose to trust and then find out that you have been lied to again? You will have a decision to make: Either separate from the relationship or start over again by choosing to trust and assume honesty. I recommend that prior to choosing to trust again, both you and your spouse seek professional help. **Anyone who lies regularly has some significant, unresolved, developmental issues. Anyone who picks a person who lies regularly also has some significant, unresolved, developmental issues.** Those issues typically cannot be resolved without appropriate help. I often successfully work with people on both sides of the problem, those who lie and those who have been lied to. If you are the one who has been lied to, a professional can also help you decide whether to go forward with the relationship.

The assumption of honesty is a foundational principle that must be adopted if a relationship is going to grow in love. You must choose to trust that your partner is being honest in all communication with you. If you cannot make that choice, then you must separate from the relationship until you can.

5. Assumption of Value

"He just doesn't love me. Dr. Van Horn, I know Mike doesn't love me. He proves it to me every day. Last Wednesday, he came home from work late. I had a wonderful meal planned. He ruined it. On Thursday, he forgot to take out the trash. Friday was our date night. Mike takes me to McDonalds. Saturday, I ask him to pick up his dirty clothes. He leaves them out anyway. How do I know that Mike doesn't love me? He proves it every single day."

"But Kathy, how do you know he wasn't late from work

simply because someone had asked him a question as he was leaving? How do you know that his forgetting to take out the trash is not simply forgetfulness? Have you ever told him you don't like going to McDonalds? And rather than say he doesn't love you, have you set up a system to help him remember to pick up his dirty clothes?

If love is the absence of personal inadequacies or mistakes, then none of us are lovers. Kathy was using practical events in her life to determine if Mike loved her. Mike regularly made mistakes so Kathy concluded that she was not loved. Kathy was not following the principle of the assumption of value.

**The assumption of value simply means
that you must maintain the belief
that your partner is truly committed to loving you.**

You must know that you are loved even when your partner is late, fails to meet daily responsibilities, or is insensitive to your pain and needs. You cannot use your partner's practical failures to determine if he or she loves you. When your partner makes a mistake, the assumption should be that he or she loves you but is not doing a good job of demonstrating his or her love for you. You must assume as a foundational belief that your partner is committed to loving and valuing you no matter what issues evolve.

Why maintain an assumption of value? Why conclude that your partner loves you when he or she is not demonstrating much love? Because without an assumption of value, sensitivity and vulnerability cannot be maintained. You will not stay vulnerable with a person with whom you doubt their commitment to loving you. Likewise, your partner will not stay vulnerable with you if his or her daily mistakes are used to validate that he or she does not love you. Questioning your partner's commitment to loving you is an effective way to sabotage the sensitivity and vulnerability critical to the maintenance of a passionate, loving relationship. On the other hand, maintaining a consistent assumption that your partner loves you will establish an environment in which both you and your partner can intimately relate to each other.

A second reason to maintain the assumption of value is to reduce the intensity of emotional pain associated with your partner's failures and inadequacies. If your partner being late means that he doesn't love you, the simple issue of timeliness is transformed into a foundational issue of abandonment or lack of love. Your experience of emotional pain will be dramatically more severe if you perceive that your partner does not love you versus realizing that he has an issue with being on time. A small issue becomes monumental. Your value, your worth, and the survival of your relationship become attached to your partner's timeliness. The failure to assume that your partner loves you can quickly lead to the destruction of your relationship. If you maintain the assumption of value, you can know that you are loved while you help your partner do a better job of demonstrating his or her love for you. Problem solving then becomes much more focused and productive and much less emotionally painful.

What if your partner is not committed to loving you? Should you still maintain an assumption of value? You should maintain an assumption of value for as long as you and your partner are working on a passionate, loving relationship. If your partner is not willing to commit to true intimacy and love, you should not accept this lack of commitment. You were created by God to be intimately and passionately loved. If you accept a lacking relationship from a partner who is not committed, you will never experience the fullness of life that is available. The assumption of value only applies to a relationship in which both partners are committed to passionate love.

What if partners claim to be committed but continue to do things that demonstrate a lack of value? Does the assumption of value still apply? Yes, the assumption of value still applies. Everyone is less than a perfect lover. You will not find a partner who does not make mistakes. You also will never be a mistake-free lover. As you productively resolve issues, you should not use the resolution of issues to determine how much you are loved or valued. You should not set up criteria that have to be met by your lover for you to believe that you are being loved. Being loved and valued has to be assumed, and working out issues is a totally separate process. In other words, when your partner makes a mistake, do not assume that it's because your partner doesn't love you. Tell yourself that "my partner loves me, but he (or she) is doing a poor job of showing it."

What if your partner is far less than a "perfect lover?" What if your partner consistently makes the same mistakes or demonstrates the same inadequacies? At what point do you stop assuming that he loves you? You should continue to assume that your partner loves you as long as he verbalizes a commitment to passionate love in the relationship and is willing to try new strategies and take appropriate consequences for his or her failures. If your partner is far less than a perfect lover but is committed to passionately loving you, then your focus should be on developing new strategies and consequences to help him win the battle with personal inadequacies.

At what point do you leave? I believe that in a truly committed relationship, you do not leave because your partner has inadequacies or makes mistakes. You leave when your partner demonstrates an unwillingness to adjust the strategy or accept consequences for mistakes. If your lover verbalizes a commitment to true love but makes frequent, repetitive mistakes in the relationship, the most common reason is that the strategy and consequences are inadequate. If a person is committed to love, has a good strategy for overcoming personal inadequacies and is willing to accept consequences, the mistakes progressively go away.

On the other hand, if you have a lover who is not willing to take responsibility for mistakes by developing alternate strategies and accepting consequences, then you can be sure that you are in a losing situation. Your partner is not truly committed. Commitment requires more than words. There must be action backing up the words. A lover who makes repetitive mistakes but will not adopt new strategies to deal with the mistakes is not committed. A partner who does not accept consequences for his or her failures is not committed. Make the decision that you deserve more in your life and pursue a loving relationship with someone truly committed.

The assumption of value is critical to the flow of love in a relationship. As long as your partner verbalizes a commitment to true love and is willing to accept new strategies and consequences for his or her failures, you must assume that he or she loves you. Do not attach your value to your partner's imperfections. He or she will make mistakes. Deal with those mistakes through problem solving in love as you enjoy the fruits of an intimate, loving relationship.

6. Process of Forgiveness

The process of forgiveness is critical to overcoming mistakes in a relationship. During the romantic phase of the relationship, most couples ignore or fail to see their partner's faults as they enjoy the pleasure of the romance. As the relationship progresses, each partner's daily mistakes become obvious. The mistakes are both *active* and *passive*.

- Active mistakes occur when partners know that they are devaluing to their partner but choose to do it anyway. Active mistakes are a result of a choice. Consistent active mistakes demonstrate a lack of commitment and an unwillingness to be a lover. Obviously, if active mistakes are a regular part of a relationship, the relationship will either be unhealthy or very short-lived.
- Passive mistakes, on the other hand, occur when people accidentally devalue their partners. Passive mistakes are a result of one's humanity. Everyone commits passive mistakes. Most mistakes in relationships are passive and can be overcome through the process of forgiveness.

To prevent a mistake, whether it is active or passive, from significantly interfering with the flow of love in your relationship, the process of forgiveness must be undertaken. The process of forgiveness has three steps:

- Act of forgiveness
- Healing of emotional pain
- Application of consequences.

Each step is significant to maintaining the flow of love in your relationship.

Act of Forgiveness

The act of forgiveness simply means that forgiveness is an act of your will. Forgiveness is not a feeling state. It is not something that you grow into or work on. *Forgiveness is something you choose.* You do not have to feel good to validate that you have forgiven someone. You simply have to make the decision to forgive and then validate that decision with your thoughts and behavior. In other words, if you have made the decision to forgive your partner, you have to speak and behave like you have forgiven him or her.

The act of forgiveness also has spiritual significance. The choice to forgive is fundamental to the experience of love. You cannot experience the fullness of the free gift of God's love if you do not forgive. Your failure to forgive inhibits your access to love. I am often asked, "Why should I forgive someone who has treated me so horribly?" The reason you should forgive someone else is for yourself. *You are the one who benefits when you choose to forgive.* You open yourself up to the healing power of love.

If you do not choose to forgive, you close yourself off to true love. Lack of forgiveness initially fogs your mind window as the pain of the past injury lingers. *Over time, your lack of forgiveness leads to bitterness, which results in your shutters closing, further blocking your experience of love.* The choice to forgive is the "smart" choice if you want to live a life full of love.

The choice to forgive does not mean that you ignore the harm done to you. It does not mean that you act as if you were never hurt and move on with your life.

The choice to forgive means that you give up your right to blame your offender for the pain that you feel when you remember how you were wronged. You take full responsibility for the pain associated with the offense while you hold the offender fully responsible for his or her actions.

From a practical perspective, forgiveness means that the pain associated with the wrong is your issue and the consequences associated with the wrong is the offender's issue.

The act of forgiveness is the beginning of a powerful process for healing after you have been wronged. You, first, choose to forgive. In doing so, you give up your right to blame your pain on the offender and you open yourself up to the healing power of love. If you then move toward love while engaging in the process of resolving emotional pain, neither the quality of your life nor your relationship will be significantly harmed by the offense committed against you.

Healing the Emotional Pain

After you have chosen to forgive, you can begin the process of healing the emotional pain. You cannot heal the emotional pain if you do not forgive and take full responsibility for the pain. On the other hand, no matter how horrible the offense, the power of love is great enough to heal your pain if you understand and apply the principles of forgiveness. I have worked with relationships where there have been horrible offenses committed, including adultery, incest, verbal and physical abuse, lying, stealing, and more. No matter how horrible the past wrong, if both the man and the woman were willing to commit to *The Seven Steps to Passionate Love*, the relationship healed and prospered.

For healing to occur, both the offender and the offended are required to understand and engage in the process of healing the emotional pain. Because emotional healing is so significant to the growth of a relationship, I have broken down this process in detail in Step 6. At this point, *I want to emphasize that emotional healing is possible no matter how horribly you have been wronged.*

Application of Consequences

When it comes to the process of forgiveness, the application of consequences is often misunderstood. The most common misunderstanding is the perception that applying consequences means that there has been no forgiveness. The act of forgiveness and the application of consequences are separate issues. As you have learned, forgiveness is a choice, an act of your will. Once you have chosen to forgive, then you have forgiven. Whether you choose to apply consequences is not an issue of your willingness to forgive. Rather, the application of consequences is an issue of your desire to help the offender.

Sounds crazy, doesn't it? When you apply appropriate consequences to the offender who has harmed you, the benefit is for the offender, not yourself. Punishing the offender does not take away the pain of the offense. You will not have any true relief from the hurt you feel if you can make your offender hurt. Your healing is an issue of what you do for yourself, not what you do to the one who wronged you.

Why, then, take the time to apply consequences? First, consequences help change behavior and are critical to overcoming faults. Without consequences, many people never get past their developmental deficits. If a person is allowed to repeat unhealthy behavior without being held responsible for the damage of that behavior, the person normally will continue with the destructive behavior. The end result is that the offender stays unhealthy. On the other hand, the consistent application of consequences will assist the offender in changing his behavior if he desires to do so.

The second benefit of applying consequences is to determine if the offender is truly committed to the relationship. It is easy for an offender to say he is sorry, but it is not so easy to stop the offensive behavior. Offensive behavior is always a part of a relationship. Everyone makes mistakes so you cannot judge a person's commitment to a relationship based on his or her mistakes. You judge a person's commitment based on his or her willingness to adjust strategies and accept appropriate consequences. Committed partners will readily accept consequences because they want the mistakes to stop. On the other hand, a partner acting repentant but not truly committed to the relationship will fight or avoid consequences in an effort to avoid the pain of changing. Avoidance of consequences ultimately will keep the relationship from maturing into the full experience of love.

For consequences to be effective, they must be objective, well-defined, specific, and agreed-upon in advance of the offense.

Tom and Jane came to my center after two years of unsuccessful marital therapy. The marital therapy was initiated in an effort to save their ten-year marriage after Tom disclosed an 18-month affair with his secretary. Jane was devastated. She agreed to work on the marriage "for the kids," not because she cared about Tom. As far as Jane was concerned, "Tom could have his bimbo and hopefully get AIDS in the process."

The previous therapy had delayed the divorce for two years but had done little more. Jane was still very upset with Tom, blaming him every chance she could. Tom was sorry he had betrayed his vows. He was sick of Jane's accusations and blaming. Tom wanted to put the affair behind him and move on. After two years of daily verbal assaults from Jane, Tom was not willing to accept any more blame.

"Dr. Van Horn, when is Jane going to forgive me?" Tom exclaimed. "It has been two years. I have done everything Jane has asked for, everything our therapist has requested

and I am still treated like I am 'whoring' around. Jane does not trust me. She accuses me daily. If I am even five minutes late from work, she starts accusing me of another affair. She yells, screams and throws things."

Jane interrupted. "Dr. Van Horn, what am I supposed to do, pretend that the affair never happened? Of course, I'm upset when Tom's late. How do I know he is not cheating on me again? I was a fool to trust him once but never again. Tom owes me. He owes me years of my life."

"Hold on a minute, Jane," I injected. "The purpose of this initial interview is not to bombard me with your perception of the problem. You will get your chance to fully express how Tom has failed you. Right now, I simply want to know if the two of you are willing to go through the process of 'true healing.' I know this relationship can be healed. I have helped hundreds of couples in your situation not only heal but become passionately in love."

"Passionately in love, with Tom?" Jane laughed as she continued. "I will settle for not getting sick when I look at him."

"I would love that, Dr. Van Horn," Tom quietly commented, ignoring his wife's insult. "I have heard you talk about the healing power of 'true love.' I want it so bad in my life. But is it really possible with someone who hates me as much as Jane does?"

"I don't hate him," Jane rebutted. "I just think he's disgusting for what he did to me and my two innocent little girls. Dr. Van Horn, I was pregnant with my daughter, Sue, at the same time he was screwing his whore." Jane started to cry as she continued, "The night I went into labor I couldn't find him for two hours. Do you know where he was? At a motel with that slut." Tears were pouring down

Jane's cheeks. "I found the credit card receipt. Can you believe it? The same night our sweet little baby was coming into the world, Tom was out cheating on his family."

By now, Tom was also crying. "Dr. Van Horn, Jane is telling the truth. What I did was horrible and disgusting! But I have changed. I am not a cheating husband anymore. I am committed to Jane and our girls. If I could take back what I have done, believe me, I would. I have begged God and Jane to forgive me a thousand times."

Tom and Jane were stuck. Stuck like many couples I have helped. Not stuck because of what Tom did, but stuck because of what both Tom and Jane were not doing. The power of love is great enough to heal any sin, any past wrong. Tom and Jane were not relating in love. They were blaming, enabling and using each other. They did not stay together for the children. They stayed together because they were too sick to leave. The children were simply an excuse to justify the maintenance of their lonely relationship.

So how could I help a couple with such a sick relationship? The process for Tom and Jane was no different than the process that I live daily with my wife, family and friends. Tom and Jane needed to learn and apply the process of forgiveness, repentance and the other principles necessary for *The Seven Steps to Passionate Love.*

Would it be more difficult to help Tom and Jane than to help another couple where there has been no sin as great as adultery? No. The ultimate quality of Tom and Jane's relationship would not be determined by past sin but by the same factor that determines the quality of every relationship: The depth of the commitment to living *The Seven Steps to Passionate Love* on a daily basis. Tom and Jane could overcome the damage of any sin if they learned and committed to a truly loving relationship.

Tom and Jane agreed. They committed to participate in a three-month process of relationship healing. The journey began with my four-day intensive workshop in Atlanta and then continued with several months of follow-up.

During the workshop, Tom and Jane learned how their families of origin emotionally cursed them both and how they brought that curse into their marriage. They also learned what "true love" is and a detailed process for living it. Most importantly, Tom and Jane were introduced to an intense experience of love during the four days. By the end of the workshop, both Tom and Jane came to believe that healing was possible and they committed to doing the work to make it happen.

The work began with letter writing and reading. Tom and Jane wrote letters to each other, which they read at my Wednesday night group. They both had the same instructions: Describe how you perceive your spouse has hurt or failed you in the relationship. Often, when there has been an affair, the "cheater" is labeled the "bad" spouse and the "cheated on" is positioned as the good spouse. All the focus is on changing the "bad" spouse. The problem with this approach is that the failures of the "good spouse" are ignored and, therefore, continue to negatively affect the relationship.

Both Tom and Jane had failed each other. Both needed to express their perception of the hurts in the relationship. Tom and Jane read their letters in front of a group of people, comprising myself and others in the workshop.

The purpose of the letters was two-fold: to "sensitize the relationship" and to "clear the table." *"Sensitizing the relationship" means uncovering the emotional pain that exists in the relationship and in the two participating individuals.* As you have learned, emotional pain inhibits the flow of love in a relationship, whether it is covered or uncovered. Uncovering emotional pain is a critical step in the growth of a relationship. You cannot heal emotional pain that is covered up. On the other hand, all uncovered emotional pain, no matter how intense, can be healed through the power of love. By reading the letters in an environment of love, Tom and Jane were able to sensitize the relationship and further the healing process.

"Clearing the table" means that both partners in a relationship must choose to forgive each other for past failures and agree not to bring up those past failures in the future. Once the letters are read, Tom and Jane have the opportunity to ask each other for forgiveness and to forgive one other. If the forgiveness takes place, Tom and Jane have a "clear table" upon which to build a relationship.

"Clearing the table" is critical to the flow of love in a relationship. If our past mistakes are used to measure our future potential as a lover, we will all be deemed a failure. We all have a past loaded with mistakes. Likewise, if our past mistakes are used to justify the present emotional pain in our relationship, we will never get past our pain. We cannot change our own or our lover's past mistakes but we can learn to flow in love despite those mistakes. The flow of love in your relationship will be determined by your and your lover's present and future commitment, not by past failures. You must choose to "clear the table" with your lover. Jane had to choose to clear the table with Tom.

"Dr. Van Horn, who should I blame?" Jane exploded. "Do you want me to blame you? Do you want me to blame myself? Do you want me to blame the 'other woman?' Of course, I am going to blame Tom. It is his fault that I hurt! When I think about the affair, I hurt. Tom had the affair. He hurt me. He cheated on me. He lied to me. You better believe

I blame Tom when I hurt! Your problem, Dr. Van Horn is that you are a man. Men just do not understand. They think affairs are no big deal."

"No, Jane, my problem is not that I am a man," I gently responded. "I do think that affairs are a 'big deal.' I think what Tom did is horrible. He betrayed you and your children in a very despicable way. Not all men are lying 'whoredogs' in their flesh. Tom was. But, now, he is changing. It is time to heal. Tom is no longer the one abusing his family. You are! You are now the one hurting your children with your blaming. Your failure to forgive is prolonging the suffering for your children, for Tom..."

Jane interrupted with a shout, "For Tom! Prolonging the agony for Tom!" Her face was flushed, her body so tense that the veins in her neck protruded. Jane was standing as she confronted me in front of the 60 people. "I want Tom to hurt! I want him to feel the pain that I have felt! I want to prolong his agony! I am not the one hurting my family! We are still feeling the pain of his affair!"

I nicely asked Jane to sit back down. She sat slowly, too angry to care what I or the rest of the group thought about her outburst. I continued in a soft, soothing voice, "Jane, as I was saying, your unwillingness to forgive is hurting you and your family. Forgiveness is necessary to heal. Forgiveness means that you give up your right to blame your pain on the one who has hurt you. You cannot heal without forgiving Tom. You cannot heal if you choose to blame him for your pain. Yes, Tom cheated on you. He betrayed you. He hurt you. I have no argument with any of those beliefs. But if you want to heal, you have to take full responsibility for your pain. If you have forgiven Tom, then he is not responsible for your pain. You are. "

Jane was flabbergasted, "Dr. Van Horn, your idea of forgiveness is crazy! Tom is responsible for my pain. I want him to know that, and I want him to hurt. I almost never feel good around Tom, but I feel my best when I bring up the affair and see him hurting."

"Jane, my idea of forgiveness is not only sane but it is also the answer to your pain. True forgiveness will enable you to heal in love. Hurting Tom will not relieve you of your pain. Love will. But you cannot experience the healing power of love unless you forgive. Forgiveness is one of the fundamental principles that must be lived if your life is to be energized by love. It does not matter if you stay with Tom or leave, you will never truly heal without love. And you will never flow in love without forgiveness. Healthy people either stay in love or leave in love. You are staying in blame. The fruit of your blame is a lonely marriage and a lonely life for you and your children. "

Jane was now much calmer. The red face was gone, her neck veins were not visible and she was talking in a quiet, controlled voice. But her distorted beliefs had not changed: "Dr. Van Horn, I was not hurting before Tom's affair. I have hurt horribly every day since he revealed his affair. Tom and his adultery are the cause of my pain. I do not care what you think!"

I looked directly in Jane's eyes and firmly said, "If you continue to believe that Tom's affair is why you hurt, you will never heal. If you continue to give him responsibility for your pain, your children will never heal. Tom will have always cheated on you, but the pain does not have to remain forever. By choosing to take responsibility for your pain through the process of forgiveness, you will open yourself up to the healing power of love. And that love will heal you."

> *Jane smiled, now very aware of her location in the center of a large group, and sweetly said, "I know you really want to help me and my family, Dr. Van Horn, but I think you are wrong."*

Jane was not willing to commit to true healing. Spiritual and emotional healing can only occur in an environment of love. Love can only flow in the lives of those willing to forgive. Forgiveness is necessary, not only in the area of major transgressions but also in the little sins of daily life. Because Jane would not commit to the process of forgiveness, I could not help her or her marriage. Jane agreed to think about it for a week. I agreed to continue to work with her and Tom if she made a commitment to true forgiveness.

Jane returned a week later with a complete change of heart. She indicated that she would forgive Tom and take full responsibility for her pain. We could now move forward in the process of healing. I had Tom and Jane hold hands, look into each other's eyes and individually say, "Please forgive me for any way I have hurt or failed you in our relationship." Tom and Jane both asked for forgiveness and forgave each other.

After forgiveness took place, Tom and Jane could begin true emotional healing and consequences could be discussed. As indicated earlier, the act of forgiveness does not mean that the emotional pain is gone. Nor does it mean that consequences are not necessary. Both Jane and Tom had years of emotional healing in their future. As for consequences, Jane believed that her six-month separation from Tom after the affair was adequate. Tom and I agreed. When asked about consequences for a future affair, Tom indicated that he would never have another affair. When pushed to identify a consequence despite his insistence that it was unnecessary, Tom concluded that an appropriate consequence for a man who commits adultery a second time is divorce. Jane adamantly agreed.

Tom and Jane's pursuit of an intimate, loving relationship was made possible through the process of forgiveness. The willingness to forgive is critical to the success of a loving relationship no matter how severe the offense. Mistakes will occur in every relationship no matter how healthy the relationship. Mistakes will not destroy the intimacy and love you desire, but the failure to forgive will.

Forgiveness means that you are responsible for the emotional pain attached to the offense, not your lover who offended you. Your lover is responsible for the offense and the acceptance of appropriate consequences. You are responsible for doing the work to heal the emotional pain. If you and your lover consistently apply the process of forgiveness, your mistakes will not keep you from living an intimate, loving life.

7. Boundaries

Boundaries were discussed in detail in Step 4. The only point I want to emphasize here is that you cannot problem solve in love without well-defined boundaries. If you and your partner have yet to establish boundaries, do so now before you start to problem solve.

8. Focus On Desired Outcome

How many times have you argued with your partner about your perception of a past event? Prior to learning how to problem solve in love, I frequently engaged in arguments with my partner that focused on our different perception of a past experience. My thought was that if she did not understand how she had devalued me, she would just repeat the mistake. I erro-neously believed that solving problems meant talking about the issue until agreement was reached concerning what happened.

Another motivation for "talking through" the problem was simply that I felt better if my partner admitted that she had done something wrong. Think about how ridiculous that position was. Does a person admitting a past mistake make the injury of the mistake any less? Obviously not. Once the insult has occurred, nothing can take it away. Another aspect of my misperception was the belief that the pain associated with the mistake was my partner's responsibility. As you now know, I had a very faulty perception of forgiveness and emotional healing. Consequently, I spent a lot of time trying to feel better by "fixing" my partner's "misperceptions."

How did I know for sure that it was her misperception and not mine? In truth, although I believed strongly in my position, I could not know for sure that I was right. Neither of us could prove our position; therefore if one of us did not surrender, the argument could go on forever. Fruitless arguments over differ-ences in perception are a common part of most couples' problem-solving process.

Focusing on the desired outcome instead of the past mistake ends these destructive debates.

Once you know that there is a difference
in perception concerning a past experience,
agree to disagree and move on to a solution.
Focus on what you would like in the future,
a strategy to obtain it and a method of monitoring.

For example, you arrive at your house for dinner at 6 P.M. Your partner is very upset, having prepared a romantic meal, expecting you to arrive at 5 P.M. You clearly remember saying that you would be home at six; your partner clearly remembers you indicating that five would be your time of arrival. Once it is clear that a difference in perception exists, stop debating perceptions and start developing a solution. The solution here would be documentation in writing of all scheduled arrivals and meetings with an appropriate consequence for each minute of tardiness.

When I introduce this concept and example in my workshop, I often here the following comment: "The person arriving late is getting off the hook. He is getting away with being late. It is not fair."

My response is as follows: "First, how do you know he was late. He may have been on time and his partner was the mistaken one. Second, if he was late, making him admit his offense will not fix anything. Third, if they establish well-defined boundaries and monitoring, either he will be on time in the future or he will receive a consequence."

Do not waste your time arguing about perceptions. Focus on the desired outcome, establish well-defined, written boundaries and monitor the process. If you do so, your time with your partner will be spent flowing in love instead of drowning in misperceptions.

The Process

Once you understand the principles, the process of problem solving in love is simple and easy. The first step is to arrive at issue time with a list of issues. Alternate presenting your issues and record your decisions.

When an issue is presented, check your boundaries to determine if it is covered. If a boundary has been broken and a consequence has previously been agreed upon, apply the consequence. If a boundary has been broken but no consequence was previously agreed upon, establish a consequence for future transgressions. If there are no boundaries that cover the issue, establish appropriate boundaries and consequences.

Do not try to feel better by making sure your partner is punished. Punishing your partner will not relieve any of the pain associated with his or her transgression. Remember, the purpose of consequences is not to punish. Consequences are used to help you and your partner stay within boundaries. In other words, the value of consequences is to reduce the frequency of future transgressions. Therefore, if a consequence has not been agreed upon prior to the offense, focus on consequences that will help prevent the offense from happening again.

What if you and your partner have a different perception of a past event? For example, you perceive that your partner spoke to you in a very harsh voice while he perceives that his voice was very soft and loving. Instead of arguing about perceptions, agree to disagree and improve your monitoring. Find a way to validate what is actually happening. If both you and your partner are seeking the truth, then the monitoring will be very helpful. Remember, we all perceive through a mind and brain window; therefore, perceptions can often be very different.

Monitoring will gradually eliminate the differences in perception. Examples of monitoring may include audio and video recording, a third party whom you both trust or a professional relationship therapist. Many people view monitoring as childish or insulting. In truth monitoring is simply a tool to help you and your partner move to a greater experience of love. I have watched many relationships flounder due to misperceptions. And I have also seen many relationships prosper with the use of monitoring.

What if your partner takes a position that is different from what you remember to be his original position? In other words, you remember that your partner said he would be home at 6 p.m. and he remembers saying 7 p.m. Again, agree to disagree and make sure that future boundaries are specific, objective and documented in writing.

What if your partner takes a position that is different from what you remember and you have the impression that he is lying? Assume that he is being honest, agree to disagree and clarify your boundaries in writing. Remember, you cannot have a passionately loving relationship if you question the honesty of your partner. Assume honesty until your partner proves differently.

Once you have discussed each issue, issue time is over. If all the issues were covered by boundaries, issue time will have proceeded quickly. If new boundaries had to be established, issue time will have taken longer. Eventually, however, you will have boundaries for every issue and issue time will simply be a time to accept consequences and adjust strategies.

Remember as you participate in issue time, your first goal should be to flow in love. It is also important to keep in mind that boundaries are to help you do what you want to do. Look at issue time as an opportunity to improve yourself and your relationship. If you do, you and your partner will enjoy a progressively enriching experience of love.

Assess and Adjust

The Seven Steps to Passionate Love have been lived and experienced by hundreds of couples. I have spent the last ten years teaching many of those couples how to maximize their experience of love. In doing so, I have looked for ways to simplify the process so that individuals and couples can successfully mature in love without my help. An important aspect of maturing in love is regular assessment and adjustment.

Regular assessment means monitoring the flow of love while adjustment means making appropriate changes to insure that maturation continues. Regular assessment is not a complicated process. I have found that there are only four main areas that need to be assessed on a regular basis:

- *Maintenance of Value.*
- *Presence of Sensitivity.*
- *Absence of Blaming.*
- *Personal Health.*

Assessing your **Maintenance of Value** means evaluating whether you are engaging in the necessary relationship activities needed to promote the flow of love. Those activities are covered throughout this book and summarized in the appendix. If you participate in your daily and weekly passion builders, you will not have to worry about maintaining value. Those exercises work to promote the flow of love.

Assessing the **Presence of Sensitivity** can be a deceptive task. The only way to truly assess sensitivity is to first be sensitive. Because I regularly lead groups designed to promote sensitivity and also participate with my wife in a very sensitive support group, I maintain a very high level of sensitivity. Therefore, I am very capable of assessing sensitivity among other people. Most people, however, spend much of their time in very insensitive environments and are, therefore, not very capable of assessing sensitivity.

The answer to this dilemma is to regularly participate in sensitizing activities. If you are daily doing the holding exercise with your partner and weekly crying in a sensitive setting, you can assume your sensitivity is adequate. The best way to insure appropriate sensitivity is for you and your partner to participate in a support group with sensitive people. The sensitive environment of the group will enable you to both assess and enhance your sensitivity.

Blaming kills the flow of love. I cannot say that too many times. Blaming must not be a regular part of your life or you will never flow in love. Regularly assessing your relationship for the **Absence of Blaming** is a must. Both you and your partner should commit to helping each other avoid blaming.

Remember, behind all blaming is emotional pain. The answer to your emotional pain is love. Whenever you feel like blaming, ask your partner to hold you and cry in his/her arms. Crying in the presence of love will de-energize the drive to blame.

Finally, **Personal Health**—physical and mental—must be regularly assessed to insure that you are an effective channel of love. You are not your flesh but you experience and share love through your flesh. A sick flesh can significantly interfere with the flow of love. Make sure that your body and mind are in the best shape to promote the flow of love.

If you desire to maximize the flow of love in your relationship, make sure that you regularly assess the **Maintenance of Value**, the **Presence of Sensitivity**, the **Absence of Blaming** and your **Personal Health**. Make the appropriate adjustments and the benefits will be obvious.

Drills for Step 7

Exercise 1: List everyone who has offended you in the past who meets one or both of the following criteria:
- You have yet to forgive them.
- You still experience emotional pain when you think of the offender or offense.

Once you have created your list, make the decision to forgive anyone you have not forgiven. For the offenders or offenses that trigger pain in you, apply the following emotional healing process:

Start by writing a sad letter expressing the pain you experienced with the offense. Read the letter to your partner or in your support group. After reading the letter, create a card that lines your thinking up with the truth of love. Read the card twenty-five times daily until you are able to think about the offense and experience the fruits of love. An example of an effective card a woman concerning a father who abused her would be as follows:

I am a beautiful, wonderful woman of God. I am no longer an abused child. I am a spiritual being who is being healed by the Spirit of God. Thank you God for the wonderful healing power of your love. As I access the Spirit of God, I will experience the warmth and power of love despite my past abuse. God has a wonderful plan for my life.

You do not have to rush the healing process. Grieving in love slowly de-energizes the painful memory circuits while card reading directs your brain energy toward healthy memory circuits. You may desire to read several sad letters concerning the same offense and/or read a card more than twenty-five times per day. If you stay focused in your spiritual growth process, you will progressively experience the benefits of love.

Exercise 2:   Once every week, both you and your partner independently grade yourselves and
each other in the four main areas of assessment. Use a grading system ranging from
zero to ten with ten being an excellent
score. During issue time, compare your
scores. For any score below ten, list some
objective changes that need to take place.
Develop a strategy for those changes;
establish expectations and consequences;
and, finally, monitor.

The purpose of this exercise is to assist you
in your spiritual growth process. You will
always be an imperfect lover, however
regular assessment and adjustments will
limit your imperfections.

Exercise 3:   Engage in the problem-solving process
daily during issue time. If you establish
well-defined, objective, specific written
boundaries and both commit to meeting
your responsibilities, you will quickly discover that problem-solving is a quick an
easy process. If my wife and I follow the
principles of problem-solving in love and
avoid blaming and arguing perceptions,
our issue time takes less than five minutes
per day. That leaves us a lot of time to be
passionately sharing love.

Summary

CONCEPT SUMMARY OF THE SEVEN STEPS TO PASSIONATE LOVE.

The goal of *The Seven Steps to Passionate Love*: To energize your relationship with the highest quality of love.

Basic premise:

- Men and women are inherently the same: sensitive, vulnerable spiritual beings created to intimately experience and share love in relationships.
- Love results from specific decisions made and actions taken by individuals in a relationship. Love grows when individuals grow beyond their developmental issues. Love matures when individuals mature emotionally and spiritually.

Why this process works:

- Because it aligns you with the purpose of your creation as a sensitive, vulnerable spiritual being prospering in love.
- Because it teaches you exactly what you need to do on a

daily basis to experience and maintain passionate intimacy and love in your life.

The Seven Steps at a Glance

Step 1: Know What Love Is: Discover the full nature and qualities of love.

Step 2: Know Who You Are: Learn the truth that you are a spiritual being experiencing the world through a body and mind and how to return to the spiritual state in which you were created to live.

Step 3: Love Factors: Explore the five critical factors that determine the flow of love in your relationship.

Step 4: Establish A Foundation: Take the steps to secure the foundation for your passionate, loving relationship.

Step 5: Communicate Love in Words and Touch: Build on your foundation through the promotion of loving communication, the elimination of destructive communication and the consistent experience of daily touch and heavenly sex.

Step 6: Heal your Emotions: Acquire a new view of feelings, thoughts and emotions and an effective plan to eliminate the emotional baggage of your past.

Step 7: Problem-Solving in Love: Protect your intimacy and love by turning relationship problems into an opportunity for maturity and growth.

Step 1: Know What Love Is

- Love is the nurturing spiritual energy that enables spiritual beings to experience lasting fulfillment and value.
- **The characteristics of love:**
  Love is not simply a choice; it is a capability.
  Love is not an exchange system; it is a gift.
  Love is not a feeling state; it is a spiritual state.
  Love is not simply a romantic experience that fades over time; it is a growth experience that improves in quality and character over time.
  Love does not arise out of a vacuum; God provides it.
  Love is not judged by what someone says; it is judged by its fruit.
  Love, in its simplest form, is the Spirit of God flowing between two spiritual beings.
- You can only know the full essence of love through the experience of love as nurturing spiritual energy.
- Your spiritual self is YOU. You are not your flesh. Love is the spiritual food that is required for spiritual beings to thrive and mature.
- **Love Is A Capability.** The development of your capability to love requires hard work and consistent, disciplined effort.
- **Love is a gift.** Love is the free gift of the spiritual energy that resides within you that you share with another person. If you "love" with the expectation of a return, then you are not loving. You are exchanging.
- **The perception of your lover.** The perception of your partner must be energized by love, not by appearance, performance, treatment of you or any other external factor. The gift of love means **staying in love** with a committed partner and helping him with his problems. It also means **leaving in love** if your partner is not committed to both

loving you and addressing his or her issues.

- **Love Is A Spiritual State, Not A Feeling State**
Falling in love is a *feeling state* that typically fades over time. **True love is a *spiritual energy state* that matures and intensifies over time.**

STEP 2: *Know Who You Are*

- **Men and women only *appear* different.** No inherent gender differences exist in terms of sensitivity, capability of healthy, nurturing communication or commitment to the pursuit of passionate intimacy and love. It is the socialization process that promotes gender differences.
- **Men and Women are Body, Mind and Spirit:** You are a spiritual being living in and experiencing life through your flesh.
- **The Black Box:** The physical box represents your body. You are a spiritual being who lives in a body and experiences the world through a **brain window, mind window** and set of **shutters.** Shutters refer to your capability to experience on a spiritual level.
The interior of the box is part of the spiritual realm where you, a spiritual being, live.
- **Spiritual maturity** is your ability to experience true value and fulfillment through accessing and flowing in love. The greater your spiritual maturity, the better your capability to flow in the Spirit of God and the more you experience the fruits of love.
- **Spiritual emptiness** is your inherent spiritual void that is present at birth. Spiritual emptiness is the opposite of spiritual maturity.
- **The Vessel:** Spiritual maturity can be compared to an

empty vessel filling up. The only thing that fills your vessel is the intimate experience of true love. Most adults are still spiritual babies.

- **Covers:** Covers are whatever you use to numb yourself to your need for true intimacy and love, or to gain a sense of personal value. Your covers developed automatically to protect you from the lack of love in your childhood.
- **Sensitivity** is the capability to experience on a spiritual level.
- **Sensitivity and covers are opposing concepts.** The more sensitive you are, the less covered you are. The more covered you are, the less sensitive you are. Traditional male and female roles are simply covers acquired during early childhood and adolescence. The supposed inherent gender differences are actually differences in covers.
- Losing covers is necessary if you want to open up to a greater experience of love.
- **The biggest lie** regarding sensitivity is that men were created to be less sensitive than women. Men were created to live as sensitive, vulnerable spiritual beings. No woman is inherently more sensitive than any man. No matter how numb a man or a woman may be, either can regain his or her sensitivity.
- **You can't be too sensitive.** If you are lacking in sensitivity, realize that you are being cheated. Sensitivity opens you up to a greater experience of love. A greater experience of love brings you a greater quality of life.
- You must value passionate love more than anything else if you desire to experience the highest quality of life possible.
- Most men and women are either **motivated by feelings or maintaining covers** when they pick or stay with a partner.

- **Motivated by feelings** means you are either **moving toward pleasure or moving away from pain,** or a combination of both.
- Motivated by covers means that people choose partners based on each other's covers, They choose a partner with a matching cover or a partner with the same cover as a parent who he or she admired or a partner with the opposite cover of a parent who he or she disliked.
- **Lasting value** can never be found in covers.
- No matter what inspired you to match up with your partner, you can develop a relationship based on love.

STEP 3: Love Factors

Five critical factors that determine the flow of love in a relationship are:

1. **The presence of the power source, the Spirit of God.** Love requires not only the presence of the Spirit of God, but also the capability to access and flow in the Spirit of God
2. **The clarity of the mind windows.**
3. **The openness of the shutters.**
4. **The clarity of the brain windows.**
5. **The quality of the IHR** (*intimate, healthy relationship*) **Bridge.**

The five ingredients to an intimate, healthy relationship (IHR):
- **Time.**
- **Loving Communication.**
- **Loving Commitment.**
- **Loving Touch.**
- **Loving Perception.**

STEP 4: Establishing a Foundation

Establishing your relationship foundation requires the following six steps:

1. **Establishing a time of commitment.**

2. **Adopting foundational values.** The hierarchy of values needed to fully experience of love are:
   - **Value #1: Intimacy and love with God.**
   - **Value #2: Intimacy and love within at least two adult relationships, your partner being the most significant.**
   - **Value #3: Intimacy and love with your children.**
   - **Value #4: Providing for and taking care of your immediate family.**
   - **Value #5: Maximizing your God-given talents.**

3. **Clearing the table.** "Clearing the table" means that both partners in a relationship must choose to forgive each other for past failures and agree not to bring up those past failures in the future.

4. **Securing a support system** means developing intimate, loving relationships with people other than your partner who are also committed to *The Seven Steps to Passionate Love.*

5. **Setting boundaries.** Boundaries are the framework within which you and your partner interact. Boundaries are divided into five main categories:
   - **Values** are defined as beliefs or positions on life issues that you are not willing to change.
   - **Preferences** are defined as beliefs or positions on life issues that you are willing to change. Preferences are not absolutes. Preferences are choices that you make based on your feelings.

- **Expectations.** Expectations are simply what you expect of your lover in the relationship.
- **Responsibilities.** Responsibilities are what you perceive that you are responsible for in the relationship. "Appropriate independence" simply means that you should let your partner deal with his or her responsibilities as he allows you to you deal with yours.
- **Consequences.** Consequences are future behaviors, activities or losses that you are willing to engage in or accept if you fail to meet your responsibilities.

6. **Start regaining your sensitivity.** Regaining your sensitivity requires uncovering pain and moving toward love in the midst of that pain. The uncovering process begins with four foundational decisions.
   - You must decide that you believe in *The Seven Steps to Passionate Love.*
   - You must choose to accept the premise that intimacy and love require sensitivity and vulnerability.
   - You must decide that the benefits of love are worth the suffering associated with uncovering emotional pain.
   - You must decide to do whatever is necessary to return to the sensitive, vulnerable state in which you were created to live.

For greater sensitivity, you must be willing to access emotional pain. You know you are accessing emotional pain when you **cry and grieve**.

STEP 5: *Communicate Love in Words and Touch*

Communicate Love in Words and Touch means communicating in a manner that promotes, enhances and maintains the flow of the Spirit of God in your relationship. The ultimate value of loving communication is a greater experience of true love for both you and your lover.

- **The five specific values that a Loving Communication offers:**

  1) **Clarity of brain windows.** Eliminating arguments, blaming and other forms of negative communication, along with the regular use of positive communication, will significantly reduce the stress on your brain and reduce the risk of a fogged brain window.

  2) **Clarity of mind windows.** Blaming, criticism, and distortions are just a few ways that your mind can get fogged. Communicate Love in Words and Touch will help you eliminate that fog by assisting you in maintaining healthy thoughts and feelings.

  3) **Promotion of sensitivity and vulnerability.** People blessed with an abundance of positive communication and free from the pain of negative communication are more likely to live with open shutters.

  4) **Maintenance of four spans of the intimate, healthy relationship bridge.**
  Four spans—loving communication, loving touch, commitment and loving perception—all require that you Communicate Love in Words and Touch.

  5) **Reinforcement of Trust.** Trust cannot be maintained unless you Communicate Love in Words and Touch.

- **Promoting positive communication involves:**
  1) **Sincere Affirmations.**
  2) **Regular Expression of Gratitude and Appreciation.**
  3) **Healthy Discussion of Life Events.**
  4) **Problem Solving In Love.**

- **Eliminating Destructive Communication:** Destructive communication is defined as communication that moves you away from love.

Problem Solving in Love

- Forms of destructive communication include:
  - **Absence of communication**
  - **Sarcasm and joking**
  - **Complaining and blaming**
  - **Indirect and passive**
  - **Deceitful or lying**
  - **Screaming and yelling**
  - **Gossiping and splitting**
  - **Using the past to predict the future**

- **Loving Touch involves:**
  - Daily touch is the consistent loving touch that should occur throughout your normal day.

- **Heavenly Sex** includes four factors:
  - Lifelong Commitment
  - An Attitude of Giving
  - Consistent Communication
  - Sexual Time

STEP 6: Heal Your Emotions

Releasing stored emotional pain: Grieving in an environment of love means having intimate relationships with people with whom you can cry and experience love in the midst of your tears.

Definitions of terms involved in healing emotional pain:

- **Feelings—Bodily sensations arising from electrical memory circuits stored in your right brain, over which you have limited immediate control.**
- **Thoughts—Visual and verbal mental representations of previous experiences.**
- **Emotions—The dynamic interaction of your thoughts and feelings.**

- **Trigger—Anything that turns on a brain circuit.**

Fundamental Principles for Reprogramming Your Emotional Computer:

- **Principle #1: When you hurt, you hurt because your brain is firing and you are experiencing your spiritual emptiness.**
- **Principle #2: You are totally responsible for all your feelings.**
- **Principle #3: You must be capable of feeling your feelings.**
- **Principle #4: You must think and behave based on the power of love.**
- **Principle #5: You must trigger the emotional pain as frequently as possible and respond to it appropriately.**

- **Reprogramming Your Emotional Computer: General Concepts**
  - CONCEPT #1: What you know and believe is determined by decisions. Lovers make those decisions based on love not feelings. You can immediately change what you know and believe by making different decisions.
  - CONCEPT #2: What you like, want and desire are determined by decisions. Lovers make those decisions based on love, not feelings.
  - CONCEPT #3: The thoughts and feelings programmed in your mind are not determined by reality. The programming of your mind is determined by your conscious thinking patterns.
  - CONCEPT #4: When your brain is firing, focus on the power of love. Do not focus on the trigger or the automatic thoughts.

- CONCEPT #5: The foundation for reprogramming your mind is a foundation of decisions.

Decisions determine destiny. Decisions determine the programming in your mind. Make decisions that guarantee that your mind will be energized by the power of love. Your destiny will then be a life flowing in love.

Four Steps For Reprogramming Your Emotional Computer
    Step #1: Feel the Feeling.
    Step #2: Tell Yourself the Bad Feeling is a Lie from your Right Brain.
    Step #3: Tell Yourself the Automatic Distorted Thoughts are Lies from your Left Brain.
    Step #4: Think and Behave Based on the Power of Love.

STEP 7: Problem Solving in Love

Eight fundamental principles of problem-solving in love:
    1. Love first.
    2. Issue time.
    3. Personal honesty.
    4. Assumption of honesty.
    5. Assumption of value.
    6. Process of Forgiveness
    7. Boundaries
    8. Focus on desired outcome, not past failure.

- The process of problem solving in love involves:
    1. Arrive at issue time with a list of issues.
    2. Alternate presenting your issues and record your decisions.

3. When an issue is presented, check your boundaries to determine if it is covered.
4. If a boundary has been broken and a consequence has previously been agreed upon, apply the consequence.
5. If a boundary has been broken but no consequence was previously agreed upon, establish a consequence for future transgressions.
6. If there are no boundaries that cover the issue, establish appropriate boundaries and consequences.

- **Process of Forgiveness:** The process of forgiveness is critical to overcoming mistakes in a relationship.
  - Active mistakes occur when partners know that they are devaluing to their partner but choose to do it anyway.
  - Passive mistakes, on the other hand, occur when people accidentally devalue their partners.
  - The process of forgiveness has three steps:
    - Act of forgiveness
    - Healing of emotional pain
    - Application of consequences.
- The act of forgiveness simply means that forgiveness is an act of your will. It is something you choose.
- "Clearing the table" means that both partners in a relationship must choose to forgive each other for past failures and agree not to bring up those past failures in the future.
- Emotional healing is possible no matter how horribly you have been wronged.

PASSION BUILDERS

DAILY	SUN	MON	TUES	WED	THURS	FRI	SAT
KISSES AND VERBALLY AFFIRM—Initiate 2 kisses each per day lasting 5 seconds per kiss outside of the bed and separate from hugs							
HUGS AND VERBALLY AFFIRM—Initiate 2 hugs each per day lasting 5 seconds per kiss outside of the bed and separate from kisses							
POSITIVE COMMUNICATION—15 minutes or more per day—hold hands							
ISSUE TIME—Must hold hands, maximum of 15 minutes per day							
HOLDING—10 minutes each in cradle position							
AFFIRMATION CARD—25 times per day, include affirmation of partner							
MEALS TOGETHER—2 per day							

Weekly Assessments: 0-10 (excellent)   Values: _____   Sensitivity: _____   Blaming: _____   Health

Weekly	SUN	MON	TUES	WED	THURS	FRI	SAT
FUN TOGETHER—Activity we do for minimum of 2 hours per week (can be four 30 min. times)							
RELATIONSHIPS—2 hours per week with other IHR / 5 min.a day on phone							
LETTER READING OR SAD MOVIE—Goal is to be able to cry together—may read sad letter or watch a sad movie together once per week							
ASSEMBLY WITH SUPPORT GROUP—1 time/week							
CASUAL DATE—3 hours (minimum) can double date, movies or public place OR (one day per week, alternating casual/romantic and who plans)							
ROMANTIC DATE—3 hours (minimum) must be alone so can talk intimately, no movies/friends							
MAKING LOVE—Minimum of three times per week scheduled.							